LOVE CONQUERS NOTHING

BOOKS BY EMILY HAHN

Love Conquers Nothing

Purple Passage

A Degree of Prudery

England to Me

Miss Jill

Raffles of Singapore

Hong Kong Holiday

China to Me

Mr. Pan

The Soong Sisters

Love Conquers Nothing

A GLANDULAR
HISTORY OF
CIVILIZATION
BY

Emily Hahn

DOUBLEDAY & COMPANY, INC., GARDEN CITY, N.Y., 1952

Foreword

BIBLIOGRAPHIES are growing overornamented. If we do not look out they will suffer the fate of the trilobite, which committed race suicide by adding more and yet more trimming to itself. The same danger threatens the customary author's acknowledgment, which is getting sillier and sillier. "Thanks are due the gallant public libraries of Maryland, Louisiana, and Vancouver. Thanks are due my courteous, loyal typing agency, without which this book would never have been typed."

It is high time to ask the question: what should a bibliography be? If only critics would get their ideas sorted out on the subject, I would be less confused when preparing mine. I've always thought a bibliography is there to show where the writer got his source material. It need not be a dump heap of all the books from which I may possibly have extracted vague bits of atmosphere, nor a list of titles included in the name of general culture. A bibliography is not intended for showing off, on either the author's or reviewer's part. According to my ideas, it's included for the convenience of that forgotten man, the reader.

Anyway, I've now worked myself into such a temper that I am not going to use a bibliography at all. The list would be too long and pretentious, considering the number of characters discussed in the text. After all, any reader who wants to can employ a library card index. I did. Let it be understood between us, then, that I've read a lot, though not nearly everything there is to be read on my subjects.

A few comments, nevertheless, seem to be in order. Grudgingly I vouchsafe the information that I used E. V. Rieu's translations of Homer for the Helen chapter. My husband found me the material on Nzinga, mostly in Dapper's *Africa*. Thanks are due my husband.

The direct quotation in the Cleopatra chapter I owe to Weigall.

The Sappho translations come from various anthologies. Two are from the Lindsay *Homage to Sappho*, which, for some incomprehensible reason, is on the restricted list of the British Museum Reading Room, and so must be read very close to the main desk, under the attendant's suspicious eye. It really isn't as shocking as all that. Thanks are due the attendant.

EMILY HAHN

Preface

MOST DECIDEDLY, love does not conquer all. Why we have all grown up believing the tarradiddle that it does, handing it on to our children as an article of faith, passes my comprehension. It should be banished to a corner with such other quaint oddities among proverbs as "Early to bed and early to rise," or "Cold hands, warm heart." Love seldom conquers anything; it only makes a mess of arrangements once in a while and for a little time.

History proves it with negative evidence. Where did love conquer? Who are the great lovers we immediately think of, when we are asked to think of great lovers? Well, there are Cleopatra and Antony, for two; there are Tristan and Isolde, and Dante and Beatrice, and so forth. Cleopatra and Antony, when you come down to facts, were a political and economic merger. I cannot swallow that famous saying about the length of Cleopatra's nose. It might have been a good deal shorter or longer for all Antony would have cared. Egypt, not her nose, was what Antony admired about Cleopatra. Dante and Beatrice were hardly a love affair; had they been, we would never have had Dante's poetry; there would have been a lot of little Dantes

7

instead. Tristan and Isolde, I grant you, are a model couple and everything lovers ought to be—fated to meet, constant if not faithful through long years of separation, clinging to hopes of each other, and dying tragically at the end for their love. But, alas, they never lived in fact. They are myths, like most of the other great lovers.

Not for a minute do I wish to deny that love meddles in things. It does. It swings the course of events this way and that way, so that history runs like a meandering river and not the neat canal we always try to build. Love does not, however, deflect the river so far as to carve out a new path that winds somewhere, unlike Swinburne's, to a different sea. It would take a mighty love and a long-lived lover to do that, and humanity affords neither. The longer the river the easier it is to see the unflattering truth that we are puny people, with truncated lives and swiftly passing loves even shorter than our lives.

This, I grant you, is a pity. It would be a better thing for the world if love did conquer, for then all the captains and the kings would forget to go out and make conquests of their own. Love instead of power! It is not a new ideal, but it never seems to be attained. All the world loves a lover, and with reason, for a genuine lover is not a dangerous nuisance. Soothed and happy, or at least hopeful that he will soon be soothed and happy, he wanders harmlessly under his own bright star and doesn't try to hurt anyone, or grab things. The other sort of lover, the type who goes in for short fierce affairs, like Henry VIII or Napoleon, is not a lover at all. He is love's archenemy, the maker of history.

I have tried in this book to give a few examples of the struggle that goes on ceaselessly between love and ambition, and how it affected, or was affected by, people whose ambitions won the argument. There will be some characters you recognize, and perhaps a few who are unfamiliar. All of them, however, made a splash in their time. All of them played a part in spoiling the line, the neat, canal-like river bed of history as it might have happened. All, fortunately or unfortunately, had their weaknesses as well as their strength. Otherwise, who knows where we would be now? Catching cold, perhaps, in More's Utopia, or doing each his bit in an artificial fertilizer factory dreamed up by H. G. Wells.

The thoughts of might-have-been are endless, but the facts are these: we are still, as we have always been, caught between two strong desires—love and ambition. Ambition still wins in the long run, as it always did.

Love does *not* conquer all. It tries to, but as far as we can make out from the archives, ambition is forever slamming doors in love's face. Love in history usually runs a bad second. When it does win the race you have no history at all. Happy men do not make history.

II

LOVE CONQUERS NOTHING

Unhappy Helen

BASED ON E. V. RIEU'S TRANSLATION
OF THE *Iliad*

CONSIDERING that the gods on Mount Olympus are not ours, we are well acquainted with them. There is good reason for our fondness for Homer; the ties between the godlike company and us are many, though our feelings are those of fellowship rather than worship. We know where we are with those imposing rapscallions. We do not know where we are, in the same way, with God, and that is as it should be. The Galilean, in spite of all the centuries we have spent trying to understand Him, remains an enigma; perhaps it is because of the centuries rather than in spite of them, but there it is. Save for those clear moments of exaltation vouchsafed to very few humans, we are left to wonder. There is, of course, no comparison. Jesus was born of woman, but He is God. The gods of the Greeks were human. Certainly they were too unpleasant on occasion to be anything else.

In those enormous beautiful bodies dwelt correspondingly enormous passions; pride, greed, jealousy, and lust. Their lives and those of the mortals they directed (with great interest in the smallest detail) evoke in us delighted sensations of recognition and agreement. That is, they have this effect when we reread the Iliad, but unfortunately we don't read it much, because it's a classic. It is very bad luck on Helen's memory that her story should have become a classic; one is apt to forget the true versions of such literature. Helen and Paris have become stereotyped characters, great lovers in the worst sense of the phrase. White Helen is a cliché. This is not fair. Helen was better than that; she was a personality and a riddle; she had a most unfortunate life, but not a banal one. (For my purposes of argument, as the reader must already be aware, Homer was retailing history, not fiction. I cannot see that at this late date there is very much difference between the two.)

Helen, the daughter of mortal Leda and immortal Zeus, was a very pretty woman. I say "pretty" rather than "beautiful" deliberately, because of an idiosyncrasy which I may possibly share with my readers; the word "beautiful" in such a connection immediately bringing to my mind cold white marble, a broad waist, and one of those straight noses that make the ancient Greeks seem so heavily in earnest. Helen could not possibly have looked like that. She was a very pretty woman, then, and she was married to Menelaus, who was brother to the great Agamemnon, King of Argos. They had one child, a daughter, and were presumably happy enough together—though one feels that Menelaus may have been rather too old for his wife—until Prince Paris appeared on the scene. Yet sometimes I wonder how happy an intelligent woman could have been with Menelaus, or any other Greek king of his stamp.

If her husband had been able to make of her an important queen, Helen might have calmed her restlessness with pride of power. But Menelaus wasn't head of the family; he deferred to his elder brother Agamemnon, and no doubt Helen's secondary position as his wife was irritating. It wasn't very amusing at best to be a married woman. The households of ancient Greece were always crowded with females as a matter of course, over-flowing with wives and handmaidens who occupied themselves endlessly with weaving cloth, sewing it, and washing it. Life was dull for women, as it is apt to be in a polygamous society; their only outlets were domestic or sex intrigues. Helen, like the other females, was a chattel, something to be seized by the conqueror after a war and sold for a slave with the rest of the weaklings in the community.

Slaves, of course, enjoy certain advantages. Even a male slave is free from responsibility; someone else must see to his keep. And a Greek woman, who was always something of a slave even though she might not be in legal bondage, was not held responsible for her virtue. There was a certain amount of lip service paid to the ideal of chastity, but no girl seems to have been blamed when she was abducted. Abduction is a term which is significant in itself; women were not seduced so much as carried off. The term "seduction" places on a woman the onus of choice, and the Greeks never took a woman's choice into consideration. (N.B.: The name of Helen came to my mind in the Belgian Congo, when a native girl accused a man of her village in open court, saying he had raped her. The white magistrate asked her to describe the crime, and she said, "I met him by chance on the forest path and he asked me to sleep with him. I refused. Then he asked me again. Again I refused. Then he asked me again, and then he slept with me." "But why did you allow it?" "Bwana, I have just told you. He asked me *three times*.")

Very well, then. The situation was hopeless from the start. Helen, a famous beauty, was married to a dull though able man, and languished among her looms and laundresses. It is difficult not to believe that Paris was merely a means to an end, that if it hadn't been Paris it would inevitably have been someone else. Moreover, we must not forget the gods, who were forever meddling with the Greeks. Aphrodite less than any of them would have let Menelaus alone in domestic bliss. She was a restless goddess at the best of times, a snapper-up of idle mortals;

she fidgeted, owing, I think, to a strong sense of inferiority. One can scarcely blame her for this. The other goddesses, perpetually jealous, never missed a chance to snub Aphrodite, and the male gods were not much better in their own way. Though they were swayed with admiration and desire of her beauty, they balanced these occasional moments of weakness with an attitude of affectionate contempt for Aphrodite. They were always telling her to stick to her own line and not to attempt any other activity. It was enough to annoy any goddess, and set her to experimental mischief-making.

As a bribe for his bestowal on her of the golden apple (we all know that story) Aphrodite had promised the beautiful youth, Paris, the most desirable prize in the world, which was Helen. It was not playing fair to get the apple in this manner, of course, and it was gratuitous besides. Aphrodite would have been entitled to it in any case, but that fatal sense of inferiority overwhelmed her judgment and robbed her of self-confidence, and so she stooped to bribery. Alas, the gods hardly ever did play fair, and that is one reason, no doubt, why humanity eventually deserted them in search of a less human code of honor. However, in those days they still flourished, which was convenient for mortals, because they always had an excuse for unpleasant behavior. Paris, for example, was not just a cad. He didn't abduct Helen, the wife of his host, merely because he suddenly wanted her, or because of the evil in his heart. It was Aphrodite who put the idea into his head.

As moderns we are apt to deprecate his action the more, perhaps, because he did not content himself with Helen. He took as well all of Menelaus's portable property that he could manage to get aboard his swift-sailing ship: the cooking pots and spears, the lumps of iron, the gold drinking cups and fine linen, all those valuable goods which meant wealth to the Greeks. Today we feel, in keeping with our code but erroneously, that what Helen did with her person was her own affair, but that it was shocking for Paris to steal caldrons and clothing. We forget that Helen wasn't responsible. Like the rest of Menelaus's household utensils she was, quite simply, stolen.

I am sure she enjoyed it, nevertheless.

What was Prince Paris like? According to the book, he was very beautiful; supple, young, and foppish. He departs from the customary pattern of the time; the usual Homeric hero was bigger than Paris and less volatile in his emotions. I feel, though I do not speak with authority, that Menelaus and Agamemnon and Hector and the other great warriors cultivated their beards and were proud of the resulting growths, whereas Paris, with more sense of the aesthetic, kept himself clean-shaven. As a child, no doubt, he trotted after his brother Hector in the nursery. He had a wide selection of companions, Priam having begotten fifty sons, but Hector was his chosen hero. Hector must have been pleased and flattered by this preference, and so he made a pet of his golden-haired baby brother. The women petted him, too, with the inevitable result: Paris grew up a sissy. He wasn't a weakling; he was good at games, and his enormous vanity kept him up to the mark at fighting, but he was unstable emotionally.

A good many women adored him. This fact is not in accordance with the Greek conventions, which decreed that women should prefer great hulking males who habitually knocked down other enormous males and abducted their wives in proof of superiority. It is obvious, nevertheless, that women loved Paris. Nor should we wonder at this, knowing as we do that Aphrodite herself once fell in love with Adonis, a beardless boy. Besides, why should not any girl like Paris, who was lovely and sweet-smelling and sympathetic? In the monotony of household life, would not any woman welcome a man who obviously preferred her company to that of his companions-at-arms? Paris loved women and was not ashamed of it. He didn't merely use them for mating; he loved to talk to them about things they understood—personal comment on their friends, linen, fur, jewelry.

He must have been the complete antithesis of Menelaus, and thus a great relief to Helen at the moment.

At the moment only, mark you. Here, undoubtedly, we come to the heart of the matter, and here, too, we must pause to consider Helen's character, which was not that of an ordinary woman. She had been endowed with certain gifts at her birth; she was practically a professional charmer, with whatever a charmer needs and nothing she doesn't. Helen aroused desire and admiration in all men, evidently, but she did not in turn desire or admire all men. She liked powerful men, not ingratiating, pettable creatures. She liked men she could respect. She was not like the women who had brought up Paris; Paris was not really her type.

Nevertheless, she must have been infatuated with him at the beginning. She was carried away, figuratively as well as literally. Her captor's person must have appeared to her in a glowing light, and besides, there were all the trappings of royal abduction: the excitement of flight in the dark, the blessed sense of escape from all the cats in her husband's house, the speeding ship cutting the water and throwing up phosphorescent foam. Then the delight of a stolen honeymoon must have been intoxicating. Honeymoons come to an end, however, and so did Helen's. Once more she found herself an inmate of a king's palace, weaving and embroidering and sitting all day indoors with the women. It was then that she first looked with clear eyes at her new husband, and realized that she had committed herself to a flighty stripling. It must have been an unpleasant shock.

To love a pretty boy like Paris one wants a strong maternal instinct. As far as I can see, Helen was devoid of all that sort of thing. Her emotions went into love-making rather than motherliness; she had run away from home, for instance, without giving a thought to her baby daughter. If such a thing had been permitted to females in those days I would dare to say that she was more in love with herself than with any man, and she naturally wanted her mate to be worthy of her. As a Greek she could enjoy certain qualities only by proxy—position and power and strength—and yet she was now farther from them than she had been with Menelaus. Paris was a younger son, like Menelaus, which status automatically deprived him of position and power. His strength lay more in amorous talents than anywhere else, and Helen was not sensualist enough to find complete satisfaction in bed. The unfortunate woman must often have looked wistfully at her brother-in-law, mighty Hector. Hector would have been the perfect answer to all her longing thoughts.

I am sure that Hector knew how Helen felt about him. He may have agreed, secretly, that he should have been her husband. He, above all Priam's other sons, knew how weak Paris really was; many a time he must have pitied Helen. We know that he was very decent to her, though there was never a breath of scandal against those two. There would have been no reason for scandal; Hector was always a gentleman. Besides, Andromache suited him. It was only that he would have pitied any woman Paris married.

Considering everything, her chagrin, her disappointment, her suppressed admiration for Hector and all the rest of it, Helen behaved remarkably well in Troy. Priam's women never had cause to complain of her manners. She was a well-bred woman, and had learned patience in a hard school. Besides, it must have been some alleviation to her boredom to know that for nine long years the Achaeans besieged the city of Troy, ostensibly on her account, though according to my ideas the abduction of Helen was only a small match flame to a fuse that set off the big fireworks. I think that the Achaeans, with the exception of Menelaus, would never have fought so long merely for a woman, and she another man's wife they'd never even have a chance to abduct. No, they fought first in hopes of sacking the rich town of Troy, and later because they would have looked very silly if they had stopped. Then there were all kinds of private feuds mixed up in the affair, and they grew in importance as time lengthened, until every single officer's honor was somehow bound up in the siege. The war became a habit, and Helen, the original cause, was nearly forgotten.

Even Menelaus must have had to remind himself sometimes that he was a cuckold and that his honor demanded repair. Never for a moment did he lose sight of his dearest wish, to carve the heart out of Paris, but it was only to be expected that his mind should dwell more on that satisfaction than on the loss of a wife. Also he probably thought of his property, his wealth, now dispersed among the tall pillars of Paris's house, and then he would grind his teeth and look forward to getting it all back with interest. But to think of the siege of Troy as a clear-cut example of a love battle is, I am sure, a gross oversimplification, and equally gross flattery of Helen.

Fortunately for her spirits, that lady did not have to remain cloistered and immobile for the duration. The cold war waxed hot at last, Menelaus sensibly suggesting a private duel between Paris and himself, and pledging that he would stand by the result, whatever the outcome. But Helen's bad luck in marriage continued. She was invited to the Scaean Gate to witness the encounter, and she went forthwith, tears of homesickness running down her cheeks. It would have been far better for her pride not to be in the public eye at that particular time, for, ultimately, Paris did not show up well.

It began in an orderly manner enough. After a considerable amount of palaver and ceremonial sacrifice, for the ancients were a talkative people and the gods resented the slightest neglect, the duel began. Paris won the toss as to who should have first chance to throw his spear, but Menelaus parried the blow with his shield. The King's spear had more effect; it came very close to killing, but Paris swerved and saved himself. Menelaus's sword broke on Paris's helmet, and then, mad with rage, the wronged husband leaped at his rival, seized him by the crest of his helmet, and started to drag him back to the Achaean lines. "Paris was choked by the pressure on his tender throat of the embroidered helmet-strap," and Helen would have seen the end of her pretty lover then and there if Aphrodite, with her customary unscrupulousness, had not broken the strap and whisked him off, wrapped in a dense mist. She put him down in his own perfumed bedroom and went back to Helen, who was still sitting over the Scaean Gate, trying not to betray her humiliation and fury.

"Come!" Aphrodite said. "Paris wants you to go home to him. There he is in his room, on the inlaid bed, radiant in his beauty and his lovely clothes. You would never believe that he had just come in from a duel. You would think he was going to a dance or had just stopped dancing and sat down to rest."

If Helen was irritated, one can well understand and sympathize. There she sat, bitterly absorbed in homesick remorse, and as if that were not bad enough, she had to swallow the unpalatable fact that Menelaus, her despised and discarded husband, had just proved himself a far better man than Paris, whose property she had become. Hardly a tactful moment, one would say, to suggest amorous dalliance with that same Paris. Helen lost her temper.

It was not often that any goddess received the tongue-lashing she now gave Aphrodite. All her frustration and shame came pouring out in hot words. Perversely, she gloried that Menelaus was evidently still interested in her and would be willing to take her home.

". . . Go and sit with him [Paris] yourself," she said at last, wildly. "Forget that you are a goddess. Never set foot in Olympus again, but devote yourself to Paris. Pamper him well, and one day you may be his wife—or else his slave. I refuse to go and share his bed again. . . ."

As might be expected, there was an explosion from the furious Aphrodite. She threatened the arrogant mortal until Helen was somewhat cowed and consented at last to an interview with Paris. Reluctantly she left her place on the tower; sulkily she accompanied the goddess to her own bedroom. There Aphrodite pushed home her victory: she seized a chair, carried it herself across the floor to the waiting Paris, and plunked the refractory Helen down on it.

Even then Helen showed spirit. She was still so angry with Paris that she could not refrain from scolding him, as bitterly as she had rated Aphrodite. And as she was never a hypocrite she continued to talk of Menelaus, that great soldier.

Was Paris perturbed? Did he hang his head in shame? Or, better still, did he shout at her to hold her tongue, nor mention Menelaus again? Not he; he replied quite calmly and sweetly. Next time, he assured her, he would win. One couldn't always win. In the meantime——

"Come, let us go to bed together and be happy in our love," he said. "Never has such desire overwhelmed me, not even in the beginning—never until now have I been so much in love with you or felt such sweet desire."

The unfortunate Helen could only obey him. Out on the battlefield Menelaus searched in vain for Paris. Once more he had been balked of his revenge.

Some moments later Hector came in haste to his father's palace, panting and sweaty with the effort of fighting, hot with anger against his young brother.

"I wish the earth would open and swallow him up," he said to Hecuba, his mother. "The gods brought him to manhood only to be a thorn in the flesh of the Trojans and my royal father and his sons. If I could see him bound for Hades' halls, I should say good riddance to bad rubbish." Hecuba did not demur. It would have taken a reckless woman to argue with Hector just then; besides, she probably agreed with him.

The hero stormed over to Paris's house next door and stamped up to the bedroom. There, as he had expected, he found Paris, at his ease with Helen and a number of handmaidens, examining his armor with the anxious eye of a fop, but showing no urgency to put it on again. Vigorously Hector delivered himself of his opinion of such behavior. Helen's presence did not deter him. He probably felt that she was his ally; I think she may have signaled her approval to him with a flash of her lovely eyes.

Even Hector, however, could not stir Paris to more than a good-natured, half-sincere apology. Yes, he was probably right, said Paris. The whole thing had been regrettable, but Athene had obviously been on Menelaus's side. Better luck next time. Yes, he realized it might look rather odd that he hadn't gone right back to the fighting—Helen had just been saying the same thing, as a matter of fact.

"Brother," interrupted Helen, "I am indeed a shameless, evil-minded, and abominable creature. I wish I had found a better husband."

Altogether one of the most miserable of family scenes. I pity Helen from the bottom of my heart.

The war dragged to its close, and all that the gods foretold came to pass. It was a bloody conclusion. Hector was killed and so was Achilles, who had killed Hector. Ilium was sacked and burned; during the final fighting Paris fell. But Menelaus lived to sail away to Argos in triumph, Helen regained.

One wonders what her opinion was of all this. The *Odyssey* gives us as sequel an attractive family scene, a conversation piece which reminds us of an eighteenth-century painting. It is just as artificial in its way as any Zoffany. Helen, sitting in her high-backed chair, reigning over her household gathering, recognized a likeness to Odysseus in the newcomer Telemachus. She became reminiscent. She referred calmly and cheerfully to the bad old days.

"Shameless creature that I was," she said to her husband mechanically, in passing reference to the ten years' war.

I cannot help feeling that things were not quite on this good-natured basis when she and Menelaus found themselves alone. Even after several years' time he must have lost his temper when he thought of his wife's abduction, and there were no doubt plenty of quarrels, inconclusive as such altercations always are, with the pattern monotonously repetitive.

Menelaus would refer to the best ten years of his life wasted in regaining his wife. Helen would retort that any man who called himself a man need not have taken such a long time about it. Followed a lively discussion as to Paris's merits and demerits, with due attention to the fatal day when Menelaus had him on the run, to the great detriment of Paris's dignity. Doubtless Menelaus called Paris a pansy, or the Greek equivalent thereof.

"Muscle isn't everything," Helen retorted.

"Yet if memory serves me," said Menelaus, "you admired Hector's."

One thing led to another, and the quarrel always ended, I am sure, in exasperated tears on Helen's part and a slammed door on Menelaus's. Really, one doesn't know which to be sorrier for.

I hope that when they grew old they made it up for good. I like to think of them then, taking care of each other when they had rheumatism or stubborn summer colds.

The Warm Voice

Lo! love the looser of limbs stirs me, that creature irresistible, bitter-sweet; but you, Atthis, have come to hate
the thought of me, and run after Andromeda in my
stead.

And what countrified wench in countrified clothes fires
your breast, though she knows not how to draw her
gown over her ankles?

So I shall never see Atthis more, and in sooth I might
as well be dead. And yet she wept full sore to leave me
behind and said: "Alas, how sad our lot; Sappho, I
swear 'tis all against my will I leave thee." And I answered her: "Go your way rejoicing and remember me,
for you know how I doted upon you. And if you remember not, O then I will remind you of what you
forget, how dear and how beautiful was the life we
led together. For with many a garland of violets and
sweet roses mingled you have decked your flowing
locks by my side, and with many a woven necklet made
of a hundred blossoms your dainty throat; and with
unguent in plenty, both of the precious and the royal,

*have you anointed your fair young skin in my bosom,
and upon a soft couch had from the hands of gentle
serving-maids all that a delicate-living Ionian could
desire; and no hill was there, nor holy place nor water-
brook, whither we did not go, nor ever did the crowded
noise of the early spring fill any wood with the medley-
song of nightingales, but you wandered thither with
me. . . .*

A CHINESE WOMAN I KNEW, who had a
brilliant career at Oxford and specialized in Greek, once said to
me, "Chinese poetry can't compare with Greek. It's not only
poetry: Chinese literature in general isn't comparable with Greek
literature. Don't believe the scholars who tell you ancient Chinese
is rich and beautiful. They don't necessarily think so themselves.
After spending all their lives on it, though, they aren't going to
admit they've wasted their time."

She was particularly fond of Sappho's poetry, and insisted that
no one in early China ever wrote anything so fresh, passionate,
and spontaneous. Of course, I told myself, she herself has spent a
lifetime on Greek. By her own reasoning, she would not wish to
admit— Still, I see her point about Sappho, however dimly
through my own ignorance of Greek.

The Lesbian poetess, you may argue, has no place in this book,
because she had no effect on history. She caused no war, no
political reform. Her love affairs, being Sapphic, were sterile; we
do not even know exactly who her beloveds were, or, save for
Erinna the poetess, what they did. I can only reply to you that
Sappho is history. Most of her life is unknown, but that doesn't
matter: she is the first human being whose voice we actually hear.
She talks through the ages straight to us, and we understand her.
That is inexpressibly important to the world's story.

Beyond her on that long road leading back to antiquity the
forms we see are indistinct. It is too long ago. All we can swear
to is that there were people in those days, and it is for some

reason comforting to be sure even of that much. Since they were people not unlike us, I tell myself, they must have loved and quarreled and eaten and slept as we do. Still, one cannot wonder that some races thought and still think of the ancients as monstrously different from themselves—mountain-hurling giants, or many-armed creatures with extra eyes in their foreheads. The innocents know no better, for they have not heard Sappho. She is not a part of their love tradition as she is of ours.

> *The moon has set, and the Pleiads; it is the middle of the night and time passes, time passes, and I lie alone.*

The warm voice is heard across twenty-five centuries, as if it were ringing today in the ear. Sappho is as miraculously akin to you and me as is that Dordogne hunter with his buffalo, brightly colored after all the dark years he has endured on the cave wall. Poem and picture reassure me; I am not to be left in solitude, after all, to face the whistling emptiness of Time.

And I am not the only one she speaks to. Everyone who has listened to Sappho takes possession of her and builds an image of her, usually in reflection of his own. All of which is, I suppose, natural, but it makes discussion of her difficult. The minute you talk about Sappho you step on toes. People are touchy about her. People are touchy in any case about what are generally called The Classics, and when you ask for more trouble by mentioning so controversial a topic as Sappho's love life, you find yourself floundering in very deep water. Helen of Troy is a far less disturbing subject, but then Helen is a symbol, whereas Sappho is a woman. Symbols are always simpler.

Examined in clear cold light, without anyone's theories to confuse the issue, the facts about Sappho are sparse but explosive. She lived about the end of the seventh century B.C., she wrote poems, she loved women. Some of her poems were about girls she loved and others were not. Those others, by our lights, were the

conventional ones, but the poems she wrote to women may have
been, by her lights, far more conformist and natural. I don't know.
You don't know. He or she does not know. It doesn't matter.

The Greeks do not seem to have thought it mattered either.
They admired Sappho's poems when she wrote them and for at
least seven centuries thereafter. But when Jesus Christ had lived
and died and the Church took hold of His memory, Sappho, like
other early Greeks, came under a cloud. Every writer who had
worshiped the pagan gods was suspect. Their literature was suppressed by methods unhappily familiar to us today; their scrolls
were burned, and the priests did their best to expunge all memory
of pagan poems from the people's minds, regardless of intrinsic
beauty. These censors did a lot of damage, as censors so often do,
but in spite of their most earnest and well-meaning efforts a few
of Sappho's writings survived.

If the essential Sappho has herself survived in some afterworld
or otherworld, she may wonder ruefully if these remnants would
not have been better undiscovered. She could not deny that they
have been the source of sententious foolishness among scholars
and readers. The world we inherit has changed. It is still recog-
nizably the same world; we realize that whenever we come upon
cave drawings and ancient poems. Nevertheless, there have been
changes, and one especially becomes glaringly, painfully evident
whenever Sappho's name is mentioned.

Today we do not think women should love women, or men,
men. We carry it further; in the words of the etiquette books,
such love simply is *not done*. Of course you know what etiquette
books are: this statement does not make sense. It *is* done, actually.
Indeed, such love adds up to reams of pages in best-selling novels.
Psychoanalysts all over Europe and America (I don't know about
modern Greece) spend a good part of their working days trying to
adjust the facts of such a love to a world which does not officially
admit them.

It is possible that this state of affairs annoys Sappho's shade.

But I prefer to believe it doesn't worry her as much as something else does: the way her name is taken in vain as patron saint of a number of crackpot modern institutions. The word Lesbian itself—what vision does it conjure up? A stocky woman in tailor-made coat and skirt, collar and tie, and heavy brogues, who possibly breeds dogs. I have never understood what in the name of Heaven she has to do with Sappho. She rejects beauty, which Sappho loved. She is a misfit, poor woman, and Sappho was more than accepted as a member of society; she was admired and honored. Our modern Lesbian imitates men, and Sappho never thought such imitation necessary.

I have arrived too swiftly, as one always does when one talks about Sappho, in the region of conjecture. Was she officially a poet, a government laureate as it were? It seems likely. Did she run a school, an academy, where she taught younger people to write and dance and sing for the temple ceremonies? I am sure of it, not only because many savants seem to think so, but because of what is called "internal evidence," which as far as I can figure out means one part solid evidence to about five parts intuition. (This shows my amateur status. Real scholars never refer to intuition; they prefer to call it "interpretation.")

Here is the slender anecdote which set my mind working. Alcaeus, a brother poet of Lesbos, wrote an ode to Sappho in which he said, "Dark-haired, pure, sweet-smiling Sappho, I would like to say something, but shame holds me back."

This, I repeat, was part of an ode intended for publication, and not of a private letter. Even twenty-five hundred years ago there was a wide difference between the two. Sappho, as any modern poet would have done, pleasantly replied by the same method of communication.

"If what you wanted had been good or noble," she retorted, "shame would not show in your eyes; you would speak of it frankly."

The rest of you may interpret this exchange as you will; for myself I think it proves conclusively that Sappho was a school-mistress. What could be more schoolmistressy than that? Poor snubbed Alcaeus!

She was head of an academy of young poets, then, who tried their hands, collectively or in competition, whenever an ode was wanted in commemoration of important Lesbian occasions. Probably Sappho's academy was the source of supply for dancers and musicians at all the temple celebrations, and they sang their own songs as they danced. One shudders to think of the rivalry, the heart-burnings, the mutual accusations of favoritism that must have preceded first nights among these ambitious fledgelings. If Sappho was paid a salary for this work, we can safely declare that she earned it. Some of the young women to whom the head-mistress wrote her passionate lines may have been members of the institute: Erinna of Telos was referred to as Sappho's pupil. What we know about Erinna is interesting if scrappy. For one thing, she was a very good poet; at least contemporary critics said so. (Her works were burned in the Church reformist holocaust.) For another, she did not return Sappho's love, and Sappho wrote a poem complaining about her coldness. Yet did Sappho really love Erinna? Does a poet necessarily adore the person he addresses openly, in words he intends to endure for centuries? He loves his poem and he uses a name for it, but the interpretation is not always so sweetly simple as all that.

Sappho was fashionable on Lesbos and beyond. All the literati of Greece knew her work, and they claimed, at least, to appreciate it. She was compared to the best writer they knew—to Homer, who even in those distant days was considered an ancient. No one was sure when he had lived, or knew any incontrovertible facts about him. It was rather like us with Shakespeare. There was even a Baconian school of thought which argued that Homer wasn't Homer at all.

But let us get back to Sappho. It was inevitable that among the praises there should be upraised here and there a dissenting voice. After all, asked one of the critics, a man and himself a writer— after all, what did one learn from Sappho save how to make love to maidens?

It was a sour remark. We will never know just what frustration or jealousy prompted it. It is, as I have said before, too long ago. The speaker may have suffered from an unkind criticism Sappho had made of his work, or perhaps he genuinely disliked her style, or maybe he considered that his own poetry was unjustly neglected because everyone was running, sheeplike, after her. The only thing we can be sure of is a negative one; he was *not* expressing prudish disapproval of Sappho for loving maidens. It would not have occurred to him to condemn her for that. The Greeks didn't disapprove of that sort of thing.

In fact, if homosexuality were as dangerous and contagious as it is believed nowadays to be, there wouldn't be any human race left on the planet by this time. The Greeks would have died out for lack of reproduction, and the races subject to them would have adopted these habits wholesale, and then they too would have died out, and so *ad infinitum*.

Sappho and her academy were only a small, unimportant part of society: it is to be feared women in general played an unimportant part in the Greek scene, as they have in many another epoch of history. If we believe the intellectuals of the time, the leading men of Attica and Aeolia hadn't much use for women anyway. They liked boys. Boy love wasn't just one of those weaknesses which can be winked at, either. On the contrary, it was supposed to be a good thing. It stimulated heroic sentiments, the Greeks said. The boys naturally would want to be popular, and they worked hard at the gymnasium trying to improve their physique. Any boy who had a name for beauty, charm, modesty, and all the rest of it was followed around by crowds of respectable statesmen, philosophers and other V.I.P.s. It was a most extraordinary state of affairs. Under such circumstances it is small wonder that the habits of Sappho and her little group did not attract more attention, or stimulate more resentful criticism.

At that, she didn't get off scot-free. Even twenty-five centuries ago, the literati were capable of malicious gossip. Some wag, years after Sappho's death, deliberately made up a story about her, alleging that she had fallen madly, hopelessly in love with a character named Phaon. She was portrayed pursuing Phaon unavailingly, and committing suicide at last because he would have nothing to do with her. People began to believe the silly story after a few years, and the cliff from which she was supposed to have jumped was pointed out to visitors on Lesbos as "Sappho's Leap." The longer the tale was bandied about, the more people believed it. Within a hundred years of the real Sappho's death (which presumably was not by suicide, and not for love), there were at least two comedies written on this theme, both of which represented Sappho as a grotesque, comic figure. The truth could not possibly have resembled the travesty in any particular. Phaon was a mythical character, a comic in his own right: he appeared in other plays and legends as well.

It is an unhappy fate to become grotesque in the minds of posterity. Taken all in all, I think Sappho's shade has a thin time of it. She couldn't have had a very good time even when she was alive. In the first place, she was a woman who loved women, in a world made by men for men who prided and preened themselves on loving other men. In the second place, she was a schoolmistress. Schoolmistresses are not always treated with the courtesy they deserve, it being generally supposed that they lack humor and resilience. She would not have dared to take herself too seriously, and I think people must often unwittingly have hurt Sappho's feelings. It would be a great mistake to think that she lived in an atmosphere that was all rose leaves, vine leaves, music and song.

There must have been compensations, of course. She must have known what a good poet she was. Even the rest of the world, imperceptive though it was, knew that.

And for all the cruel plays men wrote about her, they went on knowing how good she was. Down to Plato's time they talked about her in admiration. Plato called her the tenth Muse.

There were in the beginning of the world, said Aristophanes, three sexes, male, female, and hermaphrodite. Each male had two faces, four arms, four legs, and two identical sets of procreative organs. The females likewise had two faces, two sets of limbs, and, like the males, two sets of private parts, exactly alike. The hermaphrodites, however, were different: their double reproductive organs were not twins but each creature had one of each.

In a world cataclysm, all these creatures were split into two, and the resulting people were just as we see each other now. Throughout our lives, says Aristophanes, we seek each his original other half. The descendants of the hermaphrodites seek their opposite sexes. It is the descendants of the males and the females who seek their identicals.

Sappho must have been one of these.

I love all delicate things
and Love for me
has the shining, has the beauty
of the Sun.

And I love, dreamily,
to lie beside a shady spring and leaning
touch the cool fronds of its murmuring:
to let loose captive birds and kisses let loose

into a wheeling sky of gold
on wider wings than any bird has grown
and vanishing:

raspberries, and dark lashes to pale eyes,
violets: and then girls
going tired to bed
undressing in the dark without a word,
knowing their own nakedness so well—

the rustling and the quiet hands are heard,
then only nakedness, as the night breathes
and hands reach out to seek . . .
stripping the darkness too as they go stroking
for Beauty by the mind's rose-lanterns fed
yet carven on the cheek:

I love all delicate things—
O Andromeda, bare your body to me.

Very Unpleasant Characters

HALFWAY down the stairs, much nearer than Helen and Sappho to the foot where we stand gaping up at all these figures, stands Cleopatra, Queen of Egypt. At first it may be difficult to recognize her. Cleopatra's role in history was altered strangely long after her death, by an impertinent man named Shakespeare. He took a strong-minded woman who had the almost legendary qualities of a true sovereign, stripped her of the extraneous emotions and thoughts which cluttered his story, and transmuted her into a Great Lover. So vivid was Shakespeare's Cleopatra that she quite outshone the real one. The Shakespeare Cleopatra was, first of all, a *woman* (how one slips inevitably into Hollywood speech, discussing her!) whose state and power were merely background to the stirring tale of her passion for Antony. It is rather a shock to turn away from this lovely single-minded creature in tan grease paint, to regard with as unprejudiced an attitude as we can muster, after a lifetime of theater, the human being Cleopatra really was.

Shakespeare's Cleopatra was a much *nicer* character than the real one. That is my point.

Perhaps, however, I should qualify these sweeping statements

I am making about the real Cleopatra, because I haven't much to go on. The one in the play was born over three hundred years ago, in the seventeenth century, whereas the original lived some years before Christ. Facts, like royal trappings, decay and are lost in sixteen hundred years, and many facts about Cleopatra have disappeared in that fashion.

Somebody had occasion only the other day to sum up what is called "source material" on the Egyptian queen. After ruthlessly discarding all secondary comment, he was left with a few words in Egyptian, a little in Greek, and several gossipy paragraphs in Latin; not very much considering Shakespeare and Otway and Shaw and all the others who have used her story. There is an argument that because we know something of Julius Caesar and Antony, we also know something more of Cleopatra than is written in the sources. But do we? Can one deduce a woman's character from the sort of lovers she chose? And, if it comes to that, *did* Cleopatra choose her lovers? Not really. In her position her choice was too limited to be called choice at all. Her lovers were selected for her by accident of birth and international politics.

For that matter, one may well ask if Caesar was, in fact, her lover at all. It is not a new question. His Anglo-Saxon champions say indignantly that he was not. They say everybody knows the Romans were frightful scandalmongers, and Cleopatra was a vulgar little social climber who merely boasted, for her own advantage, that she had enjoyed his favors. Caesar was a gentleman, they protest; the greatest man in Rome. He wouldn't have had anything intimate to do with a questionable character like Cleopatra.

Let us study the portrait busts of these two people. Cleopatra looks like an intelligent, handsome Greek woman. Caesar's face is humorous, clever, and moody. Both appear eminently respectable; admittedly, sculpture has that effect on most faces.

Remember, you must be wary of ascribing your own tastes and

codes to Cleopatra, and Julius Caesar, and Mark Antony. After all, whatever happened took place a long time ago and a long way off. We are always being brought up short, even by living peoples like Eskimos, or Indians, or Russians. They are not, we suddenly observe, at all like us. Then why do some of our scholars continue to invest the ancient Romans and Greeks with characters so very much like their own? The spectacle of Mr. H. G. Wells turning up his nose in fastidious disapproval of Cleopatra, as he does in the *Outline of History,* becomes rather funny when one reflects that the lady is about two thousand years his senior. It's a rash thing to do anyway. If she were able to read his *Outline* it would doubtless shock her grievously. Perhaps it would clear the air if we admitted from the very beginning that the ancients, from our point of view, were very unpleasant people.

In those days when the world wasn't crowded, people in power, those who made up the aristocracy, were few. There was only one set of wealthy rulers. One gossip column, had there been such columns, would have been enough for everyone who could read. Most of the Continent (and Britain as well) had heard of Julius Caesar the Consul, and knew who he was. But they hadn't heard of Cleopatra in 48 B.C., except in her own country. She was only twenty-one the year she met the Roman general.

Queen of a fabulously wealthy country, she was nevertheless rather weak. In fact, she had just been dethroned, which is why Caesar paid attention to her to begin with. Rome was responsible for Egypt; she maintained a kind of protectorate over the African country, and so the status of Egyptian royalty was of direct interest to a Roman official in Caesar's position.

Cleopatra's father had named her, who was his eldest child, and her younger brother Ptolemy as joint heirs to his kingdom. When Ptolemy was old enough he would be his sister's husband in accordance with the custom of all Egyptian rulers, who in the national tradition were gods. Only god could wed with god, and so prince married sister princess, without breaking whatever incest tabu the Egyptians may have observed among their commoners.

Cleopatra and Ptolemy would marry and rule Egypt together: such were the King's plans, and on the face of it they were sensible. However, if he remembered his family history he probably reflected that plans might go astray. Intermarriage had intensified certain awkward traits in the Ptolemies. The royal annals were full of parricide, matricide, and fratricide, not to mention much other treachery. Cleopatra heartily disliked all her siblings, and they had no love for her either. As soon as the old King died there was hell to pay. Stirred on by palace slaves, his four children were soon involved in a lively civil war over the succession. When Julius Caesar, himself pursuing the last stages of a Roman civil war, alighted on the beach at Alexandria, he found Ptolemy and the younger Princess Arsinoë in control, with Cleopatra driven out and missing.

Strictly speaking, it was not so much Ptolemy and Arsinoë as their favorite palace eunuchs who were in control. The three children were too young to be more than puppets. Had any one of the party in power known where Cleopatra was, she would have been assassinated.

To Caesar the consul, such quarrels among colonials and other barbarians were nothing new. It was a routine part of his work to stop these people fighting and make the Egyptian throne firm before returning to Rome. He was probably prepared, after studying the question, to take Cleopatra's side, even before he met her. She was the rightful heir, and when Caesar had nothing to gain he plumped for impartial justice. But to tell the truth, Caesar was too busy with Roman affairs to worry much about Egypt's domestic troubles; he had not come on purpose to settle them. He was on another mission, which had just come to an ignominious end. His enemy Pompey had fled to Alexandria, and Caesar had pursued him there. It was most vexing to be met on his arrival with the news that Pompey had been murdered, as he disembarked, by overzealous Egyptians led by Ptolemy's eunuch, who hoped thus to put themselves in Caesar's good graces. They had made an awkward mistake. In spite of their differences, Caesar held Pompey in great esteem, and the murder, a dingy and dishonorable death for a great general, really grieved him. He was out of temper with both Ptolemy and his apple-polishing eunuch Potheinos.

Now, while he sat in the palace and scowled, Alexandria seethed with Pompey's troops, who kept stirring up trouble with the consul's escort. For days there had been riots and little battles in the streets. Potheinos walked softly and everyone was very polite to Caesar.

One night Cleopatra, under cover of dark, sailed over from her hiding place in Pelusium, with her faithful attendant Apollodorus, in order to interview Caesar. Being, quite naturally, afraid of capture on the way to the great man's rooms, she and her slave evolved the stratagem which was to become so famous. She rolled herself up in a bundle of rugs and was carried past the guard in that undignified posture.

What happened once she got into Caesar's apartments has been the subject of much bitter argument among historians, and it all sounds extremely silly to modern ears. In the parlance of the woman's page, did Caesar fall in love with Cleopatra on sight? Did she set out to win his favor? Was Caesar at fifty-four too old a man to be caught by passion and sentiment? Or was he a libertine, taking advantage of a poor unsophisticated little girl of the provinces? Was he not a tired, dissipated roué, too old to seduce her? Weren't there a lot of snickering allegations that he was "queer" in any case, and much preferred generals and pretty princes to young ladies?

One cannot but wonder what these people are talking about. Read any account of Caesar's life. No matter how you may admire him, or how obvious it is that his enemies exaggerated and traduced him, the school of Emily Post would not have approved of the real Julius Caesar. Possibly the allegation wasn't to be taken seriously; possibly it was just like passing the time of day in Rome when they hailed young Caius Julius Caesar as Queen of Bithynia because he stayed such a long time with King Nicomedes. It was no doubt merely a rough pleasantry when they called him Queen of Rome to Pompey's King. That sort of remark was lightly tossed about. But whether or not Caesar was doublegaited, it was no mere allegation that he adored women; many wives of his friends could bear witness to the truth of it. Moreover, he was very vain, and must have considered the conquest of the twenty-one-year-old queen of Egypt a challenge to his masculine pride.

On Cleopatra's side there were overpoweringly good reasons why she should cajole the consul. Caesar was arbiter of her fate. With his good will she would be restored to the throne, and without it she must spend the rest of her life in exile. Perhaps she liked him anyway; most women did. He was much older than she, and many young girls find older men attractive. But even if Caesar had not been an accomplished and practiced lover, even if he had been a drooling, revolting specimen, I feel that Cleopatra would willingly have taken him on. She was no sentimental little thing, but a bold, determined queen. None of her family seems to have been of the tender, delicate type. It was an aunt of hers who got cross with her husband, cut up their son, and sent the pieces, pickled in brine, to his father as a birthday present. No, Cleopatra was no sensitive plant; she came of a stock which never hesitated to commit the bloodiest sort of crime in order to gain power. She really did long to see her sister Arsinoë killed and out of the way. Nobody will ever convince me that she was capable of harboring modern middle-class yearnings for a virtuous life, or of waiting for the right man to come along.

In addition, we must not forget that failing the civil war and Caesar, she was destined to share her bed with a brother seven years younger than herself. She grew up fitted for a life of which we can appreciate little or nothing. How then can we pretend to understand Cleopatra enough to praise or blame her? Praise her if you wish for qualities we recognize and admire, for cleverness and courage, but let us not try to judge her sex morals. If we do that we must condemn not only Cleopatra but all the ancients. Let's repeat it: they were *very* unpleasant characters.

Caesar, not being handicapped by our code, probably understood Cleopatra well enough, and liked her very much. Anyway, he promptly espoused her cause. Her claim to half the throne was water-tight, as he pointed out to the disgruntled young Ptolemy, her reluctant partner. Because the consul willed it, the sisters and brother settled down to dwell together in the palace like the big happy family they were not. Naturally, this peace did not last long. Potheinos, still intriguing for Ptolemy, stirred up the people outside to rebel, and for several weeks the palace was in a state of siege.

The war made little or no difference to Caesar and his young queen. They presided at banquets and other merrymakings quite as if a rebellion were not going on at all. Caesar had plenty of leisure to spare for a honeymoon, and as word had just come from Rome that he had been promoted to dictator he must have felt all the more like celebrating. Strategically, a long stay in Alexandria, consolidating his position with Cleopatra, was a good thing for his career, for it meant he had Egypt's enormous wealth and power at his disposal. Caesar was a shrewd man; the portrait painted by his enemies of a lazy debauchee who neglected Rome merely to indulge in sensual pastimes was no more accurate than one would expect of politicians.

Nor was he as blind as he pretended to the dangers of the situation. Despite the gay parties, the canny Roman kept an eye on Ptolemy and Potheinos. The minute he got the chance he shoved the boy out of the palace, advising him to join and lead his own troops against Cleopatra, since he felt so strongly about it. Just as Ptolemy's elder sister had hoped, he was soon killed in battle. The tiresome Potheinos was done away with quietly and tactfully at a banquet. As for Princess Arsinoë, she ran away and joined Cleopatra's enemies. At the end of the siege she was captured and became officially what she had long been in fact, a prisoner of state. Scarcely a model family group, one reflects, nor does Caesar appear to have behaved to the children like Santa Claus. The protests of historical writers that the dictator was above reproach and that Cleopatra was merely a designing little woman who behaved like a village drab, quite gratuitously accusing that greathearted man of fathering the baby she now bore, fall strangely on ears which have already heard this much of the story.

"He didn't!" cry Caesar's champions stoutly. "He never had a thing to do with that woman. Julius Caesar wouldn't do a thing like that. Caesarion? He wasn't Caesar's son. Never mind what she said; a woman like Cleopatra would say anything. She was a *loose woman.*"

No matter what his fans may say, Caesar did not deny paternity of the child, nor object to its being named "Little Caesar." He had probably already gone through a form of marriage with Cleopatra. The Egyptians recognized him as a ruler with as much right to the title as any Ptolemy's. It is true that he was already married, and that his Roman wife, Calpurnia, awaited him at home. But Calpurnia herself was his third wife. Divorce in Rome was simple, and Caesar, I repeat, was *not* a present-day Englishman in his habits. He was a much-divorced man, he was an experienced co-respondent, and Rome was a long way off.

However, all holidays, all honeymoons, come to an end. After nearly a year's stay in Egypt, the dictator returned to Rome. There he found a large accumulation of things to do, among which was a punitive expedition to North Africa. In Mauretania he had an affair with Eunoë, the Queen, which nobody, not even Eunoë's husband, seems to have resented very much. The person who might well have resented it fiercely was Cleopatra, the young mother, but she, like Eunoë's husband, seems to have borne no grudge. Men were like that, and her mind was set on other matters. Caesarion was a newly born baby, but Cleopatra of the Ptolemies saw him as king of the world. Her plans were ready and waiting.

As soon as he was a year old, Cleopatra set out for Rome. She arrived in time to witness Caesar's triumph, in the procession of which her sister Princess Arsinoë, according to the unpleasant custom of the time, was forced to march through the city in chains. The Roman populace was allegedly shocked that Caesar should have treated in this manner a girl who was practically his sister-in-law. They were also said to be shocked that Cleopatra should have approved what he did. But the Roman people, whatever their other qualities, were not notoriously tenderhearted, and it is not on record that anyone stayed at home and missed the triumph out of principle. Very likely what the Romans really felt was a loyal indignation on Calpurnia's behalf that Cleopatra should have come to Rome at all.

Cleopatra, it is scarcely necessary to say, didn't care what the Romans thought. A queen who had ignored rebellion in her own city could not be expected to turn sensitive about the opinion of a lot of Italian foreigners. She moved into a villa on the Tiber and settled down, living there in apparent contentment for two years.

Two years is a long time for a sovereign to stay away from home, but Cleopatra had her reasons, and again I do not think they were sentimental ones. She wanted Caesar to make Caesarion his legal heir. Perhaps she played a part, too, in Caesar's slowly growing desire to assume the crown. Caesarion as the baby son of a dictator would not stand much chance of stepping into office, a Republican government being run, presumably, by people who were selected, not born to office. But Caesarion as son of a king, or an emperor, would be assured of his position. Even Rome might respect the hereditary rights of a prince, no matter how young. Cleopatra's reasoning and misunderstanding of Roman mentality might be full of holes, but that was probably the way her mind worked. It was the way she had been brought up.

Caesar, however, would not agree. He clung to his original idea of handing over his office to his nephew Octavian. He made a will to that effect, and refused to change it. No doubt he felt that Egypt should suffice for Caesarion, and that Octavian as a Roman would be more likely to know what was good for Rome.

Then he was assassinated, and there was Cleopatra, without her august protector, alone with her little son in a city of hostile foreigners.

Unexpectedly, one of them was not hostile after all. This was a man named Mark Antony, one of Caesar's most loyal followers, who stepped to the fore after the murder and cleverly whipped up public hatred against the conspirators. Just which way the tide would finally settle down to flowing was difficult to say, but in the meantime Antony was building up a name for himself. One day in the Senate he made a statement which must have been gratifying to Cleopatra, declaring that the martyred Caesar had himself recognized Caesarion as his rightful son. Such a remark, annoying as it was to the senators, frightened and enraged Octavian even more.

Octavian and Antony were sworn enemies, though each was committed against the same two men, Brutus and Cassius, leaders of the conspiracy against Caesar. These men and their assistants had been hastily got out of Rome until things should settle down. Until they were able to gather their forces and attempt to come back, it was a question which of the two remaining on the battlefield would come out ahead, but Cleopatra could not afford to wait and see, nor was she particularly interested. She fled with Caesarion back to Egypt, reassured yet hastened on her way by the anger which Antony had stirred up in the city when he named the baby Caesar's heir. Her feelings about her new friend must have been mixed.

Mark Antony's character has tempted many a novelist and play-wright to use him as a hero, and it is easy to understand why this should be. He is a familiar type. He sounds just the sort of man we have all known in our time, hearty and good-natured, brave and reasonably loyal, good-looking in a big healthy way, and, though far from stupid, not subtly clever. Antony's cunning and craft were just a bit ahead of the mob's. When young and self-confident he must have been lovable. Certainly his soldiers loved him. He possessed many qualities of a leader, not least of which was his talent for oratory.

His portrait bust shows a big man, large-featured, with very curly hair. One can imagine his prototype nowadays going a long way on charm. I see him as the favorite boarder in a lodginghouse where the landlady saves him titbits and does his laundry and mending free of charge, or a swaggering strike leader in some car factory, or perhaps a lifesaver and swimming instructor at a public beach, surrounded by admiring girls and little boys. The one thing I cannot imagine is Mark Antony as ruler of the entire Western world; yet that is what he was for a space.

He achieved his eminence by temporarily dropping his quarrel with Octavian. It had become evident to him that without some-one like Caesarion or Octavian to connect with, he had no good excuse for shouldering himself to the top. Which star should he hitch his wagon to? One can easily imagine him weighing them up and deciding that Octavian as a grown man, named in the will, was far more likely to succeed than the little Caesarion. Antony dropped the vexed subject of Caesarion and made an alliance with Octavian.

A third man, named Lepidus, having been brought into the partnership, they called themselves the triumvirate and briskly took hold of Rome's affairs. It was high time someone did, for the Senate had been floundering ever since the assassination, and Brutus and Cassius were on their way back to make their long-expected attack. Antony led out an army and defeated the enemy at Philippi, and at that battle both Brutus and Cassius were killed. "Now," said the triumvirate, "we must consolidate."

First of all they must collect funds from Egypt. Whenever Rome needed money she turned toward Egypt. So Antony set out for the East, by way of Greece and Asia Minor, to see what could be done about broaching the treasure cask once again. At Tarsus he sent word to Cleopatra, requesting that she come that far to meet him for discussions. He hinted at a threat, in preparation for his demands. Had not Cleopatra been suspected of aiding and abetting the conspirators who killed Caesar?

Possibly she had, since everyone of prominence in Rome was always suspected of a part in every conspiracy. Cleopatra wasted no time in indignant denials: that sort of thing was routine, and could be attended to when she encountered Mark Antony in person. After all, he was the man who had stood up for her son's rights in the Senate, though now he followed the hateful Octavian. There were possibilities in the situation, so Cleopatra made her preparations and set sail for Tarsus.

The meeting between these two people was not without its humorous side. Deliberate pomposity is always funny to modern eyes, but it played a large part in pageantry among the ancient kings, and Cleopatra took very seriously her plan to overawe Antony. He on his part was determined to impress the Queen with his power and importance. The two proceeded at stately measure to the game of face-winning.

When Cleopatra's fleet sailed up the Cydnus, Antony arranged himself in state in the market place to receive her. He waited a long time. The royal ships came to anchor near the opposite bank, the sun passed its zenith, unofficial reporters brought news that the Egyptian's slaves seemed very busy aboard, but nobody landed. Finally the idle market-place crowd deserted the waiting Romans and drifted down to the riverside to watch the more interesting newcomers. Antony was left like a wallflower. At last he swallowed his pride and sent an invitation to Cleopatra to come to dinner.

The messenger returned with a counter-invitation from the Queen, to come aboard ship as her guest.

Antony accepting, the first of that famous series of banquets was duly arranged. The royal galley was brought across the river to fetch him. "Across the water, in which the last light of the sunset was reflected, the royal galley was rowed by banks of silver-mounted oars, the great purple sails hanging idly in the still air of evening. The vessel was steered by two oar-like rudders, controlled by helmsmen who stood in the stern of the ship under a shelter constructed in the form of an enormous elephant's head of shining gold, the trunk raised aloft. Around the helmsmen a number of beautiful slave-women were grouped in the guise of sea-nymphs and graces; and near them a company of musicians played a melody upon their flutes, pipes, and harps, for which the slow-moving oars seemed to beat the time. Cleopatra herself, decked in the loose, shimmering robes of the goddess Venus, lay under an awning bespangled with gold, while boys dressed as Cupids stood on either side of her couch, fanning her with the coloured ostrich plumes of the Egyptian court. Before the royal canopy brazen censers stood upon delicate pedestals, sending forth fragrant clouds of exquisitely prepared Egyptian incense, the marvellous odour of which was wafted to the shore ere yet the vessel had come to its moorings."* Cecil de Mille himself could have done no more.

Antony, his retinue, and the local men of importance who were fellow guests were staggered. Rome in all its glory had never been like this. But Cleopatra was not done with her showing off, which she must have enjoyed hugely. After dinner Antony expressed his wondering admiration of the ship's banqueting saloon, where the couches and walls were festooned with rich embroideries and the

---

*Life and Times of Cleopatra, Queen of Egypt, by Weigall (Putnam, 1914).

goblets and dishes were made of jeweled gold. The Queen said in offhand tones:

"It's not worth talking about. Do take all this as a gift." Then she ordered the whole array, the plate and silk and furniture, to be packed up and taken ashore to Antony's quarters. It was a party favor well worth bringing home.

On the second evening Cleopatra entertained again. This time every one of her guests was given a souvenir. Each of the important men took home with him the couch and the plate he had used, as well as a litter complete with slaves to carry it and torch-bearers to walk before. The less important guests had to be content with gifts of mere horses, outfitted in gold.

So it went, the whole time the Queen remained in Tarsus. Antony did his best to keep up appearances for his side. When he was host he managed to spend a fortune, but he never outdid the Queen. Still, he enjoyed trying. He loved to be prodigal; he was a generous, extravagant man with a large appetite for sensuous pleasure, and this political game was much to his taste. Thus both competitors came out ahead. Antony had a wonderful time, and Cleopatra succeeded in her design of showing the Roman that Egypt's wealth was to be respected and desired. It is no wonder that Antony, when he thought it over later in Rome, wondered why he should not desert the triumvirate and join Cleopatra for good. It would be wonderful to defeat Octavian once and for all. He could use Caesarion as a rival heir to Julius Caesar's power, as once before he had meant to do.

There was another temptation to leave Rome: Antony's wife Fulvia lived there. We know all about the excellence of Roman matrons, and Fulvia must have had her share of good qualities. It has always been this writer's opinion, however, that the typical Roman matron, although a good mother and an excellent manager, might possibly have been just a bit forbidding. At any rate, Fulvia was. She treated Antony rather in the manner of a combination sergeant major and stern great-aunt. A man not easily squashed, he did his best to assert himself against Fulvia's granite personality; he would hide in dark corners of the house and jump out at her, yelling "Boo!" But life with Fulvia could never have been really jolly or stimulating, whereas Cleopatra was beautiful, witty, brilliant and subtle. Also rich and powerful.

In 41 B.C., without committing himself, Mark Antony went to Alexandria.

At this point in Cleopatra's life there comes a happy moment for the moralists who judge her from their own century with such puzzling results. Mark Antony lived with the Queen, loved her, and gave her every hope of carrying on her early plans for her son. Then, six months before she was brought to childbed, he left her.

He had several good reasons. News arrived that Fulvia and the leaders of his faction had been forced to flee from Rome, owing to an outbreak of the smoldering quarrel with Octavian. This meant war. Antony was urgently needed. Whatever he may have promised Cleopatra and himself for the future—marriage and world conquest—would have to wait. Antony went to Greece and rejoined his Roman wife; in the space of a few months Fulvia had died, Antony had again made peace with Octavian, the uneasy triangle was re-established, and Cleopatra forgotten. Antony was named master of the eastern provinces and promised to leave Italy to Octavian. As an earnest of their friendship, the two men arranged a marriage for the widower, Octavian giving his sister Octavia to his erstwhile foe. They were married at the time Cleopatra, in Egypt, was giving birth to twins, a boy and a girl.

Seldom has queen been so snubbed. Whatever her sentiments toward Antony, whether or not she had been actuated by love as well as policy, Cleopatra must have been bitterly angry when she heard of his marriage to Octavia. Perhaps the great blustering boy signed his death warrant by that act, though before the tragic end he was to be reconciled with his Egyptian Queen.

Four years passed. Octavia bore a son to her husband, and in Alexandria Cleopatra bided her time. Success had gone to Mark Antony's head. He was drinking more than his judgment could support, and dreams of further glory heated his imagination. In time he remembered the wealth of Egypt and reflected on how useful it could be now for his purpose. Why should he not consolidate the East into as great an empire as Octavian's? Why not make it even greater? Why not, in fact, pick up his alliance with Cleopatra where he had dropped it, and conquer Octavian? Abruptly, Antony sent Octavia home. Then he met his deserted royal mistress at Antioch, and they talked it over. A fresh alliance was formed. Cleopatra dissembled and showed no resentment. Antony had perjured himself many times over, but he was Antony, and as such was still Caesarion's best chance.

From that time on Mark Antony behaved like her legal consort. They were actually married according to Egyptian law; he was given the title of Autocrator, and spoke in his letters of his wife Cleopatra. Many of his eastern domains were turned over to the Queen by treaty, in exchange for her future help in his campaigns. Whatever her true thoughts may have been, Cleopatra at this time pretended to trust her husband absolutely.

The first step in Antony's program of triumph as they planned it was to be the conquest of Parthia. With an enormous army he set out, full of confidence, Cleopatra accompanying him a part of the way. But she was again pregnant, and when this was discovered she turned back to Alexandria. Confident in the outcome of the war, she passed the time there quietly, and at length gave birth to her fourth and last child, a boy who was, like most Egyptian princes, named Ptolemy.

In the meantime, in spite of his splendid equipment, Antony's campaign had come to grief. He managed by tremendous effort to bring the remnants of his army into Syria, being like many other men at his best in adversity, but by the time Cleopatra was able to sail in and rescue him, her husband, who had been waiting miserably in a Syrian seaport, had taken refuge in drink. The blow to his masculine pride had been a severe one. He probably dreaded meeting Cleopatra, and the meeting was every bit as painful as he had expected. The Queen naturally decided he had muddled matters and did not conceal her contempt.

Shall we trace in detail the story of Antony's progressive degradation after this? It is hardly necessary; this is not a military report. In any case, after the Parthian debacle he had great success for a while, and his stock rose another time when Octavian was making overtures of peace and Antony's discarded wife Octavia almost persuaded him to rejoin her. Cleopatra had to work hard; it took a lot of histrionic ability to hold Antony then to the treaty he had made with her in Antioch. We can hardly suppose that this humiliating affair increased the Queen's love for him, but she was not playing the game for love. After this final capitulation to past promises—though Mark Antony could not possibly have stood by all the contradictory promises he made in his life—he seems to have settled down and devoted himself wholeheartedly to his Egyptian wife. In my opinion, this was not so much a tribute to Cleopatra's attractions as a sign that he was losing his grip. He continued to drink too much. He floundered, and as he grew weaker in will he grasped at her, clinging like a drowning man to his wife's strength.

Cleopatra was more than ever eager to defeat Octavian and install Caesarion in Caesar's place. That ambition was one of the few bonds which still remained between herself and Antony. As soon as the triumvirate treaty expired, the Egyptian army and navy set forth, with Antony and Cleopatra in close attendance. Antony urged his wife repeatedly not to stay with the forces, to go back to Egypt, but she did not dare leave him to his own devices. She was in the quandary which many another drunkard's wife can well understand: was the man who had failed in the Parthian campaign capable of doing this job without her? Probably not. And even if he had been, could she trust him to remember her interests in the hour of victory? He had let her down that way, too, more than once in the past. Decidedly, Cleopatra would not go back to Alexandria. She was still aboard her flagship when the great engagement began.

The decisive battle, a naval one, took place near Actium on the Ambracian Gulf. Antony had deliberately elected to meet his foe in full force on the water, for he was strongly supplied with Egyptian ships, whereas the Roman land army might well be superior to his own land forces. As it turned out, Egyptian superiority on the water was too great; it constituted an embarrassment. Antony's ships were huge armored things, comparatively impregnable but very slow-moving. Octavian's vessels were small and agile, too light for ramming the big ships. Instead they set upon the enemy in clusters, like dogs attacking a stag.

The day wore on, and still the strange clumsy battle continued. By slow degrees it became evident that Antony was losing. Then suddenly something took place which no one expected. Cleopatra the valiant, Cleopatra the long-suffering, the Queen who had taken back a faithless lover after four years of ill treatment—Cleopatra deserted Antony. She gave her orders, called together her ships, and set sail in a favoring wind for Egypt. It was not at all the traditional thing to do, and must have shocked the onlookers, but Antony's behavior after that was even less orthodox.

When he saw what was going on he leaped into his galley and pursued her, leaving his men to their fate. Seldom has such an outrageous performance been perpetrated by a hitherto valiant leader. The indignation of those few who grasped what was happening can be imagined. For a moment, when his fast galley overtook the Queen's flagship, the crew must have expected Cleopatra to scorn the craven, to refuse to take him on board. However, even a queen could not quite do that, one supposes. She gave her orders and Antony, frantic and panting, was hauled up on deck.

Without a word to him, Cleopatra retired to her cabin. For

three days she stayed there, ignoring him, while the ship flew on toward Egypt. For three days he sat motionless in the prow, in abject disgrace, sunk in confused despair. Then at last Cleopatra admitted him to her cabin, but the rift had grown too wide to bridge: it must have been one of the most miserable of reconciliations. We cannot envy either one of the unhappy pair. Antony had lost his last spark of pride. He was finished, and they both knew it.

News of the abandoned battle came trickling in, further disheartening Queen and consort. On land, Antony's forces had done far better than had been hoped, but as soon as word went out that their leader had deserted, they naturally surrendered to Octavian's army. Greece was lost to the Roman ruler, and so, in time, was Africa. Once Antony attempted in a halfhearted way to commit suicide, but he was restrained, without difficulty, by friends, and he didn't try again. This was thoroughly shameful. Nothing could be more contemptible, in the opinion of the ancients, than to fail in an honorable suicide, unless it was to avoid committing suicide altogether. Under the circumstances, Antony *should* have killed himself. It was most embarrassing.

The Queen returned to the royal palace at Alexandria, but Antony, who was not invited to accompany her, took refuge in a piece of maudlin play-acting. He moved into a lonely little house on a pier in the great harbor, within view of the palace, and announced that henceforth he would live in imitation of Timon of Athens, the misanthrope. There, he said, he would end his days, cut off from all men, hating his kind. And there for quite a long time he actually stayed, solacing himself with wine and forgetfulness.

Followed a weary, unedifying period during which the actors in this drama went on behaving in their characteristic ways, quite as if Fate would be forever delayed in closing in on them. Like nobler Achilles, Antony sulked in his little hut. Cleopatra, ignoring him, planned new forays, started new fortifications, and managed her unwieldy kingdom as best she might on her own. All the while the pursuing Octavian drew nearer and nearer to the final inevitable scene, the conquest of Egypt and vengeance on Antony, that many-times turncoat.

Then came the climax. Octavian fell upon the Egyptians, but it was not a clean, dramatic battle, for he knew his enemy's weaknesses and he preferred to lure the Army to his side. It was easy, he found, to bribe most of the officers, and the Queen automatically became his prisoner as soon as her army was won over. There are various versions of what went on during the interview between Octavian and Cleopatra.

I find it difficult to believe, as some historians tell us, that the Queen refused to give up Antony to the conqueror in exchange for her own safety with honor. I don't think he made any such offer. Octavian did not have to ask the helpless Queen for custody of Antony. The Roman renegade was his in any case, sooner or later, for the taking. Nor can I swallow the Shakespearean version of her message which went wrong by accident. There was Cleopatra, still alive and well in the royal mausoleum with her women. How could any message passing from the mausoleum to the fugitive get so garbled on the way that he was led *by mistake* to believe that she was dead? I am sure Cleopatra sent the lie on purpose.

She knew what she was doing; deliberately she tricked him, knowing he would commit suicide. There could have been no grief in her heart when she did it. Vengeance and honor were her motives. For months, every day Antony lived had been a fresh reproach to Cleopatra. He was her husband, and honor demanded that he die by his own hand; death, indeed, was long overdue. Sodden coward though he was, there was still the chance that he might kill himself if his one remaining prop was withdrawn. Quite coldly, I think, Cleopatra withdrew it, and I for one respect her for the deed.

Afterward, when she realized that Octavian would not spare her public humiliation, or allow her children to live in the style to which she was convinced they were entitled, she calmly killed herself as well. That part, I feel, was one of the easiest tasks Cleopatra fulfilled in her far from easy life. "Very well done," the dying Charmian said, and Charmian was right.

Henry the Inevitable

OF COURSE there is Henry VIII. One cannot leave him out of any history of the Western world, though, to be quite frank, this writer had a good try at doing it. My reluctance was twofold; first, I felt that Henry has already been discussed and interpreted far more than most monarchs, and second I dislike him so intensely that it was an effort, at the beginning, to polish up my knowledge. Early thoughts are often erroneous, however, and mine in this case are no exception. I am glad now that I had to reread so much about Henry VIII. One forgets that there is much more to him than the Charles Laughton performance, memorable though it be.

What he did to history was not so important as *how* he did it. If Henry VIII had not broken away from the Church of Rome, someone else would have. It had to be: not even the Church could hold onto the entire world. England was, to the Pope, a distant colony, and the Pope must have seemed to colonies and colonials a far-off tyrant, an absentee landlord. As people grew up on the periphery of the Holy Empire they inevitably began to think for themselves, and from this thought to chafing against the unknown Holy Father's strictures was a short step. Sooner or later there was bound to be a breakaway. Had it not been caused by Henry's divorce the rupture would have been brought about by another quarrel and perhaps another king. However, it was Henry VIII who did it, which was unfortunate not only for his victims but himself as well. It is doubtful if any other sovereign, even in those unprincipled days, would have shown the strain to such disastrous effect. The National Gallery portrait of this man as a stripling invariably brings the visitor to a halt, while he stares incredulously. Can this lovely youth possibly be Henry? There must be some mistake. Whatever can have happened to turn him into the mean-faced fatty of Holbein's picture?

Of course, as we know, plenty happened, and it cannot be wondered at that Henry's face should have changed. Oscar Wilde may well have seen those two portraits when he thought of Dorian Gray.

The worst thing about Henry was not that he was a murderer, a coward, and invariably false to his most faithful friends, though all of these are true. By far his most revolting trait was his self-complacency. That is what shows in the Holbein portrait, is-landed in the middle of the heavy oblong face—the prissy, cruel, pursed little mouth. This is not to say he was always happy about himself. He had moments of self-questioning, like everyone else; especially must he have smarted heavily under the shame of discovering how his fifth wife Katheryn had married him not for love, but to be Queen. But he never thought that any of these things were his fault.

Incidentally, most women will wonder how he could have thought his wives were actuated by any motive but ambition. Presumably he looked at himself in the glass. . . . But they will not wonder long, if they know men. Henry VIII was a man whose normal masculine failings were magnified by his royal status to—well, to king size. Thus, he was self-complacent enough to marry again and again, comfortably confident each time that his wife adored him, until Katheryn spoke with such calamitous frankness before the chopping block.

Henry is not the only man by far who has done the sort of thing he did, but he is just about the only one who managed to kill so many outside people in the process. It wasn't only the women directly involved who suffered. Haroun-al-Raschid, in that case, would have more than matched Henry. But out of his first petulant defiance of the Pope grew the schism between Rome and England, and directly as a result of that schism came Henry's bloody crimes of execution. He murdered, robbed, betrayed, schemed; yet the worse he became the less did he think he was at fault. The world might betray him, the very Pope might misinterpret God's will, but Henry stood firm. He consulted his conscience, buttoned up his nasty little mouth, and went ahead, destroying whatever he thought stood in his way. He was romantic, sentimental, poetic, like a weeping rhinoceros. One doesn't mind an ordinary murderer so much, but he was a sanctimonious sneak. The horror of the picture is increased a hundredfold by that mouth.

Really, one's sympathy for Henry can be evoked only at the beginning of his kingship, when he had not yet fallen into the habit of being sorry for himself. It is at the most a mechanical, anachronistic sympathy. We happen to live in a civilization in which marriage is supposedly based on love, or at least on personal, free choice. This conception of marriage is so important to us that even our dwindling supply of monarchs is ruled by it to some extent. Thus a prince or princess who marries according to government arrangement is invariably declared to have made a love match. Admittedly, when a prince or princess does actually make a love match *not* arranged by the government the reaction of the public is not one of wholehearted approval. Usually the offending royalty is pushed out of the way to end his days in some neutral sunny clime. But this does not in the least affect the pretty fable. Kings and queens nowadays, we firmly declare, marry for love. It is really quite simple; any king with his country's welfare at heart need only remember to fall in love with an eligible girl rather than an ineligible one. And I must say, when one thinks of Henry VIII there is something to be said for our point of view.

When Henry was only ten his elder brother Arthur, the fifteen-year-old heir apparent, was married to Catherine, daughter of Ferdinand and Isabella of Spain, because it was the best political move his father Henry VII could think of at the time. It was the custom to go through the religious form of this sort of marriage as early as possible, since on one side or the other, whichever had most to gain, there was eagerness to get the contract settled before some other principality should step in and steal the prize. Mere betrothals could be broken; they were friable contracts. Marriages, however, were hard and fast. The Pope saw to that.

Sometimes these marriages of state took place when the bride, or groom, was too young for sexual intercourse, and it was because of such a situation that Henry's first troubles with the Church were to arise. Catherine was sixteen and mature. But was Arthur capable? He was only fifteen and rather sickly, but the court let Nature take its own course. Just what course Nature took still remains undecided by public opinion, there being two schools of thought on it, one led by those who believe Catherine and the other by Henry's supporters. It is strange that any ambiguity should ever have attached to the question. Delicacy would not have restrained courtiers from finding out every detail of the wedding night, after the young couple had been undressed and put to bed together; delicacy in such matters was unknown in 1501. Arthur's potency, moreover, was of legitimate interest to all his prospective subjects. Unfortunately, however, there *was* ambiguity, and the question was to become burningly important on two occasions, once before Henry's marriage to Catherine, and again, to an intense degree, when he tried to get a divorce. The truth must have been known to a number of people, but after some years and under bullying they forgot it. Even Catherine might possibly have forgotten. Such lapses of memory in girls are not uncommon.

One of the attendant nobles told a silly little story, it seems, the morning after the wedding night. Arthur, he said, on awakening, called to him from the curtained bed and demanded a cup of warm wine, announcing that marriage was thirsty work. The Prince of Wales added, "Last night I was in the midst of Spain." Whether he really said it or not, this trivial bit of schoolboy prurience was to rock the world before it was forgotten.

Arthur was consumptive. He died a few months after the wedding, and now the second son Henry was Prince of Wales, and what on earth were they to do with Catherine, that childish widow? An embarrassing question. She had brought a good dowry, according to the agreements, when she married Arthur, but only half of it had actually been paid. Ferdinand and Isabella, bargaining to save that half, argued that she should now marry Henry, Prince of Wales, but the English retorted that it was very much against Church teachings that a man should marry his brother's wife. And they were right: according to Leviticus 20:21 it was impurity. ". . . he hath uncovered his brother's nakedness; they shall be childless." One doesn't know exactly why a man's sister-in-law's nakedness should be his brother's nakedness as well, but there it was in the Bible, mysterious and terrifying. There was only one way out: very likely even that was blocked. Had Catherine and Arthur had sexual intercourse? If they had, all was settled; but if they hadn't, then they hadn't really been man and wife, and it would not be sin for Catherine to marry Henry.

Catherine said she was a virgin. A report was made after examination; Catherine *was* a virgin, said the examiners. So that was all right, said the Spaniards triumphantly.

But it didn't clear the way, for Henry VII was not sure he couldn't do better for his son this time. For eight years he wavered, never quite committing himself, scheming with his confidant Wolsey, the chaplain, and changing his mind with every wind that blew on Catherine's sails. Sometimes her prospects of power-inheritance brightened, sometimes they dimmed. Her position at court was intolerable, but she had to tolerate it nevertheless. In the meantime, the prince was growing up, cheerfully accepting the possibility that he might one day marry Catherine. There was no reason not to be cheerful: he found no lack of amusement during the interim of bachelorhood.

Poor Catherine could wish for no happier way out of her embarrassment than to be married to Henry, or indeed to anybody. As things were, her father-in-law snubbed her, Ferdinand never sent her any money, and the court neglected her. Any woman's lot was pretty miserable in the sixteenth century, but even lower-class women were better off than were princesses. According to all reports but Thomas More's, Catherine was no beauty. Stocky and fair, with a broad blond face and pale blue eyes, she was passable—just a nice, eligible girl.

The eligibility happened to outweigh other considerations at the time Henry VII died, and so Henry VIII, amiably enough, married her at last.

For a long time things went well for Catherine. In marrying the King she had fulfilled her destiny as she had been taught to do, but after a while people began to wonder what was to come next. There were grave disappointments. Though the Queen conceived readily enough, she had miscarriages almost as readily. The first boy she bore alive managed to go on living only six weeks. She did produce one baby, Mary, who survived, but Mary was only a daughter, and the much-desired sons did not live. It seemed gravely dangerous that England might be governed by a queen. Elizabeth had not yet been born to prove how effective a queen can be.

· Everyone knew, and often cheerfully referred to the fact, that the King had syphilis, but they did not know enough to link up cause and effect regarding all those stillborn boys. Barrenness or Catherine's kind of ill luck was always assumed to be the woman's fault. However, Henry didn't reproach Catherine. At that time he had good manners toward his wife. He was jovially certain with each pregnancy that it would be all right this time, and that a healthy boy would be born. He was jovial even when Mary was born and survived; if he and Catherine could produce a daughter, he said, they could yet produce a son as well. Besides, the baby, female though it was, was still a baby: it disproved all the clucking old women who had begun to recall the Leviticus business about a man's brother's nakedness and the curse of childlessness. Henry was glad and eager to disprove all that, until he met Anne Boleyn.

He was to marry four women after Anne, but she is the one we all remember. That is because she made the most trouble and was the woman for whom he quarreled with the Pope. We remember her as well for being the prettiest, with the most character. It wasn't a very nice one, but it was vivid.

The story need not be told again in all its detail; it is probably as well known as any in history how Henry suddenly realized he had been living in sin with his brother's wife for eighteen years, and how he insisted it was his conscience and not his lust after Anne Boleyn that made it imperative he be divorced, and how the Church stood firm in refusing. Henry would probably have let matters drift there, for his nature was not capable of sustaining long-drawn bouts, and he had gone to bed with his girl anyway. But Anne Boleyn pushed him farther and farther; she would not allow him to back down.

She was a determined and very confident young woman. Knowing how Henry was later to develop, we in our superior knowledge are sometimes appalled by her presumption. She was not only very sure of herself; she was fond of her royal lover, though not fervently in love, as she had been with young Percy. Henry was still attractive. The world must have appeared all her own property. The disease of swelled-headedness afflicted Anne Boleyn just as it did Henry himself, and for a long time it looked as if her estimate of her own value was correct.

Anne and England believed that for love of her the King deserted Wolsey, who died of it. For love of her Catherine was set aside and her solemn marriage denounced as if it had never existed. For love of her, Henry split with the Papist Church and robbed its possessions wherever he could lay hands on them, and in time set up his own church. So thought Anne Boleyn in her simple, direct, sixteenth-century way. Actually, it was only his own desire Henry loved, as Anne was to find out. And so, in sorrow and violence and trickery and terror, the Church of England was born.

"What laws have been enacted, what noble and ancient monasteries overthrown and defaced . . . how many famous and notable clerks have suffered death, what charitable foundations were perverted from the relief of the poor unto profane uses. . . . If eyes be not blind men may see, if ears be not stopped they may hear, and if pity be not exiled they may lament the sequel of this pernicious and inordinate carnal love. The plague whereof is not ceased (although this love lasted but a while)." Cavendish wrote this in his *Life and Death of Thomas Wolsey.*

Everyone who had nothing to gain by the sack of the monasteries felt the same way, and blamed the proceedings, not on the King—it would have been impious and dangerous to do that—but on the object of his "pernicious and inordinate carnal love." The people remained disinclined to accept Henry's own version of his nobility of spirit, his conscientious scruples. His arguments seemed all the more muddled in the face of the well-known fact that for five years he had been enjoying an affair with Anne's older sister Mary Carey before he transferred his affections.

There was something in the Bible against a man lying with women who were sisters, just as there was against a woman having relations with men who were brothers. People couldn't, then, subscribe wholeheartedly to Henry's arguments against the spiritual authorities. Like Anne, they were simple and direct; they blamed it all on her.

Cynically they watched her grab Wolsey's magnificent house and all the other property she could get. Sympathetically they watched Queen Catherine, proud and stubborn, retiring from the world. Flashing and preening herself, the dark-eyed Anne queened it at Hampton Court. It was too much, even for a people not yet Puritan. They did not love Anne Boleyn.

Yet I think she must have been lovable; gay and pretty and laughing. The relentless spite with which she pursued her enemies did not dim her black eyes nor dull her glistening hair. She was sure of herself at first, so sure that she pitted herself cheerfully against the almighty Church; so sure that as soon as she thought herself pregnant, long before the marriage had taken place—which was bigamous at best, insisted the Pope—she blurted the news to Wyatt, openly, in the hearing of everyone. She was triumphant. It would be a boy. It was sure to be a boy.

In the last long weeks before she was delivered, however, even cocky Anne grew nervous and jealous, as women do. She accused Henry of infidelity. Then, to her amazement, he gave her full warning of what was to come. For the first time he turned nasty.

"You close your eyes, as your betters did before you! You ought to know that it is in my power in a single instant to lower you further than I raised you up!"

Perhaps she felt a chill. I think she did; she was very intelligent.

I have said that Henry had the usual masculine faults, magnified by his position. One of them was a surplus of conventionality. Henry was a very conventional man; that is why he kept marrying his mistresses, and losing interest in them when they became

wives. He was like the man in the case history who could make
love only in brothels, or that other man who was unable to have
his wife unless she first took off her wedding ring. Without the
conflict of sin versus duty, Henry had little urge. Anne, as soon
as she was his by law, even though it was a law he happened to
have made himself, became just another wife.

Then on top of all that, she outraged him by giving birth to a
daughter.

It was very thoughtless of her, Henry could not help but feel,
a typically selfish thing for a wife to do. As befitted a king, he forgave her, but he had been badly used and he could not forget it.
The golden bowl was broken. Mildly at first, and then with in-
creasing sharpness, that conscience of his began to ache. He was,
after all, a conventional man. *Should* he have married this
woman? Was it legal?

God, who never let him down, soon gave him a sign. Anne's
next pregnancy ended prematurely, with a stillborn boy, just
about the time that Henry fell in love with Jane Seymour.
Obviously a change was indicated. Opportunely, miraculously,
Heaven Itself working through the agency of Cromwell, it was
discovered that Anne had committed the treasonous crime of infidelity. And not only once, and not only with one lover. There
had been three ordinary lovers, with her own brother thrown
in to give the proceedings that added dash of horror and disgust
which is necessary when a queen is to be killed. They were all
promptly thrown into the Tower, Queen and lovers alike.

Whatever else one can say about Henry VIII, he gave his
people circuses. Here was something they could chew on in lieu
of bread for a long time to come. Anne the wicked sorceress, the
merciless dethroner of queens, was come to this, and it served her
jolly well right.

Still, it was not so easily dismissed a matter that a queen's head
had been cut off, and when the thing was done and everyone had

subsided, there came a natural uneasy revulsion. People had to reassure themselves. She *was* awful, they reflected. Which may account for the persistence of the rumor, even today, that Anne really did all those things she was convicted for. Plenty of people believe it. One modern writer has gone so far as to explain Anne's "nymphomania" as a post-puerperal frenzy of some sort.

I simply cannot understand this belief. Look at the facts! Look at Henry's record! He had never wanted for lackeys willing to swear themselves black in the face telling lies for him. That delicate conscience of his kept him from telling lies for himself, but as he was King it wasn't really necessary that he do it. He had Cromwell to think up Anne's crimes, Cranmer to condemn them, and men-at-arms to carry out his just commands, once the framework was established. Most exquisite dispensation of all, he need not give direct orders; he need not know anything about it. He could face his Lord shining with virtue on the Day of Judgment —not that the Lord would ever be impertinent enough to insist upon judging Henry VIII!

That is the first and most glaringly obvious reason for questioning the case against Anne Boleyn. The second one lies in Anne's character. It was, I repeat, not a nice character, but it wasn't weakly foolish. On the contrary, she had played her game with amazing deftness, outguessing the most astute politician at court. Nor was her feat a flash in the pan. She campaigned for years without taking one seriously false step. She knew the material she had to work with; she knew men. Admittedly she became overweening in her first pride, but that self-confidence soon suffered a severe blow when Henry began to snarl at her within a mere five months of their marriage. She knew what that meant. She knew, too, that he was having affairs. After the birth of Elizabeth, she went so far as to try to pick out his mistresses for him, selecting people she could trust. She was aware of Jane Seymour, after he met Jane, and the threat the new infatuation implied. Anne was chastened long before the deadly crisis. Only an imbecile would have dared take the risk of a love affair under these conditions, let alone several love affairs, and Anne was no imbecile.

The third and last argument is that her accusers in their zeal outdid themselves. Had they settled for one lover, the easily intimidated "base-born" Mark Smeaton, we might have believed it. He was a dancer and musician; musicians were traditionally suspect because they were always hanging around the women, armed with the sentimental appeal of sweet song. Anne was a neglected wife and all that. Mark Smeaton was just possible. . . . But the accusers piled on the agony well beyond him. The tale of two more lovers, which she allegedly switched around night by night with monotonous regularity, begins to strain credulity. And then to cap it all they brought out that old chestnut about incest with her brother George. Incest was the thing unimaginative people always thought of when they wanted to smear others. It was the great crime; it was the conventional shocker; it was handed down from the ancient Greeks and so, they felt, it must be good. And so they put it into Anne's dossier.

No, no, one feels like saying to the historians, don't give me that. What do you take me for?

They were not all so silly in Anne's day. Unpopular as she was, some of the people resented what had happened to her, knowing why. An inn that stood on Boleyn land took for its sign, "The Bullen Butchered," and not for some time did the proprietors moderate it to "The Bull and Butcher."

Anyone who thinks Anne Boleyn guilty of the crimes she was killed for simply wants to believe it for his own pleasure, or else because of that long-standing, widespread, nitwitted conviction that once a woman is no better than she should be, she is bound to do anything and everything. Not that all this matters now to Anne Boleyn, who died with dignity four hundred years ago. She was a bad girl, but she died better than had the whimpering Wolsey, whom she had helped to kill

Henry's sentimental career thereafter becomes just a bit tiresome, like the long roster of marriages which characterize a film star's life. We remember Jane Seymour chiefly because she was neither killed off nor divorced, but tactfully managed to die after giving birth to Edward. Anne of Cleves was an awkward mistake and hardly counts. Henry found her so unattractive that he couldn't consummate the marriage, and the well-oiled divorce went through with more speed than Reno's litigation could provide today.

But Katheryn Howard provides a break in the monotony, as one might expect from a cousin of Anne Boleyn. Pretty—at least so we are told, though her portrait makes her look like a very plain abbess—light and vivacious, and much younger than Henry, she married him because it seemed to the Howards such a good thing. By that time any wife with sense would have realized that her chances of survival were slim, but Katheryn didn't have much sense. As for the crimes of treasonable infidelity with which she was taxed, unlike her cousin Anne Boleyn she actually committed them. She was in love with her kinsman Culpepper, as she had been in love before with other pretty boys. She slept with Culpepper as she had slept with others. She loved him. Artlessly, she said so at the execution block. Unnatural wench, her mind was not on herself when she died. We cannot say as much for the others.

"I would rather have had him for a husband than be mistress of the world, but sin blinded me and greed of grandeur; and since mine is the fault, mine also is the suffering, and my great sorrow is that Culpeper should have had to die through me. . . . I die a Queen, but I would rather die the wife of Culpeper. God have mercy on my soul."

Poor, pretty child. Through her very lack of desire to wound, she gave Henry the most exquisite torture he had ever experienced. Betrayed, cuckolded, and, worst of all, forgotten! He, the magnificent Henry VIII! He had cut off her head, but he could not cut that memory out of his heart. Of all the tears Henry shed in his emotional life, these were the most sincere and painful. Not only herself, but three other wives were avenged. I don't think we have ever given Katheryn Howard enough credit.

We could go on to the next Queen, the third Catherine and sixth wife, Katharine Parr, but I prefer to take leave of Henry like this, sobbing his heart out for lost pride. It is a scene to remember. It moderates my feelings when I look at the mouth in Holbein's portrait.

The Warrior Queen

OUR CODE OF MORALS is what we, or our ancestors, or a combination of the two, have made it. Such as it is, we come by it honestly. We may not always like it, but we are used to it and would scarcely attempt to meddle with the main outlines. People who depart from it are called immoral, as if there were only one possible code, that which we accept. We don't admit that these others have a code at all. When they cling to their own stubborn notions, therefore, we call them not only immoral but unnatural.

It is unnatural, we feel, for a man to have relations with his sister, as every Ptolemy did in Egypt. We believe this firmly, and invoke a mysterious thing called "instinct" when we need help in convincing unbelievers. There are a few things that we have changed our minds about, as a matter of fact: until a recent act of Parliament, for example, it was unnatural for a man to marry his deceased wife's sister. It was also, of course, illegal.

"I could not look my wife's sister in the face without blushing, when I go home tonight," thundered a furiously shocked M.P., "were I to vote against keeping this law."

Yet all of a sudden it has become all right for an Englishman to marry his deceased wife's sister, and people everywhere, M.P.s included, look their sisters-in-law in the face without blushing.

Nevertheless, we have not gone completely mad on reform. Far from it. Some taboos are still retained, and they don't look shaky. It is still immoral, and presumably will continue to be so, for a man to own more than one wife at a time. It is even more immoral for a woman to own a lot of husbands simultaneously; we do not approve of that at all.

Because of limited space and time I hardly dare begin to discuss the myriad non-sexual aspects of morality, but we can mention a few. There is our strange predeliction, for example, for the truth. Perhaps we don't always tell it, but we know we ought to. Representatives of other civilizations distress us when they tell lies. First we are dismayed at their whoppers, and then we become righteously indignant. And there are other things we do not always see eye to eye about when we encounter foreign tribes. There are the food taboos. Some people are disgusted because we eat oysters, and other people disgust us because they eat human flesh. We cannot let these differences pass with a tolerant shrug. We become shocked; we cling to our morality, blindly faithful.

This, I am sure, is as it should be. Some virtues can go too far, and tolerance, possibly, is one of them, though to be quite frank, I have yet to see that particular virtue carried to excess. Sometimes, thinking of the rigors life held for the early Christian explorers, I feel wrung with pity. Think of the emotions of Portuguese adventurers, faced with the new spaces and races they discovered! They have always been a proud, assured, inflexible people, easily shocked. Yet it was they who first made the discovery which still can render us so uncomfortable, centuries later, that the world is full of human beings who don't subscribe to our moral code. Their horrified protests ring out with sincere anguish, even today, when we unlock the archives. But the Portuguese did not sit back and accept these differences in any impotent spirit of tolerance. They grasped the nettle and set to work, teaching the one true code. Nothing discouraged them, and in the end they usually had their reward, even against tremendous odds. Such a triumph was won in East Africa, early in the seventeenth century, and this is how it happened.

When the new Portuguese governor arrived in Loanda he received a surprise.

No doubt he was prepared for a certain amount of unconventionality in West Africa, though not so much as he was to encounter. João Correa de Sousa, for that was his name, had been assigned from Lisbon to this post in a colony not quite fifty years established. The white men could scarcely be described as safely installed, but Loanda itself was a large, well-built city, though unhealthy, and Portuguese influence had spread far into the fastnesses of the mainland.

Some native chiefs had by now come over to the Portuguese and willingly embraced their faith, giving in return the important amenities of a free hand in slave capturing. Others had not. The most powerful of those who resisted was Ngola Nzinga Mbandi, great King of Ndongo, whose territory the white men called Angola, after his title or rank "Ngola." ("Angola" was to remain the name of a district the boundaries of which have radically shifted.)

João Correa de Sousa was aware that he was stepping straight into a war of long standing with this King; it was one of the affairs he most desired to settle.

It would, of course, be far better for the Portuguese not to be forced to waste their men and ammunition in such futile struggles. The governor was willing to be reasonable with the King of Ndongo—even to placate him to some extent—both because he hoped to be able to spread the holy word of God a little farther into the dark continent, and because peace would give an added impetus to slave export. A large part of Portugal's wealth depended on Loanda. Sincerely in the name of God, the Portuguese traded profitably with the Negroes, exchanging for slaves commodities which natives highly prized—cowries from the fisheries on the island opposite Loanda, cloth from Europe or native palm cloth, brandy, salt, and horse tails. Cowries were used for native currency; cloth was used for their scanty garments; brandy intoxicated more thoroughly than palm wine and was much in demand. Salt in large crystals was rare in Africa; it is still as good as money or better in certain isolated districts of that continent. Horse tails, like elephant tails, yielded hair which the Negroes fashioned into magic rings or bangles, as they do today.

To obtain these luxuries, chiefs would go out on expeditions and collect prisoners, which they handed over to the whites. The Portuguese hastily "converted" their miserable captives, loaded them in crowded ships, and sent them off, chiefly to Brazil, though some were shipped to other South American ports and to Lisbon. The cruelty of these voyages was unbelievable, but it was a lucrative trade which satisfied almost everyone but the victims concerned. The black slave dealers had no qualms; slave trading was an old African institution, though admittedly before the arrival of the Portuguese it had never been practiced on such a grand scale. Some of the Portuguese themselves, however, felt compunctions, and a few of them, usually missionaries, now and then wrote protests against the methods and even against the entire institution of slavery. When criticism became too loud, the traders grudgingly instituted a reform of sorts; they sometimes sent priests along on the slave ships in order to administer last rites to the dying. The trade continued to flourish; it was important to Portugal that it should flourish. João Correa de Sousa, as governor, had his orders: the trade should not suffer longer from the interference of Ngola Nzinga Mbandi or any other native ruler.

So it was a relief to learn upon his arrival that this troublesome King had actually made overtures for an end to hostilities, and was rumored to be sending an ambassador to discuss a peace treaty. Ngola Nzinga Mbandi was a force with which it would be wise to compromise. He headed a formidable army of the dreaded Jaga people, and though not a Jaga himself, he had from all accounts adopted many of their most terrible habits. Of the cannibal Jaga we shall have more to say in due course.

Ngola Nzinga Mbandi was a usurper. True, his father had been King of Ndongo before him, but the rightful heir was another son whose mother had been Queen, whereas this King's mother was only a slave. When the old King died—by common consent of his people, who assassinated him when his tyranny became too severe—Ngola Nzinga Mbandi went earnestly to work and won the throne for himself. He was not elected; he was a self-made King. He slaughtered his way to the throne, executing his opponents and competitors, in his zeal killing not only his half brother but his nephew as well, the son of Nzinga, one of his three sisters. As soon as his position was secure he began harrying the Portuguese, just as his father had done.

He had not had it all his own way, as a matter of fact; he had been forced by the Portuguese and their allies to flee into the interior. The white men's troops still sporadically attacked and plundered his villages, carrying off the inhabitants and selling them at the coast. His strongest adherent and dependent, the King of lower Ndongo, had been so badly whipped that he paid tribute to the invaders; a hundred slaves every year. Knowing all this, the new governor had every reason to feel hopeful of good results from the projected interview with Ngola Nzinga Mbandi's envoy. He was also curious, for the envoy was a woman, the Princess Nzinga, sister to the King, and to a seventeenth-century Portuguese such a situation was astonishing. Portuguese women were not at all independent.

The lady arrived and was received with all due honor by the city garrison drawn up under arms. She was lodged at the house of a prominent citizen and a few days later had her first interview with Correa de Sousa.

This meeting was not, incidentally, a romantic encounter, whatever the hopeful reader may for a moment expect. In 1621 Nzinga was forty years old. From the European point of view she could never have been a beauty, even in early youth. She had taken a good deal of trouble with her appearance, but she had not been motivated by any ordinary feminine spirit of vanity in so doing. She was dressed simply, but as befitted a person of royal blood. Correa de Sousa, as a newcomer, was no doubt unfamiliar with the finer points of the national costume of Angola; he was probably unaware that Nzinga was dressed as a man. But she was. A bark-cloth skirt or apron covered her privates in the masculine fashion rather than the feminine, which in itself was significant of Nzinga's personality. A royal leopard skin hung down from her waist, which was bound with a belt of buffalo tail. Above the waist Nzinga naturally wore nothing—no Negro did—but a sort of skimpy mantle of palm cloth covered one arm. Her hair was uncovered, though several ornaments were stuck into it. Her nose was bored straight across from one nostril to the other, and, in honor of the occasion, she had probably placed decorative plugs in the holes.

It is tempting to pause here and imagine to the full the stupefaction which must have possessed those Portuguese gentlemen. The governor was new to the colony, but the others had no doubt lived long enough in Loanda to have picked up many of the extremely elegant habits which were remarked and derided by world travelers. A plethora of servants, a vast amount of easy, cheap authority, the excuse of Loanda's insalubrious climate had made the colonists languid and lazy and delicate; each of them was followed by a concourse of attendants who carried handkerchief, mantle, even comb. Nzinga, in her unclothed hauteur and with her latent ferocity, seemed a more vital, virile figure than any of them.

The minute she arrived, followed by a retinue of male and female slaves who stood at the door, the unexpected occurred.

In their preparations the Portuguese had innocently slighted their diplomatic guest. The governor sat in a chair, but no chair had been provided for the princess; instead, two gold-embroidered cushions lay on the floor, for her use and that of the interpreter. In Portugal ladies did not sit on chairs; they always crouched on cushions. But Nzinga was no Portuguese lady; indeed, as Correa de Sousa was soon to discover, she did not like to think of herself as a lady at all. She glanced at the cushions; she glanced at the governor's chair. Then, without saying a word, she turned and looked at one of her female slaves. The woman promptly advanced to the center of the room and got down on her elbows and knees. With unperturbed dignity Nzinga seated herself on the level back thus presented, and signified that she was ready to begin with business. Swallowing their various emotions, the Portuguese officials tried to concentrate on the matter in hand.

Their wonder grew. The woman Nzinga proved herself intelligent, shrewd, and unexpectedly diplomatic. To tell the truth, she was not the first African female to occupy an important position in public affairs. Royal blood in her country was a powerful thing, and there had been famous queens in the Congo and Ndongo, in her own family as in others. None of the rest of these women, however, went so far as did Nzinga in demanding and holding a man's place in warlike or hunting activities, nor did the others ever achieve a reputation like hers. Her greatest fame was still to come, but during her stay in Loanda she made her personality felt.

During the preliminary skirmish which this conversation proved to be, the governor asked how much tribute the King of Ndongo was prepared to pay. The King's sister professed herself taken aback by such an inquiry; he was not prepared to pay anything, she said. Tribute is paid only by a conquered nation to the nation which has conquered it. Her brother Ngola Nzinga Mbandi was not a vanquished king suing the victorious Portuguese for peace. The situation was quite otherwise: she represented a power which was willing to treat with another, equal, power on the subject of amicable relations.

Nzinga had a strong case. One of the things which her brother considered a grievance was that his dominion was often invaded by unofficial raiders from the Portuguese colony, parties made up of mulattoes, Europeanized Negroes (who were called *Negros calçados*—shoe-wearing blacks), and their leaders, who were ordinary white slave traders without portfolio, so to speak. These people had stirred up so many battles with their lawless expeditions that the governor in office before Correa de Sousa admitted their undesirability, and passed a law decreeing that only *pumbieros descalços,* which is to say shoeless hawkers, were henceforth permitted to penetrate the interior in search of slaves. But formulating a law was one thing, and enforcing it quite another.

Obviously, many questions would have to be discussed before the treaty was arranged, and Nzinga's stay in Loanda would be a fairly protracted one. The first interview came at last to a close. The ambassadress rose to take her leave. She had already started for the exit door when the governor noticed that the miserable slave on whom she had been sitting remained crouching on the floor, quite motionless. He called out:

"You've forgotten your woman!"

Nzinga turned her head slightly and said over her shoulder, "Oh, my chair? But of course I don't carry furniture about with me! You may keep it."

She was gone. The woman still crouched in the middle of the room at their feet. The elegant white gentlemen were left staring at one another.

Probably one influence which formed Nzinga's character, and not the least, was that of the Jaga with whom her brother waged his wars. She spent most of her time with them.

It is not easy to decide what one should call the Jaga, for they were not in the ordinary sense of the word a tribe or race. They drew their numbers from all or any sources. The only thing they passed along from one generation to another was their ferocity and their peculiar brand of philosophy. It is not even known where they originated; theirs was a name to terrify the other Africans, and inevitably many apocryphal stories were told of them. Some anthropologists say that they originated in East Africa, others say they came from Sierra Leone; when the Portuguese first encountered them (to the cost of the whites) they were ensconced in Central Africa and roamed wherever they wished, killing and robbing as they went.

The Jaga were true cannibals. Other Africans were part-time cannibals who ate human flesh for ceremonial purposes or as a change from their everyday diet, or in the excitement of victory after battle, but the Jaga were cannibals as a matter of habit, convenience, and conviction. They kept no flocks nor indulged in any other agricultural pursuits. They were purely nomadic robbers. A man named Andrew Battell, who got back to England about ten years before Nzinga paid her visit to Loanda, lived eighteen months with these people after he fled to the interior from the Portuguese, who were keeping him captive.

"They rise in harvest," he told Purchas, who afterward hastened home and made a record of his reports, "and invading some country, there stay as long as they find the palms, or other means of maintenance, and then seek new adventure. For they neither plant nor sow, nor breed up cattle, and, which is more strange, they nourish up none of their own children, although they have ten or twenty wives a man, of the properest and comeliest slaves they can take. But when they are in travail they dig a hole in the earth, which presently receiveth in that dark prison of death the newborn creature, not yet made happy with the light of life. Their reason is that they will not be troubled with education, nor in their flitting wanderings be troubled with such cumbersome burthens. . . . For of the conquered nations they preserve the boys from ten to twenty years of age, and bring them up as the

hope of their succession . . . with education fitting their de-
signs. These wear a collar about their neck in token of slavery,
until they bring an enemy's head slain in battle, and then they are
uncollared, free'd, and dignified with the title of soldiers; if one
of them runs away he is killed and eaten; so that, hemmed in be-
twixt hope and fear, they grow very resolute and adventurous,
their collars breeding shame, disdain, and desperate fury, till they
redeem their freedom as you have heard."

These were the people who were Nzinga's playmates in her
youth, companions in her maturity, and bedmates presumably all
the time. Later she maintained a kind of male Jaga harem, or
bodyguard of masculine concubines, rather in the reputed fashion
of Catherine the Great. Knowing all this after the event, one may
be inclined to wonder a little at something she did before she left
Loanda, where she lived the better part of a year, concluding a
good workmanlike treaty which did not include a tribute clause.
Nzinga joined the Holy Roman Catholic Church. Yes, she did.
In the process she was baptized Dona Anna de Sousa, João
Correa de Sousa acting as her godfather.

The ambassadress enjoyed the whole affair. She thought the
Church such a good idea that she returned to her brother the
King full of ideas to convert him as well. She met with success up
to a point, for he was infected enough by her enthusiasm to ask
the authorities at Loanda to send him a priest. His request was
promptly granted, no doubt too promptly, because those responsible did not take into account the imperious pride which was
characteristic of Nzinga's family. Instead of sending on the mission what the King expected as his right—a Portuguese priest—
they nominated a subject of Ngola Nzinga Mbandi himself, a
native who had been ordained there at Loanda. Not unnaturally,
the King took umbrage at this action, which he considered a
deliberate snub. He scrapped the treaty his sister Nzinga had so
laboriously made with the governor. He went back to war. But

bad luck pursued him. He was beaten off, his army deserted, and he fled to Ndangi, the island where his ancestors were buried.

There he too was buried with his fathers. Some historians say that he was murdered by a vassal of the Portuguese, but others think Nzinga poisoned him, in revenge for his murder of her son. If she did kill her brother, and for that reason, she certainly concealed her resentment for a long time. It is more likely—in fact, it is exceedingly likely—that she coveted the throne for herself. Moreover, she carried her brother's bones around with her for the rest of her life; they always accompanied her to battle or religious ceremony thereafter in a silver casket she had procured from the Portuguese. But this practice of carting one's family remains about with one was a custom common to her tribe and need not be taken as a sign of affection. Nzinga's emotions do not seem to have been consistent, in our sense of the word, so perhaps she had harbored a grudge against her brother even when she was representing him as a loyal ambassadress; if she *did* poison him it might have been because of her dead son. One cannot without effort think of Nzinga as a loving, mourning mother, but anything is possible.

At any rate, we know that she followed her brother's example when at last she mounted to the throne in 1623. She killed *his* son.

The new Queen also announced that she was no longer a Christian, and though one might be excused for remarking that she had never behaved very much like one, even at the supposed heights of her pious phase, she seemed to be doing her earnest best to live up to this, her latest resolve. The beginning of her reign, like that of her brother's, was marked by a number of political murders apart from that of the heir presumptive. She cemented her cordial relations with the Jaga who had followed the late King until they saw that his power was on the decline.

Then she got down to serious business and declared war on Portugal.

The Portuguese immediately counterattacked, diplomatically, by commanding the King of Ndongo (as they called him—he was that same vice-king of lower Ndongo who had long paid tribute to them) to fight his dangerous neighbor on their behalf. Yet if Nzinga had been willing to make a deal with the Portuguese by calling off the war in return for the vice-king's territory, which she claimed as hers by right, they would not have hesitated to betray him. Nzinga would not agree, however; she much preferred, always, to fight.

A strong force of Portuguese promptly set out to subdue the impertinent female. They made their way to Ndangi Island where Nzinga was encamped with her forces among the tombs of dead kings. The Queen, following the Jaga fashion, asked the spirit of Ngola Nzinga Mbandi for advice, and he seems to have told her not to give battle. She therefore fled before the pursuing Portuguese. They caught up with her army and beat them badly, taking her two sisters prisoner. Nzinga, however, escaped into further reaches of forest toward the east and stayed hidden with the remnants of her troops until the Portuguese went back to Loanda. Then she returned to her old camp on Ndangi Island to meditate fresh forays.

The two sisters were kept in Loanda, where they were of course converted, and baptized under the names of Dona Barbara and Dona Engraçia. Later they escaped.

For the following eight years Queen Nzinga carried on a harrying war against the Portuguese. She would have gone all out in a direct campaign, but a rival Jaga, Kasanji, had taken advantage of her temporary retirement to build up dangerous strength, and he distracted her attention and kept her forces employed against his own, rather than the Portuguese. As a side line which met with more success, she attacked and vanquished a neighboring country, Matamba, which like her own was ruled by a woman, though Muongo Matamba, the other queen, was not of such stern stuff as was her conqueror. When Nzinga branded her royal captive as a slave, Muongo Matamba died of grief. Her country became for a time after that a battlefield between the two fierce Jaga leaders, Nzinga and Kasanji.

In 1636 the Portuguese governor managed to get in touch with Nzinga through two missionaries, and a rather precarious peace was declared. It was not to last.

Quite naturally, the amazing woman had by this time become a household word of terror throughout Central Africa. Her eccentricities became more pronounced through the years, and a most interesting account of her has been left by the Dutchman Dapper, who, like Purchas, collected and published a number of travelers' tales, including this from a Captain Fuller.

"She is a cunning and prudent virago, so much addicted to arms, that she hardly uses other exercise; and withal so generously valiant, that she never hurt a Portuguese after quarter given, and commanded all her slaves and soldiers the like.

"She and her people (for the most part) lead an unsettled life, roving up and down from place to place, like the Jagas; Before any enterprise undertaken, though of meanest concern, they ask counsel of the Devil; to which end they have an idol, to whom they sacrifice a living person, of the wisest and comeliest they can pick out."

The following description of this ceremony is not unlike that given by Andrew Battell, who told Purchas some years earlier that he had witnessed a human sacrifice made by a great Jaga chief Kalendula. However, Battell says that the Jaga had no idols, only fetishes, and his report is probably the more accurate. Queen Nzinga sacrificed not to an idol, but to one or all of her five favorite ancestral spirits, including Ngola Nzinga Mbandi. His bones, remember, were always there with her, in their silver casket.

"The Queen against the time of this sacrifice, clothes herself in man's apparel (nor indeed does she at any time go otherwise habited) hanging about her the skins of beasts, before and behind, with a sword about her neck, an axe at her girdle, and a bow and arrow in her hand, leaping according to their custom, now here, then there, as nimbly as the most active among her attendants; all the while striking her *engema,* that is, two iron balls, which serve her instead of drums.

"When she thinks she has made a show long enough, in a masculine manner, and thereby hath wearied herself, then she takes a broad feather and sticks it through the holes of her boar'd nose for a sign of war.

"She herself in this rage, begins with the first of those appointed to be sacrificed; and cutting of his head, drinks a great draught of his blood. Then follow the stoutest commanders and do as she hath done; and this with a great hurly-burly, tumult, and playing upon instruments about their idol."

A curious note follows close upon this, the more curious when one recalls that Nzinga at that time was at least fifty-five years old. "The Queen keeps fifty or sixty young men instead of husbands, each of which may have as many wives as they please, with this proviso, that if any of them be with child, themselves must kill the infant as soon as born. . . . The Queen used this very custom at that time, neither dare any of these selected young men own their sex, or mention hers; And for the more orderly concealing thereof, she clothes them in women's apparel, according to her manner, and goeth herself in man's habit, giving out that they are women, and she a man. All these have women's names, but the Queen herself a man's, especially in the army, and will acknowledge no otherwise; nay her favourites dare not say the contrary, upon peril of their heads; and as a testimony therein of their obedience and constancy to her, permits them to go freely among the women; and if they fail in their obligations, they seldom escape to tell further news."

In 1641, a few years after Queen Nzinga made her uneasy truce with Portugal, the Dutch came onto the African scene. In a hasty scramble to beat the date of a Dutch-Portuguese armistice which was soon to be signed, they occupied as much Portuguese territory as they could. Nzinga gladly offered to help these new-comers against her hated enemy, and the combined Dutch and Jaga forces held the Portuguese out of the territory they had them-selves settled until 1648. The Queen suffered a severe defeat two years before the end, however. In the worst battle her sisters were again captured by the Portuguese, and only one of them, Dona Barbara, survived this captivity. With the arrival of Salvador Correa de Sa Benavides in August 1648, Loanda was taken back by the Portuguese, Nzinga's special three hundred Dutch allies surrendered with their compatriots, and the Queen retired once more to the backwoods.

At that point anyone but Nzinga would have called it a day. The redoubtable old warrior did indeed rest on her laurels for some years. But she reappears on the pages of history in the most bizarre role which even she had ever played. In 1655, at the age of seventy-three, Queen Nzinga got religion again.

Her conscience, she said, was troubling her. She had consulted the spirits of her five ancestors, as she so often did. This time—oh horror!—they told her dolefully that they were in hell, the Christian hell, of all places, suffering orthodox tortures. It was all Nzinga's fault too. Only she could save them (and of course her-self as well) by once more joining the Holy Church, and this meant peace with the Portuguese in the bargain.

The old Queen lost no time in making overtures to the proper authorities, and they were more than willing to co-operate. First they let her ransom her surviving sister Dona Barbara, with two hundred slaves. Then they settled with her, amicably, the bound-aries of her domain, which had for so many years been the cause of battle. Even now Nzinga did not pay tribute.

Finally, when she was seventy-five years old, Queen Nzinga

was again received into the Church, and baptized just as she had been before. It was in many ways what might be called an unusual ceremony, especially as immediately after the baptism, and in the same church, she was married. The bridegroom was one Don Salvatore, probably a former member of her harem bodyguard.

Quietly now, no longer troubled by her conscience, Queen Nzinga lived another eight years. She was eighty-three when she died. All the last rites were observed. She was buried in church. There can be no possible doubt, under these circumstances, that her five spiritual counselors are now at ease with their daughter Nzinga in a Christian heaven.

Bride by Proxy

THE GOLDEN COURT of the Sun King, Louis XIV, is always a good spectacle. Louis and his people were openly grabby for wealth, self-indulgent, dedicated to a pursuit which they followed with that fervor often called religious. I do not consider their favorite game politics. That is an ugly word which falls far short of what we need. It is only a synonym for policy, and policy is a cold common-sense thing, whereas Louis's pastime was complicated and passionate. Sometimes he sacrificed reason to pure dazzling technique.

Like many other historical personages, Louis never even thought of losing the world for love, his own love or anyone else's. That does not mean that he lost love for the world, only that he never felt he need make a choice. Why not keep both?

To gain his ends, Louis used love like a master; nay, like a whoremaster. With great difficulty I am restraining myself from using two overworked similes for the pretty women he manipulated. I am resolved to call them neither puppets nor pawns. One does not mind the banality of a good simile, but I feel these are not good. Puppets need supervision for every gesture and act, whereas the girls of Louis's Versailles, once they were pushed out on the stage to play their roles, acted on their own. The King was a psychologist. Such and such a man or woman, given certain directions, could be expected to behave in this way or that. It was all a matter of foresight. Louis gave them the first shove and then trusted to remote control and early training.

Nor were they pawns. I don't know much about chess, but I have always felt that the international game as Louis played it was not subtle enough to be compared to chess. Human intrigue seldom rises above the subtlety of checkers.

The story of Affonso VI of Portugal was one of the many which Louis XIV meddled in. It bears signs of his hand, but it was only a subplot, picked up and developed when the King needed it to strengthen his position and then dropped into obscurity until he happened to think of it again. Most of the time Portugal was out of the main stream. She was a long way off. Travelers neglected her, with the notable exception of England's Charles II, and her own great men neglected the rest of Europe. As a result, she had a highly individual little court, formal in ways unexpected to other Europeans, and then suddenly informal in just as unexpected a manner. Her people were a mixture, in blood and in culture, of North and South, East and West—Iberian, Celt, Moor, and Oriental, with the Roman Catholic Church holding sway over all.

Marie Françoise, who was juggled and bounced in the fountain of Versailles intrigue like a pingpong ball before she married the King of Portugal, could have been one of Louis XIV's more pitiable martyrs. A pretty, frivolous princess, thoroughly French in training, from a court that exemplified form, surface, and decoration, she might almost as well have been set down in Nzinga's savage country as exiled to Portugal. The very amusements of the two sets of courtiers made a contrast which appalled her. At Versailles they had ballet and pageants and exquisite, slow-moving plays in which the King and his followers acted, glittering in silver and pale blue brocade. At Lisbon they murdered bulls. Her husband Affonso was himself like a bull, or, rather, a bull calf.

The Queen had two strong appetites. One, for love, she was born with. The other, for power, she began to take in with her first breath and imbibe with her first milk. Had she been in a position more important to Louis, or had her kingly husband been of greater value to Europe, her fate would have been fixed. She would have had to strangle the sexual appetite and remain Affonso's Queen. As it was, however, she did not have to make a choice. Greedy as her royal master, and left alone among people she considered barbarians, the Frenchwoman accomplished a surprising thing: she ate her cake and had it too. She was a true child of Louis XIV's Versailles.

"Love or power?" one can imagine her guardian angel demanding in stern accents.

"Both, please," says Marie Françoise, reaching out and taking them.

The royal palace at Cintra stands on its mountaintop, a fairy-tale edifice with queer round chimneys, gleaming above the dark green woods and the looping road like one of those Italian castles in Renaissance paintings, from which a brilliant cavalcade winds down to the plain. When one stares up at the countless windows they seem small and faraway. When, inside, one looks out of those same windows, they are larger, but not large enough to afford a view of the full panorama. The walls are thick.

High up in the palace one August day we paused in the stony corridor, where even in the heat of Portuguese summer the air is always dank. An obedient sight-seer, I peered through a door which had a shabby red rope stretched across it, into an ancient bedchamber, not overspacious though there was a lofty ceiling. A faint mark lay across the floor; it looked like a very shallow trough in the stone.

"Here," said my friendly guide, "lived and died poor Dom Affonso VI, a prisoner for many years. He was the rightful King, but his place was usurped. To get him out of the way, they said he was mad." He frowned with an indignation which has survived in his country for more than two hundred and fifty years as he imagined the poor caged creature pacing back and forth over the stone floor. The Portuguese never let any of their history expire.

"He was *not* mad," said the guide, his voice quivering.

But was he altogether sane? It must be admitted that the Braganzas were not in general a stable family. Had Affonso's sister Catherine been more robust, the Stuarts of England would have prospered better. Affonso himself was the victim of worse than weakness. He was crippled at the age of three, when a fever of some sort, which one historian mysteriously calls a "palsie," left him paralyzed on one side. Probably he was bled too often.

He may have been an epileptic. Anyway he was odd, there was no doubt of that. His court attendants were aware of it long before he succeeded to the throne at thirteen, when his father died.

If we had enough recorded details of Affonso's peculiar antics in childhood, some psychiatrist would doubtless slap a label on whatever was wrong with him. (Apart, that is, from the state of royalty, often a disability in itself.) We must content ourselves with such data as we have, which doesn't really prove that he was certifiable according to our lights. Most of the symptoms fall into the wide ditch which lies between sanity and lunacy.

He is alleged to have said at the age of ten, when his older brother Theodosius lay dying, "that he should not be much troubled for his Death, if it should happen, since he should thereby get a Crown. . . ." In a young boy that remark is not necessarily an example of depravity, but there is no doubt it was uncomfortably honest. Throughout his life Affonso was to be awkwardly forthright. The English envoy Sir Robert Southwell, when the King was grown up, wrote about him to Lord Arlington:

". . . For as he knew nothing of dissimulation, but always spoke the truth so what evil he ever heard of any man he would in his anger upbraid him of it, without consideration of time, or place, or the person. . . ."

Considering Affonso's high position, his childhood was not unduly formal. He was neither overdisciplined nor segregated. He played as much as he liked with his little brother Pedro, who bore the title "Infant" and was five years younger than himself. He saw very little of his sister Catherine, two years his senior, but that was normal in Portugal where women lived in almost oriental seclusion. The widowed queen regent Dona Luiza, a Spanish woman with tremendous force of character, ran the affairs of the country, which was kept drained by the long war with Spain, and watched over Affonso with a close attention which was strategic rather than affectionate. No regent ever took her responsibilities more to heart than did Dona Luiza. When Affonso's childish naughtiness began to grow out of bounds, she was the first of the court to feel misgivings about his future and that of the country. She seemed actually eager to find an excuse to oust him from the throne. Most mothers are stubbornly blind to the faults of their sons, but as regards her first-born the queen regent was not. On the contrary, almost before Affonso proved himself a problem child, she was saying that he was one. Pedro was her darling. Pedro, she felt, was ordained by Nature to be the sovereign.

Affonso *was* difficult. He was not precociously vicious in sexual matters. He did not steal; he never lied, but from earliest youth he was mad on fighting. He looked everywhere for violence. His greatest pleasure was to mix in a good fight himself: failing that, he wanted to watch dogs attack each other, or bulls at bay, or men struggling. He loved mob scenes. Perhaps this taste for ferocity was aggravated by his medical history. He may have been proving to himself and the world that he was as good as any able-bodied man in the kingdom. As a little boy he often slipped the leash, ran away and stirred up brawls; he was the bane of his attendants' lives. As he grew older, he became a danger to the people of the city and to himself as well. Citizens, failing to recognize in the brawling bully their ever-to-be-respected King, sometimes blacked his eyes. Once an irreverent bull tossed him and broke a few of the royal bones. But no mishap cooled him down or tamed him, and scandal accumulated around his name in Lisbon.

Another annoyance to the queen mother was the company her royal son kept. He had no sense of dignity, an unusual lack in a Portuguese. Soon after his father's death he picked up a most unsuitable playmate, an older boy, Italian-born Antonio Conti, who sold toys at a booth near the palace. (This palace stood where the lovely Black Horse Square was later erected by Pombal.) Affonso was fascinated by Conti, for he was strong and active, the leader of a boys' mob distinguished in the King's eyes for its fighting prowess. Dona Luiza and the royal preceptors tried earnestly to break off this unconventional association, but Affonso clung to his chum. Conti often smuggled his brother Giovanni and other street urchins into the palace grounds, where Affonso spent happy hours watching the juvenile gladiators, sometimes himself taking a turn in the ring with a Negro or mulatto opponent. The gang was made up of tough boys, a motley of the nationalities that swarm over any seaport town. They introduced dog fighting as a regular form of sport, inciting to battle the mastiffs that guarded the royal precincts.

Now and then some scandalized courtier tried to lure his King's attention to a more genteel form of warfare such as fencing, but Affonso liked knife throwing better, because it was a tougher game. Whenever it came to a choice between gentlemanly brutality and the lowlife sort, the King preferred the latter.

Such behavior might have been shrugged off as a youthful

phase, but Affonso gave no signs of outgrowing his rough tastes. He grew up, but his boyish love for Conti continued to flourish. Nightly he would tear about the country with wild companions, now and then attacking some inoffensive animal. At least once he went farther than that and rushed at two harmless, unarmed citizens who were riding home in the dark. He injured no one, but the affair naturally caused talk, and it was all very awkward for his mother. Even in the seventeenth century when people were not fastidious, Affonso seems to have been beyond the limit.

Then something interesting happened outside Portugal, a long way north, in England. It was about the time of Affonso's eighteenth birthday that the court heard of Charles II's restoration to the throne. Lisbon knew Charles well; during his long years of wandering in exile he had found a kind friend in Affonso's father, João IV. Other monarchs had sometimes treated the young King tactlessly, rather like the poor relation he was, but João knew the bitterness of exile all too well for that. He had always helped Charles, and within a year after England's throne was occupied again, it became evident that Charles, urged by Clarendon, contemplated matrimonial alliance with Portugal. Luiza, excited and happy at the prospect of such a powerful connection —might not Charles even help in the dreary war against Spain?— prepared to pay over a magnificent dowry with her daughter, the Infanta Catherine of Braganza, future Queen of England.

It was significant that the queen mother managed the complicated negotiations preceding the match without once calling on her son Affonso for help or advice, though he was legally the King and had reached what should have been an age of discretion. Luiza was a managing woman, who hated to let go of her powers; besides, she was honestly convinced that Affonso was incapable of ruling. Someday, of course, she would have to give up. She knew that. But she told herself that it was for the country's good she hung on so grimly; she hoped that her second son, her darling Pedro, would ultimately take over. Affonso was delicate and likely to die young, she believed. In fact, it might happen at any time. Thus it would be best all round if Affonso should name the Infant as his heir, so as to avoid posthumous trouble. Pedro was fourteen now, a fine upstanding lad, strikingly good-looking and enormously strong. (It was said of him that he could bend an iron bar into a circle.) If she, Dona Luiza, could only manage until Affonso obligingly died . . .

Oddly, Affonso did not take kindly to this suggestion. He was unreasonable enough to take umbrage. He pointed out that he was not so delicate as all that. He rode well, in spite of the touch of paralysis. He hunted, boxed, and fenced with vigor if not elegance. He thought of himself, correctly as it happened, as a hardy specimen with plenty of life ahead of him. It was not that he disliked Pedro; they got on well together, and had compatible tastes. He simply saw no reason to be relegated to the position of an invalid ruler, always on the verge of abdication if not worse. He flatly refused to name an heir at all.

Dona Luiza, however, would not give up. She made a mistake characteristic of mothers, failing to realize that her son was a child no longer. She gave him no credit for any strength of will, and she was wrong. Though Affonso's reactions were slow, he was capable of stubbornness. Since he opposed his mother, she assumed that he was being worked upon by mischievous advisers. All she need do, then, was get rid of these undesirable influences. The leader, she felt sure, was Antonio Conti. With no more compunction than she would have felt in abstracting and drowning a litter of puppies from Affonso's kennels, she made her plans.

One afternoon somebody tempted Affonso from his apartments for an hour or so, and the Duke of Cadaval with a group of other courtiers visited the rooms during that time and carried off Affonso's gang. The Conti brothers and their chief followers were loaded aboard a ship and whisked off. Long before the King came back they were on the way to Brazil, in one of the earliest large-scale shanghai operations in European history.

Luiza congratulated herself on the neatness and dispatch with which the project had gone through, but she was not left very long to enjoy her complacent mood. The King flew into a terrifying rage. She had never thought he was capable of such rebellion, such hatred. It was to be hoped, she reflected, that he would forget about it as soon as the tantrum had passed, but he did not forget. Instead of calming down, he set about revenging himself in a highly efficient manner. He rode off to the neighboring town of Alcántara, and from there he staged a revolution against the queen mother, gathering his supporters about him and sending her an ultimatum. The regency must be dissolved, he said, immediately.

Dona Luiza had no recourse but to give in, and she did so sadly. It was a complete rout. She had not even attained her ambitions for the Infant, and now there was no question of further discussion of the matter with Affonso. He hated her bitterly, so bitterly that he could not bear even the sight of her. She had to move out of the palace and retire to a convent, and his advisers were hard put to it to conceal this shocking state of affairs from the people.

For, odd as it may seem, the people of Portugal played an important part in court decisions. They had their people's tribune, the *juiz de povo*, who was elected every year by the guilds, and the nobles were very careful to lend an ear when this tribune spoke.

Affonso was at last King in practice as well as theory, and he thoroughly enjoyed the sensations of freedom and power. He did not, however, grasp his scepter as if he knew what to do with it. He was still his old self, slow-witted and unpredictable. A good deal of the royal duty bored him, and he was all too glad to leave most of the business to his chief minister, the astute young Conde de Castel-Melhor. Castel-Melhor had his work cut out for him, managing Affonso. As long as he watched the King and counteracted the influences he did not approve, he was safe, but the King always needed watching. He was dangerously impressionable and he listened to everyone. He was quick-tempered, but short in memory.

For instance, there was that matter of Antonio Conti. Any normal young man, if he had gone the length Affonso did to avenge his friend's banishment, would at least have tried to make amends to the friend afterward. Luiza was gone and Affonso reigned supreme; why then did he not recall Conti? God knows. Probably he simply forgot the whole thing, until a courtier, to annoy Castel-Melhor, reminded him of the Italian. Then Affonso took the action one would have expected weeks before: he sent a ship posthaste to Brazil. The hapless Contis were swept up as they had been swept before, and rushed back to Portugal.

Everyone, especially the wicked courtier, thought this would mean the end of Castel-Melhor's influence. Conti would assuredly be replaced as favorite in the palace, they told each other. But they reckoned without Conti himself. The wretched toyseller's spirit was broken. He had discovered what intrigue can do to a man; he had no desire to pit himself against the whole court, perhaps to be sent off again on some mad voyage, this time never to return. Conti had had quite enough high life. Like his enemy the queen mother, he sought peace and quiet.

He went to Oporto and settled down there. I would like to know what finally happened to him. My guess is that he married and raised a family, gave up selling toys, and made wine instead. I think he bored his neighbors to death of an evening telling them tales of his escapades with his friend the King. Everyone, surely, thought he was a tremendous liar. It must have been one of the jokes of Oporto.

Affonso must marry and beget a son, for Dom Pedro was becoming a problem. The brothers were still on friendly terms, and often went out together on Affonso's beloved nocturnal expeditions, but that meant no lessening of Dona Luiza's influence on the Infant. Besides, Pedro was dangerously popular. The situation was a good example of the power of propaganda. Pedro and Affonso were always thought of by their subjects as good versus bad, white against black, Beauty and the Beast. And all this was the result of Luiza's prejudice. In actual fact the brothers were not dissimilar. Pedro was more attractive, being sound and good-looking, yet Affonso's deformity was not evident, and in his youth he was good-looking enough. Nor was there much to choose between them for behavior. Like his brother, Pedro terrified harmless citizens for his amusement, and preferred the company of hired bravos to that of courtiers. He too was fond of Negro toughs in his bodyguard. One night during a silly, pointless foray, the brothers were challenged by a civilian sentry who mistook them for Spanish soldiers, and it was the Infant, not Affonso, who grew excited and shot the man dead. But the populace persisted in accusing Affonso of the crime.

Not that Affonso could be called the good brother. My point is that they were both hard cases. It was Affonso, not Pedro, who disrupted a solemn religious procession and deliberately started a riot in which a number of people were injured. Certainly never was country so sorely beset by its princes.

For all his brotherly jollity, the Infant was beginning to feel his oats, and to wonder if the people were not right in preferring himself. Castel-Melhor, always alert, knew that the boy often visited Dona Luiza in her convent and came back to the palace puffed up with hope. Another of his suspicious actions was his deliberate propagation and elaboration of the story that Affonso was incapable of normal sexual intercourse. The Infant's followers fell upon this juicy gossip with great enthusiasm, and spread it far and wide. In effect, as Pedro well knew, it was far more than a mere joke; not only did everyone in Portugal hear of the King's impotency, but the spicy item was passed along to foreign capitals. In Versailles, especially, it caused amusement. This was all right as far as humor goes, but it hindered Castel-Melhor in his search for a royal bride, and he was particularly anxious to procure a Frenchwoman for Affonso's wife. If too many people gave credence to the rumor, the King might never marry at all. And it was not as if he were madly keen to marry, either; Castel-Melhor had worked hard to talk him into it. The minister must have wondered at times if the story of Affonso's impotency wasn't more than malicious rumor.

For political reasons, a Franco-Portuguese alliance would be best. That is, it would be best from Castel-Melhor's point of view. England was already allied with Portugal through the Infanta's marriage, and in this endless climbing game, France was logically the next power to be converted to friendship. The trouble heretofore had been that Louis XIV, listening to Mazarin, had dismissed Portugal as a weak little nation, doomed soon to fall again under Spain's domination. He had begun to reconsider his opinion only since the Charles-Catherine marriage. Now, however, he seemed to have come round completely, and went out of his way to think of suitable princesses who might wed the King of Portugal. Louis was planning to fight Spain, and Portugal, already embroiled in war with her old enemy, was his obvious ally. Besides, the Anglo-Portuguese alliance worried Louis; he wanted to break it up if possible.

His minister, Marshal Turenne, suggested they marry Affonso to Louis's cousin Anne de Montpensier, "La Grande Mademoiselle" so well known to any student of the period. Mademoiselle, however, most definitely was not having any. Always recalcitrant and independent on the subject of her marriage, she felt that Portugal was a small and insignificant country, with an uncertain future; it was altogether unworthy of her splendid self as Queen. Besides, what she had heard of Affonso—his alleged impotency and strange habits—was hardly calculated to attract any woman. Mademoiselle defied Turenne; she defied her cousin King Louis: she would not marry Affonso of Portugal.

Louis did not waste much time arguing. He had other kinswomen who would do as well. There was the daughter of the Duc d'Elbeuf, and there were two sisters, Marie Jeanne Baptiste de Nemours and Marie Françoise Isabelle d'Aumale, daughters of the late Duc de Nemours, princesses of Savoy, pretty and accomplished, and both seeking husbands of high rank. Presumably any one of these maidens would be overjoyed to be Queen of Portugal. Marshal Turenne talked it over endlessly with the Marquêz de Sande, Portuguese minister for England, whose task it was to round up candidates.

After studying Sande's reports of the three, Affonso in Lisbon put in a request for Mademoiselle de Nemours. Marie Jeanne had red-gold hair, which appealed to him.

Here, too, Turenne was checked. The Duchesse de Nemours, an old hand at diplomatic juggling, maintained that Marie Jeanne was already affianced to Charles, Prince of Lorraine. Had the duchess been keen on Affonso's offer she would have found it easy enough to ignore the previous engagement, but like La Grande Mademoiselle, she did not think much of Portugal's future.

This made the second cousin of the French King to reject poor Affonso, but no one seems to have taken such early rejections to heart. Turenne promptly and cheerfully dealt his next card, Mademoiselle d'Elbeuf. By birth she was a better match for a king than Marie Jeanne, being Louis's first cousin. Turenne explained this to the Marquêz de Sande and then brought forward a private, additional proposition of his own. Why should not Affonso's brother the Infant marry at the same time the King did? He, Turenne, had a niece, one Mademoiselle de Bouillon, of good blood and fortune, who would be an admirable mate for the young Pedro. (And it would be an admirable chance as well for Turenne's family, the marshal agreeing with the rest of the diplomatic world that Affonso was a poor risk, and that Dom Pedro was very likely to succeed to the throne.) Sande thought it a feasible suggestion, so he interviewed both young ladies and their parents, and forwarded a report, complete with pictures, to the court at Lisbon.

Perhaps Mademoiselle d'Elbeuf simply was not paintable, or the artist did not do her justice. It may have had something to do with Sande's confidential report. Whatever the reason, King Affonso did not like the idea of marrying her, and reiterated his desire to make Marie Jeanne Queen of Portugal. If Turenne could manage to overcome the duchess's objections, he said, Mademoiselle de Bouillon could marry Pedro. If not . . .

There followed a wild dance of diplomacy. The names of potential partners changed, changed again, shuffled around and whirled back to their original positions at least twice over.

Biography of the period is full of such stories. In his own life Louis did as he liked, but, powerful as he was, he was careful about his manner of doing it. Affonso, King of a far smaller country, was the exact opposite. Roughly he seized his liberty, without concealment. Affonso was uncouth. Louis was an exquisite, a cold, deliberate soul. Life at his court was like the formal ballet he patronized. Contemplating the shock that awaited any French girl who must go direct from mannerly Versailles to the Lisbon court, we are tempted even at this distance in time to cry out in warning and pity.

La Grande Mademoiselle had been too canny to be caught in the machine. Mademoiselle d'Elbeuf had been rejected. There remained the daughters of the duchess. These, playing like butterflies in the Versailles sun, were not fretting about Affonso's choice. They had embroiled themselves in a queer, pathetic little love affair; both were infatuated with the Comte de Lauzun, who had no desire to marry either of them. And a good thing too, for he was not eligible enough to satisfy their mother; she had plenty on her mind as it was. Louis was pressing her to give in and allow Marie Jeanne to marry Affonso. When Louis insisted, only La Grande Mademoiselle dared resist; the poor duchess had to capitulate. She fought every step of the way, however, and the marriage settlement was still being argued about when she suddenly died. The rest of the affair, like the young princesses themselves, was left to be disposed of by their uncle the Bishop of Laon.

This gentleman, bringing a fresh eye to the situation, at once spotted Turenne's wily plan. With shrill cries he singled it out for objection. Marry the Infant to Mademoiselle de Bouillon, or anyone else? Certainly not, said the bishop, until Marie Jeanne was well and truly established as Queen of Portugal. He refused to consider a double proxy wedding, or any double arrangement at all, before his niece should sail. A fine state of affairs, he said, if Affonso should die before they arrived. Then Turenne's niece would be Queen and Marie Jeanne would be nothing but a widow, not even a wife. The Infant might marry anyone they liked, said the bishop, as long as he didn't do it until Marie Jeanne was Queen in Portugal, sitting there on her throne. Furthermore, the bishop wanted an agreement that Marie Jeanne, if thus widowed, should have first refusal of her brother-in-law Pedro for her next husband.

Turenne naturally quarreled with this. It was his firm belief, he said indignantly, that the Nemours family was squeezing out poor Mademoiselle de Bouillon. Once Marie Jeanne was in Lisbon, what was to prevent her from persuading the Infant to change his mind and marry her own sister Marie Françoise d'Aumale? Nothing in the world.

In the meantime, what was happening to him, and what was he like, this faraway King whose wooing was so unlucky?

Anything less like Prince Charming would be difficult to imagine. At twenty-two he had lost his youthful good looks. He was very fat. Habitually he bundled himself into a large number of clothes, including several thicknesses of coats. He ate and drank intemperately, and was afflicted with an incurable acne.

One scarcely likes to think of the sex life of such an unappetizing creature, but this confused matter was to become important in his country's politics at a later date; and, as we have seen, even at the time of his courtship there was a good deal of uncertainty about it. Affonso didn't ignore women: far from it. In keeping with his swashbuckling role he spent a large part of his leisure inflicting his company on the inhabitants of the local brothels, usually bursting in with a crowd of boisterous companions, but it was whispered that his entertainments there were not of the conventional sort; that he whipped the unfortunate prostitutes, but didn't go to bed with them.

Still, he kept quite a number of women in the palace, for one purpose or another, and there was one woman for jealousy of whom he actually had a man assassinated by hired bullies. Then there was a story about a nun, Sister Maria de Saudade; no scandal touched her name but everyone knew Affonso admired her passionately. And as a crushing argument against those who tittered about the King's lack of virility—the worst insult one can offer a Latin—Castel-Melhor proudly exhibited a little girl he kept in his house, the illegitimate offspring, he stoutly maintained, of Affonso.

At Versailles the old men were still quarreling over the young women when things took an unexpected turn. Marie Jeanne, resignedly putting the finishing touches on her trousseau for Portugal, suddenly found herself being claimed by her almost forgotten fiancé, Charles of Lorraine. As if this were not enough, a third voice made itself heard above the clamor of courtiers— that of her kinsman Carlo Immanuele, Duke of Savoy. Marie Jeanne, overjoyed at the prospect of release from marriage with the dreaded King of Portugal, begged her uncle to reconsider her fate. Carlo Immanuele was a good match, so Marie Jeanne had her way, and was married to the duke.

The bishop then assured the Marquêz de Sande that the wedding of King Affonso might go on as planned, with only one slight, insignificant change—the bride. Marie Françoise was still in the shop window; she was as pretty as her sister and she would be delighted to be Queen of Portugal.

In the end that is how it arranged itself. There was another slight change as well, for the Infant Pedro turned awkward at the last minute and refused to marry Mademoiselle de Bouillon. He had not been consulted about the matter at all, he said; he had not agreed to anything; he had no desire to marry anyone, and not all Affonso's fury would move him. Turenne must look elsewhere for a nephew-in-law, but the marshal's chagrin could not hinder the main proceedings at that stage of the game. Affonso got a blond bride, and Marie Françoise a crown.

There is always something ridiculous about a proxy marriage, but nothing can surpass for sheer oddity the wedding of Marie Françoise Isabelle, Princess of Savoy, to Affonso, King of Portugal, as it was solemnized at La Rochelle before the bride sailed for her new home. Sande represented Dom Affonso, and the Duc de Vendôme stood up in the place of Mademoiselle d'Aumale. Very gravely, marquêz and duke were joined in holy wedlock by the Bishop of Laon, and there it was. Marie Françoise was a queen, a consummation she had long desired. She was an ambitious young woman, anxious for power, and she thoroughly understood that she owed all her loyalty to Louis and France. The crown was hers; now to do her duty.

Was Affonso impotent? At Versailles they sniggered and asked the question. Few marriages can have begun less auspiciously. The ship came to anchor at Lisbon, carrying as chief passenger a very seasick bride. Poor Marie Françoise, who had been miserable through the whole long, rough voyage, found no husband pacing the dock in eager expectation of her arrival. Affonso, perhaps still feeling snubbed because he hadn't got Marie Jeanne, was in the town busying himself with non-marital matters, and he had to be reminded twice that the gaily decorated barge awaited him.

Pedro was in the party which accompanied him when he went at last. This was fitting and proper, but it furnished an unfortunate contrast when the two brothers arrived on deck to pay their duties. There was Pedro, tall and handsome in his fine clothes, standing respectfully back of his grotesque, fat, trussed-up brother, who may possibly have been indulging his customary taste for wearing two or three hats on his head, one on top of another. There they stood, both of them staring at Marie Françoise in open admiration which had in it an element of unflattering astonishment. All the time the interpreter, or some Portuguese noble who could speak French (for the King could not), was chattering away to Marie Françoise, who spoke no Portuguese. At that moment, tired and disappointed, she must have regretted her bargain very bitterly, but such regrets were a commonplace in her circle.

There was no time for more than the usual long-winded courtesies. Marie Françoise had to go ashore to attend her second marriage ceremony and then set off on a wedding journey with an oafish King with whom she could not exchange a word in a common language.

The bewildered girl had at least one refuge, the ill health which everyone knew she had suffered from ever since La Rochelle. Whether or not Affonso considered himself a capable lover, he was not allowed to prove it for at least three nights. Later, the Queen was to claim that he never did prove it.

In a court one knows everything. At least one likes to have it thought that one knows everything, which is why so many attendants tell thrilling shocking stories about their royal masters. There was never any dearth of gossip at the court of Affonso, even before the pretty Queen arrived. Everyone knew, for example, about the bad feeling between the brothers, which had been gaining in strength ever since the Infant put his foot down and refused to take a wife at his brother's command. They had squabbled a good deal about the Infant's rights and his dignities. Now, with Marie Françoise in the household, they quarreled more than ever.

At a public festival during the honeymoon, sitting with the bride in full view of the large audience, Affonso and Pedro began a dispute which rapidly developed into a loud quarrel. Poor Marie Françoise, who had just begun to learn her husband's language, understood enough of the fraternal insults to be much upset. Were it not for her presence, Affonso was saying, he would kill Pedro with his sword. King and prince bawled at each other, threatening injury and death but never quite coming to blows, while between them the Queen wrung her hands. The scene ended only when Pedro flounced out.

Marie Françoise managed to bring the brothers together again, but soon there was another quarrel to resolve, and then another. At least Affonso never threatened his wife as he did his brother. He must have been fond of her in his way, although as the court gossips well knew they were not an amorous pair of newlyweds. They occupied separate bedchambers, and Affonso continued to take his pleasure, whatever it amounted to, with females he had known before his marriage.

These excursions into the sentimental should not tempt us to forget how all-important to every actor in the Portuguese drama was the world situation. Spain and the war were still with them, and Louis of France followed up the friendly gesture of marrying his cousin to Affonso by the even friendlier one of becoming Portugal's ally in the struggle.

Already there was a *rapport* between the armies of the two nations: Marshal Schomberg was virtual commander of the Portuguese forces, and Schomberg was French. That is to say, he was generally considered French, though one scarcely knows why, as his mother was English and his father German. However, it is true that he had been in the French army, among others, before Louis lent him to Affonso. Like Marie Françoise, he was the embodiment of a diplomatic gesture. Soon after the bride's arrival, the two expatriates came to an understanding that Marie Françoise be kept informed as to the progress of the war. They had to be careful to hide their sentiments from the public, for these lackadaisical hostilities were becoming increasingly unpopular in Portugal.

The Queen had to content herself with undercover activity such as this, for it was annoyingly evident that any importance Louis had hoped she would enjoy in the government was non-existent. Chafe as she might against her fate, she was a woman, and in Portugal that meant she was a nonentity in public affairs. She had been warned of this disadvantage when the marriage was first discussed, but at Versailles, where even girls had plenty of freedom, she had been gaily confident of circumventing such obstacles. Now she was giving up hope. Southwell pithily summed it up: Marie Françoise had found "a total disappointment in her bed, and a perfect insignificancy in the government."

No doubt it was galling for the new Queen to reflect that her mother-in-law Dona Luiza, herself a foreigner, had managed in spite of Portuguese tradition to make her mark and have her way. Of course she had not been hampered by a feeble-minded husband, revolting in appearance and habits. Even at that, Luiza hadn't attained her hour of strength until she became widow and regent. Was it possible to follow her example?

When two people have much the same ambition, as did Marie Françoise and Dom Pedro, it is difficult to decide which of them furnishes the first impulse to achieve it. The Infant had fallen in love with the French princess at sight. Such sentimental urges were probably commonplace in his life, and this one would have died quickly if there had not been practical reasons to hold him constant to his love. From the Queen's point of view everything combined to push her toward Pedro. He was attractive, sympathetic, and admiring. He knew better than anyone else what she had to cope with, married to his brother. Doubtless she had been briefed by Louis in the intrigues of the court, and understood that the Infant wanted to take Affonso's place. Before meeting her husband she must have thought of her brother-in-law as an enemy to circumvent. Now, after meeting the man she had already married, she began to wonder how best to help Pedro get what he wanted.

We do not know the exact steps by which she reached this state of mind, but the details hardly matter. It would give a false picture of Marie Françoise's character and of the general situation, however, if we leaped to the conclusion that she was loose or careless. She did not rush into Dom Pedro's arms. She had been well brought up by Versailles standards, and never disregarded appearances. Nor was she headstrong enough to run the risk of having an affair at that court, full as it was of enemies. I think it possible that she took Pedro as her lover later on, just before they succeeded in forcing Affonso from the throne, but even that is by no means certain.

All we know is that very soon after she was installed, during the unhappy bickering between Affonso and Pedro and her own estrangement from her husband, she and Pedro recognized each other as political allies and agreed to work together. The Infant's adherents welcomed this valuable recruit with enthusiasm. Her presence caused them to map out a new campaign to unseat the King.

First of all, obviously, Castel-Melhor must be eradicated. He was an intelligent watchdog, and unshakably faithful to Affonso. The Infant's party stirred up the public feeling which already existed against the Count, reminding everyone how the minister supported the hated war. As soon as they felt the softening process had gone far enough, Marie Françoise adroitly attacked Castel-Melhor. She picked a quarrel with him by demanding that he give her that portion of her marriage settlement which was to be her allowance; it had not yet been paid.

An outstanding debt between European crowned heads was

not at all exceptional. On the contrary, it was the usual state of affairs. Portugal herself still owed England the major part of Catherine's famous dowry, the largest ever paid—on paper. It came to nearly half a million sterling, or would have had the bride actually brought it, but the unromantic fact was that it was paid on the installment plan, and the payments went on for so many years that Charles II had long been dead before accounts were settled. Such debts were so often in arrears that the entire bookkeeping system of Europe's royalty could have done with a general moratorium.

Nevertheless, the Queen of Portugal had a case, if she wanted to make trouble. Castel-Melhor, as she expected, admitted he could not possibly hand over the sum she was demanding. Marie Françoise was loud in her complaints. News of the quarrel spread through court and country; the Queen and the minister were sworn foes. Fresh clashes occurred as fast as she could precipitate them. Marie Françoise became a termagant. Her attacks were shrewd and well timed. Soon the people began to think of her as they did of Dom Pedro, as an enemy of their enemy Castel-Melhor, and their champion.

The months passed by, and the conspiracy flourished. There was no doubt that the Queen was becoming more popular. Even the Army, she felt confident, would support her and turn against the King when the time came, for it was under the command of Schomberg, friend and ally. To make quite sure, however, she asked Schomberg to send her an up-to-date report of his men's state of mind, and other military matters. Schomberg obligingly wrote and sent to her several pages of exhaustive discussion.

Marie Françoise received this confidential report late one night and she went to bed with it, intending to read it carefully before morning. Lulled too well either by Schomberg's style or the dullness of the material, she fell asleep and left the papers scattered all over the bedclothes. Next morning she overslept, though she was supposed to attend early mass with the King. What with attendants running in to rouse her and everything being late, she went off to the chapel in such a rush that she forgot the papers. Bang in the middle of the service, she remembered. There was nothing she could do about it at the moment. Having arrived after the elevation of the Host, she would have to wait for the next mass. Terrified, she watched Affonso walk out at the end of the first ceremony.

She whispered to her confessor, and sent him up to her room, but he returned with agitating news. The King was in her bedchamber, chatting with her lady-in-waiting; of course the priest had not been able to do more than peer in, and just as he came away he had seen the King throw himself down on the unmade bed. If one of the papers so much as crackled under him . . .

The Queen was in a frenzy. On the advice of the confessor she fainted, which put a sudden end to the mass. Then she permitted herself to recover slightly, just enough so that she could totter, with support, to her room. The alarmed King leaped from the couch and scurried about being helpful, commanding that the bed be made afresh. Marie Françoise protested that she could not wait. Weakly she lay down on the muddled bedclothes. The papers were still there. For once she had reason to be grateful for the slovenly habits of the palace domestics.

The furore over Castel-Melhor had been whipped up to such a pitch that the Infant and his coterie of *fidalgos* felt safe in inviting the people's tribune, with representatives of the guilds, to come and talk things over. To these citizens they put the straight question: on whose side would the people be if it came to an open break between the brothers? Enthusiastically the citizens declared their loyalty to Dom Pedro.

All of this was immediately reported by spies to the King's party. Dom Affonso was in danger, and he was not too stupid to realize how things stood. That did not mean, however, that he was willing to do anything decisive. Castel-Melhor urged him to move out of town to Alcántara, muster his troops, and march back to make war on the Infant, but the King was averse to that sort of violence, for all his love of the other kind. Instead he rushed into the matter headlong, as he always did, upbraiding Dom Pedro openly for holding treasonous meetings. The Infant angrily retorted that His Majesty supported Pedro's enemy Castel-Melhor and was himself a traitor. If that man did not leave Lisbon, Dom Pedro said, he would.

Again Affonso would not make a decision, and by putting it off he allowed Pedro to win. The count was a good fighter, but he knew when he was beaten. As gracefully as he could, he took his leave. He knew he was abandoning his master to destruction, but as his master had abandoned him first, he had no choice.

Followed a strange and uncomfortable era in the palace. Having given in easily on Castel-Melhor, Affonso began to prove unexpectedly awkward. His Queen and her accomplices discovered that they did not, after all, enjoy the free hand with the government that they had hoped for after their triumph. The King refused to see his brother, and he would not listen to his wife's advice any more than he had before. She had still "a perfect insignificancy in the government."

Moreover, for the first time the forthright King displayed considerable talent for intrigue. He called back to Lisbon the count's right-hand man, Sousa de Macedo, to take Castel-Melhor's place, and between them they collected a large pro-Affonso party, which lost no time concocting a plot against the Infant. It was desperate in design. Pedro was to be lured to a meeting and there assassinated. However, the King's commander in chief took alarm at this idea and argued Affonso out of it.

It was Pedro's turn to take the offensive. Early one morning he burst into the palace at the head of a large body of men, and stalked into the King's bedchamber. The situation had all the makings of a good bloody battle, but this was Portugal, where most matters can be compounded in talk. It would never have done in England, but Lisbon was different. The air, instead of ringing with clash of arms, resounded with passionate speeches. Pedro, in flowery terms, requested Affonso to sack Macedo. Affonso angrily refused. Macedo was brought in and the argument continued over his unfortunate head. Hours went by. Now and then a soldier made a sort of pass at Macedo, but nothing actually happened to him, though everyone shouted a good deal.

Marie Françoise entered, and the King turned on her. In the ordinary way he was courteous to his wife in public, but this time he broke his own rule. I would not go so far as to say he threatened her; Affonso was remarkably restrained in some ways. But he did accuse her, in a childishly jealous tirade, of having walked in merely to see Pedro. An awkward silence fell at last on the group, and in the lull Macedo could be heard timidly requesting a private audience with the King. Somehow, everyone felt inclined to let him have his own way, and the others retired for a while to the anteroom. The first flush was over; the *coup* had fallen flat, and what might have been armed rebellion was petering out in talk.

Not that the talk was over; far from it. It went on for five hours more. At one point a mob gathered in the town to discuss the disturbing rumors that emanated from the palace. They worked themselves up and made a rush on the building, brandishing naked swords. However, they were a Portuguese mob and didn't really want trouble. Affonso, Pedro, and Marie Françoise hastily showed themselves in friendly proximity at the windows, and the crowd cheered them and retired. Indoors the fury of words continued unabated, to the rather macabre accompaniment of Affonso's flute, which he insisted upon playing through most of the proceedings. He said he needed the practice.

At last His Majesty tired of the affair and gave in, with reservations. Sousa de Macedo should leave Lisbon for a time, but it was to be a short time only. However, Macedo, like Conti, went away bereft of all ambition, and he was never to come back in the same capacity.

The tale had become monotonously repetitive, but now there were new developments, for Pedro proceeded to buy over that part of the Army which was still loyal to his brother. There remained a few *fidalgos* faithful to the King; Pedro's people frightened some with threats, and attempted to assassinate the tougher specimens, until one by one they all fled.

Then the conspirators engineered a demand from the Municipal Council and the people's tribune for a meeting of the *Cortes,* or Parliament. Affonso, knowing this meeting would probably be the end of his reign, held out as long as he could, but when the people threatened to stop paying taxes, he capitulated. It was arranged that the Cortes should assemble at the beginning of 1668, about six weeks thence.

Now at last Affonso dreamed longingly of doing what Castel-Melhor had begged him to do before—steal out of the palace and make his way to Alcántara, there to rally his loyal troops and attack the would-be usurper. He even tried to get out of the city by night, but Pedro's men were already on guard at every road and bridge. It was too late.

The Infant's faction may have been dubious, after all, about the temper of the Cortes when it came to the test. Marie Françoise, at any rate, did not wait. Her Jesuit confessor probably advised her that she would look less of a rat if she leaped from the ship before it began to sink. So she leaped the moment she deemed it safe, when she saw the white sails of a French fleet sailing up the Tagus to anchor. This meant that Louis XIV was backing her up in her proposed action. Determined to keep the war going between Spain and Portugal, he had decided that Pedro was the man he needed in charge of the country, for Affonso, according to Marie Françoise's latest report, planned to make peace. The fleet was his answer.

It was the twenty-first of November 1667, still more than a month before the Cortes was to convene. Quietly Marie Françoise moved out.

By prearrangement she went straight to the convent of Esperança. Once she was secure behind locked gates she sent a letter to the King. She had been so discreet that until that moment he had suspected nothing of her intentions. Beyond a vague jealousy he had no idea that she was capable of leaving him, or of making the allegations she now wrote. He was dumbfounded when he read them:

"Tell his Majesty that my conscience will not longer permit me to cohabit with him, being neither his wife, nor he my husband; that both God and his Majesty himself know, that the condition I came to him in hath not been altered; and therefore I desire the restitution of my portion, that I may return back again to my native country."

Here were shock and grievous insult combined! Affonso flew into a red fury. He took horse and rode to the convent, and there, finding the door locked, he battered wildly against it.

He had not stormed very long before the watchful Infant overtook him and began to reason with him. Affonso's rage abruptly calmed. He listened to the words "sanctuary" and "sacrilege"; he allowed himself to be led back to the palace. There he maintained dazed silence for a space. Suddenly he announced that they had all been wasting time. From that moment on, he decreed, they would speak no more of the Frenchwoman. With the air of a man who turns from trifles to important matters, he questioned his attendants about his bulls. Had they been fed? Were they being properly looked after?

Two days later the Infant's men took the final step. The King was persuaded—by what means is not on record—to sign a declaration which handed over the government to the Infant as regent, and to his heirs as sovereigns of Portugal. The meeting of the Cortes had not been necessary.

Marie Françoise, immured in her convent, waited for developments. She had entered a suit for annulment of her marriage at the same time she sent her letter to Affonso. Now, it seemed, proceedings were being held up by a mere technicality, but when she learned the nature of the technicality she grew agitated. The factotums of the Church had been busily reading their ecclesiastical law, and they had discovered that in cases like this the woman who claimed annulment on the grounds of non-consummation must submit to a physical examination. The very idea of such a thing prostrated Marie Françoise; she was overcome with maidenly horror. It was, she said, an impossible condition.

We can make whatever guesses we like as to why she was so determined. She may have been lying when she alleged Affonso was impotent; she may have had an affair with Pedro; she may not have been a virgin when she came to Portugal. Or, of course, she may really have been too modest to face such an ordeal. Anything is possible. All we know is that she refused.

The authorities, having discussed the grave question at some length, then came forward with an alternative suggestion. The formality of examination could be waived if Affonso would sign a statement that Marie Françoise was still a virgin. The question was, would Affonso sign such a declaration? The answer was, he would not. Affonso drove away the Queen's messengers with vigorous contumely. Affonso denied heatedly that his wife was a virgin. For some time he continued to deny it.

Followed a peculiar performance, a hearing of witnesses to prove or disprove, as the case might be, Marie Françoise's assertions as to Affonso's deficiencies. These witnesses were for the most part women who had been lodged in the palace before the King's marriage. There were thirteen of these, and other women too were dragged into the case from bordellos of the town. The stories of all of them depended with remarkable uniformity on whether they were called on behalf of Marie Françoise or Affonso. Marie Françoise's witnesses swore the King was impotent

and given to unnatural practices. Affonso's champions insisted he
was a perfectly normal man, capable of begetting children. Sometimes a Queen's witness convinced the judges; then some other
unfortunate drab was produced and her pro-King story swayed
judgment again. All this time Affonso refused to declare what his
wife wished him to declare, and all this time she in turn refused
to be examined.

Finally the Infant's men lost patience and convinced the King,
somehow, that his memories of his relations with his wife were at
fault. Possibly they promised him freedom, or deceived him in
some other way. Whatever they did, Affonso signed the declaration, as follows:

"To relieve the Queen Maria Francisca Isabel of Saboya, to
whom until now I have been ostensibly married, of the incon-
venience of going to law with the cause of her withdrawal to
the Convent of Esperança, therefrom to appeal for nullity of the
marriage, and for relief of my conscience, I declare that I did not
consummate the marriage with her, because she is a virgin. Thus
I swear it on the holy Evangelists, that this declaration may have
all the force and vigour necessary for the marriage which we
celebrated to be judged annulled. Lisbon 2 Dec. 1667."

That settled things, as far as the Church was concerned. The
ecclesiastics of Lisbon pronounced the marriage null, and so did
Cardinal Louis de Vendôme in Paris, who as Bishop of Laon had
married his niece to King Affonso. Marie Françoise's relatives
approved the annulment. Of course it was unusual, but really
scarcely surprising when one recalled the stories one had heard
in the old days about that man.

Now then, said the gossips of Lisbon, would Pedro marry the
girl? Some nobles were ungallant enough to doubt it. But Pedro
could hardly back out of the contract after all this, even if he had
wanted to. There was the dowry to consider; it was an awkward
sum of money to refund if the bride went home, and she could
easily go home, too, for the French fleet was still there in the

Tagus. Besides, he was probably still very much in love with Marie Françoise.

Louis XIV was the only member of our cast, apart from the forgotten King Affonso, who had cause for complaint. After all the help he had given his cousin of Savoy, after all the arranging he had done on her behalf, he was cheated of his reward. Dom Pedro, immediately after he came into power, let Louis down and made peace with Spain. To be quite fair to Pedro it must be admitted he could do nothing else; the Portuguese simply would not fight any more. Twenty-eight years, they said, was long enough for any war. Moreover, Charles II was putting on pressure as well.

So Mademoiselle d'Aumale became a bride again, only two years after the first wedding. Again she was married by proxy; again she wed the ruler of Portugal. Otherwise there was no similarity between the marriages. This time no seasickness interfered with the honeymoon. In time she bore a daughter, their only child.

Marie Françoise was reasonably happy with her second husband. She knew she had been lucky; not every princess finds satisfaction in the bed allocated to her. It is true nothing is perfect, not even for determined women like Marie Françoise who go after what they want. Pedro was a very unfaithful husband. Such a failing, however, could not have surprised or grieved overmuch a girl of Marie Françoise's background, and apart from it he was a devoted family man.

The chief vexation in Marie Françoise's second marriage was not that Dom Pedro strayed from time to time, but that she had gone down in the world. She was no longer a queen, only a princess, consort of a mere prince regent. When she urged her husband to arrogate the title as well as the powers of a king, the silly man retorted that the public would not like it. As if that ought to have anything to do with it! Still, if he felt like that there was no help for it. To be Queen of Portugal again, Marie Françoise had to wait until Affonso died, and the poor shattered creature was an unconscionable time doing that.

First they sent him to Terceira in the Azores, where he lived contentedly for nearly five years, busy with his favorite pursuits. But then there was a political upset on the island, and it was thought better to transfer him back to Portugal. Affonso spent many years thereafter in close confinement at Cintra, in the little room the guide showed me. He became dropsical and immensely fat. Also, not unnaturally, he grew more and more eccentric. He paced the floor of the room up and down, up and down, until he wore a groove in the stone. Still he went on living, and still Marie Françoise waited.

Affonso died at last, at the age of forty. Dom Pedro wept at his funeral, but Marie Françoise did not.

The Königsmarks

1. KARL JOHANN

THE BARRACK-LIKE HOUSE of Longleat stands in Wiltshire, and you may visit it, possibly under the guidance of one of the Thynne family, for half a crown. Looking down at it from the rim of the valley, or walking through the great rooms, it is impossible not to think of the past; and at Longleat you have a good deal of past from which to choose a subject for such musings. You may decide to think about Queen Elizabeth, whose cupidity and curiosity were aroused when she heard the house was being built. Or there was Bishop Ken, who left his library at Longleat: it is still there. Or Mrs. Delany of the eighteenth century, who lived there as a girl. But the outstanding tale of Longleat and the Thynne family is the murder of its seventeenth-century owner, Tom of Ten Thousand, and that is not a Wiltshire story at all. It takes us to London, where the killing took place, and to Holland, and Malta, and Hanover, and Sweden, and Venice, until we find ourselves at last in a small German church, where the wife of George I of England has been put away to rot in calculated obscurity.

Thynne, an actor in this wide-flung drama, was killed in the first act; his was not the chief name on the billboards. It is altogether a strange play, for the lead was taken, not by one person, but a whole family, the Königsmarks. They were a Swedish-German clan whose comprehensive history, still unwritten, would furnish a magnificent picture of Europe as she was for a century and a half.

The generation with which we are concerned included four people, two brothers and two sisters. They grew up in Stockholm. Grandfather, father, and uncle of these four had all toiled industriously in their own peculiar fashion to maintain the traditional role of the Königsmarks, that of very upper-class mercenary soldiering, or as they probably preferred to think of it, knight-errantry. The father, Count Kurt Christoph, was killed fighting for the Dutch in 1673, when his eldest child, Karl Johann, was fifteen.

Kurt Christoph's widow and children were not by any means destitute. They owned large estates and a comfortable fortune, but all these possessions were in Sweden, and Königsmarks seem never to have been satisfied to stay quietly in Stockholm. They had relatives on both sides of the house in various German states, and so there was always a good deal of visiting back and forth between the branches of the families in North Europe. Also, they liked to wander just for the sake of wandering. It was not only the men of the family who would not stay at home; the girls, especially Marie Aurora, traveled as well. But the men, of course, had better excuses, for as famous fighters they were offered commissions in the army of many a neighboring country. In the last quarter of that century there was always some war or other going on, and plenty of monarchs and courts to make welcome a gallant officer.

Karl Johann did not wait long after his father's death to start out on his hereditary career. Relations between Sweden and England were friendly, and so, though he aimed ultimately to visit Paris, where his uncle held the post of Swedish ambassador, he decided to look first at what London had to offer a young man on the Grand Tour. He liked the court of Charles II, and the King and court liked him in turn. Charles was always fond of a young man of spirit, remembering his own days of exile on the Continent, whereas the ladies found the Swedish count attractive in another way. Karl was stocky rather than graceful, with luxuriant golden hair which he was vain of and would not cut, nor hide under a wig as was the fashion. "He was a fine person of a man," wrote someone who saw him at his trial, "and I think his hair was the longest for a man's that I ever saw, for it came below his waist. He was very quick of parts."

The result of all this mutual admiration was a resolve on the part of Karl to return to London when he had seen more of the world. Probably he decided thus early to choose his bride in England, ultimately. He approved so much of English life and training that he made up his mind to bring his younger brother Philipp over from where he then was, in Germany, as soon as he was old enough, and put him to school in London.

Karl Johann went on his way to Paris, there to stay with his uncle Otto Wilhelm, who, though he must have complained that being an ambassador was too sedentary an occupation for a Königsmark, managed to enjoy himself thoroughly. The boy stayed long enough in France to grow up. He gained a degree of needed polish at the court of the Sun King, and then once again he was beset by the wandering itch of his breed, and traveled on his way, looking for trouble. He was, of course, a born soldier. Soon word of his daring exploits came trickling back, first from Italy and then Spain, to his friends in Paris and London. The young man distinguished himself noticeably in service with the Knights of Malta against Turkish pirates who had been harrying the islands and coast of Italy. Why he should have been with the Knights of Malta at all, as they were Catholic and he Protestant, was a matter no one investigated too closely. Any war, even a Roman crusade, was enough to attract him.

The chief anecdote from this phase of Count Karl's progress

deals with a sea battle during which he attempted to leap from one of the great Maltese galleys onto the deck of a Turkish corsair's smaller vessel. He fell short in his leap, into the sea, and was automatically given up for lost by his side, since men in seventeenth-century armor did not usually float on the waves. Karl, however, was a husky youth and he had no intention of drowning. He swam, in spite of his armor, to the stern of the corsair's ship, and pulled himself aboard.

At sight of him the pirates leaped to the natural conclusion that they were being boarded by a strong force which had somehow sneaked around to their rear. They promptly surrendered, and discovered too late, when reinforcements arrived, that they had been captured single-handed.

The saga does not end there, for later in the battle this prize of Count Karl's was blown up, and he was thrown again into the sea. This ducking, too, he survived. Whereupon, in a flush of admiration for his exploits, the Knights of Malta impulsively broke one of their fundamental laws and took him into the knighthood, in spite of his religion.

Fame continued to spring up in Karl's footsteps. From Italy he went to Spain, and at Madrid covered himself with glory, and, what is more, with *Spanish* glory, at a bull baiting. A bull baiting was a performance which had something in common with today's bullfights, but the ring was more crowded, the slaughter bloodier, and the whole thing more brutal. A number of bulls were turned loose in the ring all at once; a number of *caballeros* met them on horseback, and there were attendants all around to help the men. Karl took his place among the caballeros and picked out his bull, a strong, fierce specimen. The bull badly wounded his horse and the count had to dismount. At this point nobody would have blamed him for going out of the ring; most foreign courtiers, who were naturally inexperienced at this form of sport, would have been sensible and done so. But not so Karl Johann. Amid the wild plaudits of the onlookers, one of whom, inevitably, was his fair

Spanish lady of the moment, he stood his ground on foot and dealt his adversary a great sword wound.

No doubt about it, everyone considered Karl Johann Königsmark a hero in the best tradition of his hard-living, hard-fighting time. That he did not develop a Boy Scout sense of honor at the same time that he developed his muscles should perhaps be considered an accident of birth and class rather than an example of sheer wickedness. Yet there were principles of honor in the seventeenth century not unlike ours, and he did outrage them. Count Karl was to outlive his popularity.

At twenty-three, having finished his tour and taken the cream off such wars as he came across, the count remembered England and resolved to revisit it. His little brother Philipp was now installed in an English school just as Karl had planned. Faubert's Academy in the Haymarket was not much of a scholar's retreat; the young gentlemen there concentrated on riding, fencing, and hunting rather than books, but after all that was what young gentlemen were supposed to know about. Philipp lived with a tutor named Frederick Hanson. Karl wished to see how the boy was getting on, the Königsmark siblings all possessing the amiable quality of family affection to a high degree. It may have been in his mind, too, that he should marry now and settle down somewhere on an estate. He did not want to do all this anywhere near Stockholm; Stockholm did not interest him, but London did.

Like almost any other young spark of his world, the count did not confuse the frivolous pleasures of romance with marriage, which was a serious matter. Marriage was one method of acquiring fortune and stability, and a man chose a bride first of all for her dowry. Health, youth, good temper, and good looks were also useful qualities, but they were not so important as fortune. Karl Johann took the conventional view, because for all his wild courage he was a conventional young man. (Philipp Christoph was to prove himself more like his sister Aurora; they were romantics.) Yet Karl was extravagantly courageous and ambitious even in his right, proper desire to become a Benedict, and instead of aiming at an easy mark, he chose the widowed Lady Elizabeth Ogle. Of course there was no harm in trying—London was full of other men making the same attempt—but he had certainly picked out a difficult proposition.

The widow was a carroty-haired girl of fourteen, granddaughter of the late Earl of Northumberland and only heir to the huge fortune of the Percy family. Her father had died, her mother had married Lord Montagu, and Elizabeth was being brought up by her grandmother the Countess of Northumberland. What sort of character she had is difficult to determine, for the world's knowledge of her possessions always obscured the view of Elizabeth as a person. She had already been married at the age of eleven or twelve to a man she did not like; fortunately for her they had never lived together because of the bride's youth, and soon after the wedding he died. Now she was the greatest catch of the season, and the situation must have vexed Lady Northumberland, on whose shoulders rested this grave responsibility.

Karl Johann paid his court as best he could among all the other claimants. He was a brilliant popular figure at court, but his popularity and the King's favor did not make him any the more eligible. He was far from being penniless or lowborn, but many richer men with better titles were after Lady Ogle. Perhaps she liked him the best; perhaps she gave him reason to hope. Gossip said so when later events had transpired, but gossip would have said so whether or not it was true. I cannot think the smiles and blushes of any fourteen-year-old girl, except perhaps Juliet, would have been sufficient to inspire Count Karl to go the lengths he did. He needed no outside inspiration; his own greedy restless spirit was enough.

Suddenly the court and all London society were startled by news which amounted practically to a scandal. Lady Northumberland had bestowed her ward's hand at last, in a manner which displeased more people than disappointed suitors. She had chosen Tom Thynne to be Lady Ogle's husband—Squire Thynne of Longleat, a rich man with an income of ten thousand pounds a year, but that was all one could say in his favor. "Tom o' Ten Thousand" was dull, he was getting on to forty, he was dissipated, and though there was nothing wrong with his family history there was nothing particularly glittering about it either. Worst of all, he was the best friend of the Duke of Monmouth, who was getting a bad name for his unremitting though underhanded attacks on Charles II, his father.

Why had the countess decided on Thynne, of all people, when she had her choice of all the bachelors in London? The answer was obvious: he had bribed her. Both bridegroom and grandmother knew they might run into trouble over the unpleasant bargain. Weddings were not public affairs, and were usually carried out quietly in the presence of near relations only, but this wedding was so swift and secret and unexpected that the unhappy bride's own mother, Lady Montagu, knew nothing about it until it had been accomplished. No doubt Lady Northumberland gambled on the success of a *fait accompli,* but she was mistaken.

Lady Montagu gathered allies about her and rushed into battle. Her daughter was heartily on her side; poor little Elizabeth detested Tom Thynne, and had been dragooned into the marriage; she was overjoyed at her mother's intervention. The wicked countess found herself pitted against powerful adversaries; the King himself might take a hand in the proceedings if she went on struggling on Thynne's behalf, for Charles was no friend of any friend of Monmouth. It was too late, Lady Northumberland hoped, to undo the marriage itself, but for the moment she and Thynne had to submit to a postponement of the honeymoon. On Lady Montagu's insistence, Elizabeth was sent out of the country, to a safe distance where her husband might not be tempted to swoop down, carry her off, and take his conjugal rights by force. Later, when she was grown up—— But before that the Montagu party had hopes of arranging an annulment, or, as it was called, a divorce, on the grounds of non-consummation.

Gratefully, poor little Lady Ogle went off to The Hague under the protecting wing of the British ambassador's wife, Lady Temple, that same Lady Temple who was Dorothy Osborne. In London defrauded suitors seethed with anger and cursed Tom Thynne, and the angriest among them was Count Königsmark. Perhaps he persuaded himself, in retrospect, that his claims had been better than they really were. Perhaps he merely talked and drank himself into his wild plan.

For the time being, action was indicated to solace his disappointment. The nearest war seemed to be imminent at Tangiers, for the relief of which a detachment of soldiers was at that very moment setting out. Count Karl volunteered for service, was eagerly accepted, as he always was in such affairs, and accompanied them.

At Tangiers he fell in with an acquaintance of his, a Dutch mercenary captain named Christopher Vratz who had fought under his father, been helped out of a tight place by that officer, and retained a warm loyalty ever since for all Königsmarks. There existed a freemasonry among mercenaries unlike any other form of fellowship. War, not patriotism, was their business. Naturally they had no fixed affection for one king or cause more than any other, but among themselves they maintained a code of honor and fidelity which was shaped to fit their special case. These relationships were disjointed but persistent; friends were seldom inseparable. They would fight in the same battles for a space and then lose track of each other, it might be for several years, to meet once more and carry on the friendship just where it had been dropped. Karl and Vratz were friends of this sort, though their backgrounds were dissimilar. Vratz was a gentleman, not what Karl would consider lowborn, but he was not a noble. He was a friend and yet a follower.

Their meeting on this African battlefield was characteristic of their relations. Karl, who had no idea Vratz was anywhere in the vicinity, found himself beset by several men at once. He had just received a slight wound and was facing defeat, when Vratz, an enormous burly fellow of fifty, came to his assistance, drove off the assailants, and carried his former commanding officer's son to safety. One wonders what the accepted form of greeting was for such occasions—probably, "You here again, you old scoundrel?" They would not have wasted too much surprise on the matter; such a coincidence, they must have felt, might happen to any couple of mercenaries.

When hostilities ceased and they were again out of a job, the old veteran and the gallant young man did not shake hands and part, after their usual custom. Together they traveled to Paris. They had come to an understanding, and meant to stay in each other's company for a space. But in the light of later events, it seems unlikely that they spent much of their time going over and over their plot, or doing any polishing of the structure. As conspirators they were woefully inept; never was premeditated crime committed in a more slapdash way.

To our minds, sophisticated by the light reading of our day, the actual killing of Tom Thynne sounds about as subtle as execution by poleax. It was Sunday evening, the twelfth of February, 1682, and Thynne was on his way home from the house of his grandmother-in-law, the Countess of Northumberland. The Duke of Monmouth had been with him all evening, but was now gone from the coach, and Thynne was accompanied only by his footmen and postilion. The vehicle made its way along St. James's and turned into Pall Mall. That famous highway was dark and deserted, for in 1682 its locality was the very edge of London. It ran between the tree-shaded park called the Royal

Gardens (now St. James's Park) and St. James's Square. The coach rattled along toward the Mall's intersection with the road still known as St. Alban's. Suddenly from the south side, near Prince Rupert's residence, three men on horseback rode out to the coach and turned in next to the postilion, riding along pace for pace with him.

"Stop, you dog!" one of them cried.

The coachman probably thought fleetingly that this was a common holdup by ordinary highwaymen, but he had no time to pursue the idea, or even to come to a dead stop as he had been commanded. As for Thynne inside, he did not realize enough of what was going on to pull out his sword; he was not given a chance to do that. One of the men pushed a blunderbuss into the coach, and without further speech fired four times, straight at him. Thynne slumped from his seat as the three attackers spurred their horses, turned up the Haymarket, and galloped madly along the empty thoroughfare, shouting as they rode, to disarm possible witnesses, "A race! A race!" like young bloods at play.

Thynne never spoke again. He lived long enough to be carried to his house, and there he expired.

It was a crime that shocked London. Murder was commonplace, but the violent death of a wealthy man like Thynne was no ordinary mishap, especially as it seemed so meaningless and mysterious. The public's first hasty conclusion, naturally, was that it was somehow linked with Monmouth's unceasing intrigues. Perhaps the King knew more than he would admit. He was duly informed, first thing in the morning, a few hours after Thynne's death; bystanders commented on his surprise and regret, which seemed genuine, but one never knew.

There was no equivalent of our modern police force, but the justice of the peace for Middlesex went to work efficiently to find the criminals. His search parties were much helped by Monmouth and Lord Mordaunt and their followers. One full day had not elapsed before they met with their first success, and arrested

Vratz the Dutchman. They found him in bed, whither they had been led by informing neighbors, and he admitted immediately, with astonishing candor, that he had killed Thynne. "I wondered he should make so tame a submission," wrote Reresby, "for he is certainly a man of great courage, and appeared quite unconcerned from the very beginning, though he was very certain he should be found the chief actor in the tragedy."

Soon after the apprehension of the captain, the searchers rounded up his two accomplices. These were men who made their living as mercenaries, like the captain, but they were of a different type: ordinary soldiers, not officers, less intelligent or at least worse educated, since they spoke only their own languages (Polish in the case of one, German in the other) and the imperfect French used by most wandering soldiers. They seemed to bear a servant's relation to the captain. Nor did they maintain his courageous calm. John Stern, the German, would have confessed everything had he known enough to tell. George Borosky, the Pole, tried at first to hold out, but he soon broke down. However, with all the willingness in the world he was not able to satisfy his questioners to any great extent, during the first interview. It was obvious that Stern and Borosky had merely obeyed orders, blindly, like the well-trained soldiers they were.

The authorities were genuinely puzzled. What could have been the motive for the murder? They suspected there was nothing in the Monmouth theory, after all. Vratz placidly insisted that he had a private quarrel with Thynne, but the story did not carry conviction, for none of Thynne's intimates had ever heard of this man, and they would hardly have moved in the same circles anyway. Then the investigators came upon a new clue. One of the foreigners, it was said, upon arriving in England had asked to be directed to Count Königsmark. The elder Königsmark was not believed to be in England at all, so the foreigner had been sent to young Count Philipp, at Faubert's Academy. Pursuing their inquiries, the justice's agents too went to Faubert's, where they interviewed Philipp's tutor, Hanson. What, they asked, had his fifteen-year-old charge to do with this galaxy of continental mercenaries?

Hanson was badly frightened. From his disjointed, rambling replies the questioners quickly learned that it was not Philipp at all who had been asked for, but Philipp's elder brother, Count Karl. Karl? But he was not in England at all, said the searchers, or at least if he was, nobody knew about it. Was he in London, after all? And if so, where, and why had he kept so quiet about it?

Hanson gabbled and trembled and told them at last that Karl had lived in one set of lodgings after another, in the Haymarket, Rupert Street, and St. Martin's Lane. He had used a false name. No, Hanson did not know why. He knew only that the elder count had been in London for several weeks, lying very low and calling himself Carlo Cusk. The Pole, he was given to understand, was Karl's groom, but he had lately acted more like Vratz's servant than Karl's. Vratz? Yes, he knew the captain.

Borosky and Stern, questioned again, also admitted to knowing Karl Johann. It was too much of a coincidence. A fresh search was instituted, from the Haymarket to Rupert Street to St. Martin's Lane, but Count Karl had disappeared. By this time, however, the entire population of London was on the lookout, and Karl was found just as he was about to escape by Swedish ship, from Gravesend, in disguise. At least in his trustful aristocratic way he thought it was a disguise. He wore a black wig over his thick golden hair, but there was too much hair for the wig, and though he had wrapped it in a sort of coronet around his head, a lot of it slipped down behind, giving a very odd effect.

The report of the trial of these four conspirators is good reading, but not in the way a mystery story is good. There was little mystery about it. Even a bush Negro, had the trial been held in his language, would have seen through everyone and everything connected with the affair. Admittedly, the language difficulty did lend a note of uncertainty to matters. Neither Borosky nor Stern

spoke English; the count did, but for purposes of his own he preferred to claim that he didn't. Two interpreters were provided,
therefore; one of them, Sir Nathaniel Johnson, was not only an
interpreter, but a self-appointed champion of Königsmark and
Vratz as well. He twisted his translations, argued as if he were
counsel for the defense, and generally behaved in a most unpro-
fessional manner, but the magistrate did no more than comment,
somewhat peevishly, on his habits. The magistrates had already
been got at, no doubt, by the King's party, and knew that the
count ought to get off because Charles wanted it like that. The
other prisoners on trial, however, were to be condemned. Nobody influential cared what happened to them. Besides, they had
most indubitably killed Tom Thynne, and justice in one way or
another had to be observed.

It could not be described as a summary trial; on the face of it,
everything was more than fair. To be sure, the unimportant two,
Stern and Borosky, were so awed by the proceedings and the language trouble that they never availed themselves of such privileges as the law allowed, such as objecting to jurors as they were
sworn in. Karl Johann more than made up for this deficiency, by
excepting against one juror after another. Some of his exceptions
were quite logical, based as they were on national prejudice.
There must be no Danes or Poles or Papists on the jury, he con-
tended, for his father had served against the King of Denmark,
and against the Poles, and the Papists, and his father was a
Protestant, and served the Protestants. He also objected to Wal-
loons, "because they have always been against the Swedes." It is
worth noticing how many foreigners there seemed to be in London, that one stray scoopful of jury candidates should turn up so
many as are mentioned among Karl's rejects.

The trials of Vratz and the lesser mercenaries came first. The
prosecution got very little change out of the Dutchman, but on
the face of it his story of his motive was unlikely, from the
foundations up through the entire edifice. Vratz had quarreled,

he said, with Thynne, and so had killed him. Twice before the murder he had written from Holland, challenging the Squire of Longleat to a duel, but Thynne had ignored the messages, and at last the captain's patience was at an end. He had crossed the Channel, hired his former comrades in arms, and attacked the coach: that was all.

Pressed for an explanation as to what Thynne and he could possibly have quarreled about, he said it was not so much a quarrel as an insult. What insult? Why, Thynne had said unpleasant things about his good friend and former officer, Count Königsmark, Vratz said; so he had simply gone out with his bravoes and killed Thynne.

From a reporter's point of view Stern, who had actually fired the blunderbuss, made a most unsatisfactory witness. He was either permanently dazed, overpowered by the language difficulty, or mentally subnormal. His story was shockingly direct. He had shot Thynne, he said without amplifying the statement. They gave him the gun and he shot Thynne as he was told to do.

Borosky was the prosecution's best bet. Though he had not been present at any crucial interviews between Vratz and Karl, he did have some idea of the count's having been behind the affair, and in spite of his desire to shield the whole crew, this conviction was bound to leak out. As for facts, however, he knew only that he had been imported for some mysterious purpose, and had been clothed and armed by the count before the fatal expedition.

The count's name recurred so often in the replies of Borosky and Hanson, and was so doggedly left out of Vratz's, that when it was his turn to take the stand, most of the onlookers must have come to their conclusions long since. But Karl Johann was a quick thinker if not a solid planner, and he had his story ready. He was not very convincing about that restless secret sojourn of his in London before the murder, but he had an explanation, if a limping one. He did not feel well, he said, and was in no mood for rollicking company. He kept moving about because each place that he tried out was unsatisfactory because of smoking chimneys and so forth. For that reason he had seen only his servants and his doctor and his old comrade-in-arms, Vratz.

He had not much to say about a question Hanson unfortunately recollected his asking, "that if he should meddle with Esquire Thynne, what the consequence might be and if the laws of England would be contrary to him in the hopes or pretensions he might have to my Lady Ogle." There was another awkward question too, which his servantboy alleged he had asked on the day of the murder. "He asked me on Sunday, in the forenoon, whether people were suffered to ride about the streets on horseback on Sundays. . . . I told him, yes, before sermon-time, and after sermon-time."

At this point we are tempted to call Count Königsmark all sorts of a nincompoop. A man contemplating such a crime today, who committed such offenses against the most ordinary rules of caution as these questions were, would not be considered sane. After his trial, if not before, he would be whisked off to a lunatic asylum. But in our day the very children have become crafty. People were simpler then. It may seem incredible, but Königsmark was not, for his day and age, a stupid man. In fact, he was an astute courtier who knew his way around, and could gauge to a nicety how far this foreign justice would dare to go in risking the displeasure of his powerful connections in Sweden. He knew, too, that the King was displeased with Monmouth, and had never loved Thynne, so that Monmouth's much publicized enmity toward himself was an asset, not a liability. How far the King's private approval might extend was, of course, the ticklish question. Also, though this does not seem to have bothered him very much, he knew that Vratz was doomed, and that he was betraying a friend of matchless loyalty. The gamble had failed. But it *might* have worked. It *might* not have failed.

The circumstantial tale continued. The prosecution showed

how Karl had taken alarm at the arrests of the mercenaries, and had fled to Rotherhithe in his grotesque black wig, and found refuge that night with a Swedish ship's captain. It was worked out by means of watermen and servants how he had continued the next day to Gravesend, where the captain's ship lay waiting. There he had been discovered by two men in Monmouth's employ, who traced him to the boat.

There had been a short struggle when they took him. His wig had slipped off, and his ordinary clothes, hidden under a greatcoat he had borrowed, were disclosed. Then he admitted who he was and came along quietly, through a hostile crowd at the water front who had to be held back by his captors. A conversation he had with the two men, Kid and Gibbons, while waiting for transport back to London, was significant.

Said Gibbons, "I belong to the Duke of Monmouth."

"Why," said Count Karl, "the Duke of Monmouth has no command now; how can you take me by his order?"

Gibbons said, "My lord, I do not apprehend you by his order. You have killed a very good friend of mine, and had not Providence ordered it otherwise, you had like to have killed a more particular friend, and a master."

Königsmark seemed "very sorry at that," Gibbons narrated. "But," he said, "I don't think they would have done any harm to the Duke of Monmouth."

A little later the count said, as if to himself, "It is a stain upon my blood; but one good action in the wars or one lodging upon a counterscarp will wash away all that."

He tried to discover how much was known. Gibbons was canny, but, perhaps in an experimental spirit, he announced falsely that Vratz had confessed.

"I do not believe the captain would confess anything," said Königsmark confidently.

Going upriver, back to London, there was more conversation. "I told him that I was at Newgate on Friday, and there saw those who had done that barbarous fact," said Gibbons. "With that, my lord asked me what lodgings there were at Newgate, and whether the captain had a good lodging. I told him a very good one. He asked me whether he confessed anything; I told him he had confessed some particulars; and, said I, it is the most barbarous thing that ever was done. 'Certainly,' says my lord, 'this Mr. Thynne must have some correspondence and commerce with some lady that this captain knew, that belonged to the court, or he would never have done it.' As for the Polander, I told him he had confessed, and that he wept mightily. With that, my lord seemed very much concerned, and took up his clothes and bit them, and sat awhile up, but was very much discomposed, and then desired to lie down."

In court, having thought it over, Königsmark had some sort of answer to all this. The "Polander," he said, he had met in Tangiers, and learned that Borosky was once groom to his uncle. He had thereupon formed a plan to bring him to England, to dress his horses after the German way. In proof of this statement, young Count Philipp eagerly testified that his brother had actually sent him money from France with orders that Borosky should buy him some horses, against his arrival. As for having supplied the man with a sword, Karl freely admitted it. It was the custom in Poland for men in Borosky's position to go about with such weapons. Karl had run away after the murder, he said, because he was afraid "the common people," always ready to suspect foreigners like himself, might hold him responsible for Thynne's death, and knock him on the head.

The testimony was declared complete. Karl was told to make a speech in his own defense, if he wished (though the others were not given this chance), and he readily did so, addressing the court both in French and German. He was, he said, a Protestant; his forefathers were Protestants; they had always fought in defense of the Protestant religion and no other. Presumably no Knights of Malta were present to give the count the lie, and no one else disputed his word. He loved England and the King, he declared. As a good Protestant, he couldn't possibly have had anything to do with such a horrid crime. "And he says, that if any of his former actions can give any the least suspicion of his being guilty of this or any foul act, he is very willing to lay down his life, and very willing to have it cut off immediately."

"Immediately," added Königsmark firmly, echoing the interpreter in English.

Vratz, Stern, and Borosky were adjudged guilty. The interpreter duly reported their permitted remarks when they heard the judgment. Borosky said he prayed God to have mercy on him. Vratz said he was never rightly examined nor fairly tried. Stern said he did it for the captain's sake.

Königsmark was found not guilty. He said in English, "God bless the King and the honorable Bench!" After which he hastily departed from England.

Vratz held out to the end, rejecting all temptation to tell more about the crime than he had already done. When Dr. Gilbert Burnet visited him, as he often did, and exhorted him to repent and so forth, "He said it was his own affair, and he desired to be left to himself; but he spake with great assurance of God's mercy to him." At long distance Königsmark claimed the body, and had it put in a magnificent coffin, and caused it to be carried to Holland.

Whatever God's mercy may have proved to be, I am sure that in the afterworld it never occurred to Vratz, when Count Königsmark arrived five years later, to offer reproaches. He was a mercenary and he had his code. To Dr. Burnet it may have seemed an outlandish code, but it satisfied Vratz, and will accompany that stouthearted man, I am convinced, to the outer limits of Eternity.

2. PHILIPP CHRISTOPH

KARL JOHANN had escaped by the skin of his teeth and Charles II's prejudice. Now he tactfully withdrew from England so that public indignation might have a chance to die down, though as a matter of fact the general public cared less about injustice of the sort than did the aristocracy. Only a few of those who could afford the finer feelings maintained the principle of *noblesse oblige* on the subject of the count.

"This day was executed Colonel Vratz and some of his accomplices," wrote Evelyn, one of the conscientious gentlemen, on the tenth of March 1682, "for the execrable murder of Mr. Thynne, set on by the principal Königsmark. He went to execution like an undaunted hero, as one that had done a friendly deed for that base coward, Count Königsmark. . . ."

Karl too may have been assailed by his conscience; nobody knows. Whatever he felt, he continued to prove his incredible insolence by going straight to Holland, where he renewed his courtship of Lady Ogle. Tact was never the count's most notable characteristic. Probably he felt it unnecessary; the rich little widow had not encountered much tact as yet in her adventurous life, and she might be said to have owed him a debt of gratitude, in a way, for having killed her unpleasant husband. But he didn't get far with her. Either she had too much native common sense, or her temporary guardian, Lady Temple, advised her well. She might possibly have disliked Count Königsmark from the beginning. Whatever her motives, she sent him about his business, and Königsmark went back to the wars.

Lady Ogle's future had nothing to do with the Königsmark family, but it is interesting to know that she married for the third time, and became Duchess of Somerset, and lived a long, contented life.

In London during the weeks after the trial, Karl's young brother Philipp Christoph found his position awkward. The family name had become notorious and was execrated throughout the city, so that it was uncomfortable to go out of doors. Yet indoors he found no comfort either, since his guardian and tutor, Frederick Hanson, had borne witness against Count Karl and was under sentence of dismissal from Karl's indignant family in Sweden. The little household in the Haymarket must be dispersed forthwith.

All Karl's original plans for his brother, including Oxford after the course at Faubert's Academy had been completed, were jettisoned. Instead, Philipp was sent to the Continent to complete his military training, going from court to court in the accepted manner of young noblemen doing the Grand Tour. There was never any lack of welcome wherever he went: he was exceedingly popular. He was even better-looking than Karl, just as talented, and he showed a similar spirit in battle. As Karl had done before him, Philipp went first to visit his uncle Otto Wilhelm at the Swedish Embassy at Versailles. After that he traveled in Spain and Italy and Germany. Germany he already knew well and found congenial—his mother was half German; the Königsmarks had many connections there—and for this reason he spent much of his training period at Dresden.

In 1682, the first year of his wanderings, Philipp heard a good deal of talk about a marriage which was being arranged and was going to take place in the little German duchy of Celle, near Hanover. Philipp had lived at Celle for a while when he was a child, and he had pleasant memories of the ducal *Schloss* there, where he had played in the garden with the duke's daughter, little Sophie Dorothea. She was just his age and they had been sweethearts, fondly smiled upon by their elders. It had been a truly Teutonic idyll, all infantile sentiment. But now the little Sophie Dorothea was evidently grown up, like Philipp himself. At least she was old enough to marry. Philipp probably reacted only mildly when he heard this news; he could hardly lay claim to any serious pangs of jealousy this late in the day. But he may well have played with the idea of regretting his lost love, and sighed a few times for sensation's sake, before he continued on his travels.

To avoid confusion, we must now forget Philipp for a little while and turn our attention to the history of this bride he had known and was to meet again.

The wedding between the children of the Dukes of Hanover and Celle reunited two duchies which had previously been part of one duke's land. Father of the bride and father of the bridegroom were brothers. It was very much a family affair, and was looked upon as such by quite a few petty German princes. Not many of them realized that behind the match someone was playing a game for considerable stakes—England's throne. Though Sophie Dorothea, Princess of Celle, and George Louis, Prince of Hanover, were members of royalty, there were so many royal beings in the Empire (the Holy Roman Empire as it was called, though actually it was not much more than Germany and Austria combined) one could scarcely keep track of them.

The status of all these German and Austrian dukes and princes and electors, who were nominally subject to the Emperor Leopold, was a peculiarly loose and undefined one. For one thing, there was the fact, which seems strange in the light of our modern ideas, that such a duke or prince was quite free to ally himself with an enemy of the Emperor's if he wished, and to make war on Leopold himself, without being condemned as a traitor. He was a subject only by courtesy, as it were. Another oddity of the Empire's system of government was the assignment of hereditary rights. There was no hard-and-fast rule of succession. A prince, elector, or duke selected for himself, without reference to the Emperor, his heir and successor to his title. Many a ruler who had more than one child would divide his domain into small pieces and distribute them in his will among his sons, in a praiseworthy but shortsighted ambition to provide for the whole family. Usually, as soon as he was dead, the children set to work trying to join up the lands again, by force or trickery or marriage, for *their* children. And so wars were stimulated.

One of these reigning noblemen, a duke of Brunswick-Lüneburg, had no sons, but left his land to two nephews, George William and Ernest Augustus. Celle, the sovereign principality, came into the possession of George William. His brother Ernest Augustus inherited Hanover, ten leagues from Celle, and Osnabrück as well. Duke George William was the richer, but Duke Ernest Augustus had more land and a *much* more important wife. George William's wife was Eléonore d'Olbreuse, daughter of a French Huguenot marquis who had been exiled. Ernest Augustus's wife was Princess Sophia, one of the children of Elizabeth of Bohemia and thus niece to Charles I. Like her mother the Winter Queen and her brothers Rupert and Maurice, Sophia considered herself thoroughly English. She tried to instill in her eldest son, George Louis, a similar Anglophilia; she wanted to kindle in him an ambition to inherit England's crown, which during George Louis's childhood was being worn by Charles II, Sophia's cousin. In this endeavor she failed. George Louis persisted in thinking of himself as a Hanoverian.

Sophia was an admirable woman in many ways, with a keen intellect and a quick wit, but she was not a kind person and she had many fierce antipathies. Among them was her sister-in-law, George William's wife Eléonore. Really, Sophia was quite unfair about Eléonore. There was nothing wrong with the Duchess of Celle; indeed, most people liked her very much. But Sophia said she was low and common, unworthy to be married to a duke. The real reason for this enmity was that Eléonore had ruined the Hanover family's prospects of inheriting Celle, and though Sophia's ambitions outstripped this mere little duchy, she would not have minded getting hold of it on her way to higher things.

Her resentment was not so unreasonable as it may seem at first sight, for the Hanover faction's hopes had been raised by Duke George William himself, before he thought better of it. As a younger man he had announced that he was a confirmed bachelor, and that his brother or his brother's issue should inherit his goods. Then he fell in love with Eléonore d'Olbreuse, and when she resisted all his attempts to seduce her he made her his morganatic wife. Years of near-respectability and the birth of his daughter Sophie Dorothea softened him still farther, and he lent a willing ear to the urgings of his cousin the Duke of Wolfenbüttel, that he make everything quite aboveboard by marrying Eléonore properly. This he did, ultimately, despite Sophia's opposition. By special dispensation of the Emperor, whose powers extended this far at least, the Duke of Celle went through the necessary ceremony with his morganatic wife and she was morganatic no longer, but a full-fledged duchess. Sophie Dorothea became a princess at the same moment. Sophia could not forgive Eléonore. Her attacks were spiteful and savage, and Eléonore heartily reciprocated the sentiments of the Duchess of Hanover.

Like most wealthy little girls of the seventeenth century, Sophie Dorothea was betrothed before reaching the age of puberty. She must have been affianced even at the time she played with Philipp Christoph von Königsmark, when they were small children. But her parents, less brutal than the guardians of Elizabeth Percy, who married her off in childhood to Lord Ogle, did not carry their arrangements so far. Sophie Dorothea was still unmarried when her young man, a Wolfenbüttel prince, was killed in some war or other. She was only ten or eleven at the time, and it was generally supposed that she would ultimately marry his younger brother.

While the duke and duchess desultorily discussed the new engagement, over in Hanover the Duchess Sophia, whom the little princess had never seen, was also busying herself with matchmaking. George Louis, six years older than his cousin Sophie

Dorothea, was a valuable political pawn. He had no aesthetic appeal, no personal charm, having taken after his fat father's side of the family rather than the impulsive, quick-witted, long-legged clan of the Winter King, but he had his points; he had his prospects. Sophia entertained grandiose ideas of marrying him to Princess Anne, daughter of Charles II's brother James, who was next in line for the throne of England.

This project alarmed and angered William of Orange. He had already married Mary, Anne's sister, and intended to inherit England himself when the time came. George Louis must be got out of the way: why should he not make a less ambitious match? Let him take to wife his cousin Sophie Dorothea of Celle and remove himself from the race for England. William knew that George Louis's mother and Sophie Dorothea's mother were not on speaking terms—such chitchat was an important part of statecraft—but it was not an insuperable difficulty, he was sure. Women's preferences were usually ignored in these matters.

Naturally reluctant to put the proposition himself to the dukes involved, William went to work intriguing on conventional lines, and arranged to hire spies at each of the two German courts. Bernstorff, first minister to George William, was his spy at Celle, and at Hanover he made connections with Madame Platen.

This Madame Platen held the office of court mistress, an institution which few well-run contemporary European courts were without. We are puzzled nowadays to figure out just where society drew the line on this matter. The world allegedly considered royal mistresses bad things. According to later historians, people of the seventeenth century shook their heads and strongly disapproved of such goings on. Charles II is constantly described as having called down the curses of the people on his head for having flaunted his mistresses as he did. But the more I read, the more I wonder if these later historians have not projected their own indignations into the past. It wasn't only Charles of England who flaunted mistresses; practically every duke and prince in

Europe did the same. There couldn't have been very much serious headshaking, considering. Of course the duchesses and princesses didn't care much for the system; that is to be expected. But as for public odium—no, I do not believe it. It was much too common and popular a fashion.

Take Madame Platen, now. She was Ernest Augustus's mistress, and really he might just as well have been married to her and kept his wife Sophia as a mistress instead, for all the promiscuity he indulged in apart from these relationships. Ernest Augustus was no libertine; he was merely a bigamist, a very different thing. What is more, he was a *henpecked* bigamist, rather meek with both his women.

Madame Platen was a handsome woman with flashing eyes and one of those high square bosoms the Germans love. She was completely unprincipled. Principles were not widely distributed in her set, and we should not be censorious of her on that account, but she was perhaps more dangerous than other villainesses because she was also nearly brainless and had an appetite for power. A dominating fool can do a lot of damage. The commission she received from William of Orange to convince her ducal lover that his son should marry Sophie Dorothea pleased her. Not only did it promise to be profitable, but it gave her a chance to meddle in diplomatic affairs, and such meddling was her particular hobby.

Everything went well for William, from beginning to end. George Louis's lackadaisical wooing of Anne got him nowhere, Bernstorff found a ready listener to the new plan in the Duke of Celle, and Madame Platen, working away in Hanover, made a definite impression on Ernest Augustus. Actually, William's machinations apart, the suggested match made sense from Ernest Augustus's point of view. There was the old lure of reuniting the domains, for one thing, and for another, there was Sophie Dorothea's wealth, which would go as a matter of routine into her husband's possession. Yes, Ernest Augustus liked the idea.

So did George William, perhaps for the same reason, the attraction of reuniting the land, but more likely because he was easily led by Bernstorff. And so, in spite of the feud of the duchesses, in spite of Sophia's furious opposition at first (she gave in ultimately, however, and was active in arranging the contract) and Eléonore's tears and tantrums, Sophie Dorothea married her cousin George Louis.

Their wedding could hardly be described as an auspicious beginning to married life. The two principals had never seen each other, and had only heard the worst things about each other's immediate families. Sophia had always talked of Eléonore as a lowborn trollop, and declared her daughter was bound to be worse. Eléonore had brought up Sophie Dorothea on nursery tales about the wicked aunt at Hanover. Beaten down to submission by a husband grown suddenly stubborn and unpleasant, the Duchess of Celle, mother of the bride, wailed and had hysterics at the wedding feast. It is not surprising that Sophie Dorothea went off on her honeymoon in a pitiable state of apprehension, and George Louis was the last man in the world to comfort or soothe a girl.

To put it plainly, the Prince of Hanover was a lout. He was selfish, extremely slow in his reactions, and constitutionally sullen. His one positive virtue was physical courage; he was a good soldier, not flashy but steady and completely lacking in fear. He had not desired this marriage or any marriage, but he did not actively object, knowing it was all part of the job of being prince. Sophie Dorothea was not his type; her daintiness held no charms for him. He liked something less Latin, more Saxon. But that, in the end, need not matter. He was totally insensitive to anyone's feelings but his own. Even Sophia did not dote on him, though in general she was a fond mama to her children. She wrote about the marriage in a letter to her confidante the Duchess of Orleans:

"Ernest Augustus always had a queer head, and how such an idea could have entered it passes all my understanding. How-ver, one hundred thousand thalers a year is a goodly sum to ocket, without speaking of a pretty wife, who will find a match my son George Louis, the most pigheaded, stubborn boy who ver lived, and who has round his brains such a thick crust that defy any man or woman ever to discover what is in them."

Sophia must have been softened by the size of the dowry to lmit that a daughter of Eléonore d'Olbreuse could be pretty, but e fact is, the princess *was* pretty, noticeably so. Even had she ot been a princess she would have been admired. Certainly she as better-looking than many contemporaries of royal blood, per- aps because she was a love child, the fruit of natural selection ther than political breeding. She was small, dark, and vivacious, ith large wide-set eyes and a sweet expression. Her great interest as costume; she spent hours every day on her appearance, and hose her jewels with the greatest care and very good taste. She as properly accomplished in music and dancing and all that, id seems to have had the kittenish charm of a petted, spoiled, ily child. She could not lay claim to intellectual pretensions like iose of the Duchess Sophia, who was a true bluestocking; the ride had little interest in books. We would not have considered ophie Dorothea intelligent, I suppose, but we would have called er a nice little thing. She was gay and sweet, a singing cricket a princess. The idea of such a creature being suddenly unked down in the unfriendly, humorless and very dull Han- er court inspires pity. One thinks of a toy poodle forced to live a kennel of mastiffs.

Yet it was not too bad at first. She was homesick, that goes ithout saying, but she was not exiled; the marriage smoothed er the traditional enmity between the Duchesses of Celle and anover, and her parents came sometimes to visit, and she re- irned now and then to see them. George Louis continued to be orose and uncouth, but the mistress he had maintained before is wedding in the public manner characteristic of the Georges id been sent away by special request of Eléonore, and for some time no substitute appeared on the scene to offend Sophie Doro-thea's sense of dignity.

The life they led at Hanover sounds unbelievably tedious when we read about it. What in Heaven's name did they *do* with themselves, we ask ourselves, when they were not appear-ing in full panoply at state dinners or balls? Actually, they did just about nothing. There were no outdoor games and few urban amusements for the ladies. Sophie Dorothea spent the whole morning at her toilette, talking with her companion Fräulein Knesebeck or with such few ladies of the court as she liked and trusted. Then there was a heavy lunch, the long afternoon rest, and a sedate drive later, if the weather was fine. Then a terrific dinner, and cards or perhaps dancing afterwards—not gay danc-ing, of course. We think it a slow life, but after all it was the only tempo Sophie Dorothea had ever known, so we must beware of pitying her more than is called for.

Perhaps one of the troubles with George Louis was that he was bored and didn't know it. Like his wife, he had never known a more exciting existence, save that he sometimes went out cam-paigning. No doubt for this reason he welcomed war, as he wel-comed a good day's hunting, but life at home, the life to which duty usually called him, was a stupefying routine against which it never occurred to him to rebel.

In due course the princess bore a son, and then she produced a daughter, just as she should have done. Everyone was gratified; even the redoubtable Sophia put aside her memories of the old feud and showed her daughter-in-law a grim sort of graciousness. As for Ernest Augustus, he really melted, and became senti-mentally fond of the princess, and took to giving her presents and allowing her to accompany him on his travels to Italy. But George Louis remained his noncommittal, surly self, and the Platen was not a warm admirer of Sophie Dorothea, either.

This attitude of the royal mistress was partly the princess's own fault. As might be expected, Sophie Dorothea in her position as

gal wife and mother of a prince was prejudiced against the en-
e institution of court mistresses. It was a kind of class loyalty,
e attitude of a member of one trades union toward that of a
al organization. A clever woman might have done something
ective about this class enemy. She would have tried not
erely to annoy the Platen and thus relieve her own feelings, but
ually to undermine the other woman's influence. Sophie
orothea was not a clever woman, nor even crafty like Madame
aten. She behaved like a child; she snubbed the mistress at
ery opportunity. When Ernest Augustus advanced Herr Platen
the rank of count, the princess's resentment heightened on
neral principles, though she felt no loyalty toward her mother-
law. Just as Sophia had objected to her own mother's advance-
ent, Sophie Dorothea hated to think of this upstart becoming
ountess. She made catty remarks which were reported in rec-
l time to the other lady. The countess promptly set to work
Ernest Augustus, turning him against his pretty little daugh-
-in-law. And so it went, until the mistress thought of a better
enge.

No doubt George Louis did not need the Platen's encourage-
ent to stray from the path of monogamy; he would have found
own way into the woods in due time. Perhaps he did his own
ecting; perhaps it was only court gossip which credited the
untess with having produced the new woman who took his
cy. Her name was Ermengarda Melusina von Schulenberg,
d anyone less like George Louis's wife would be hard to
agine. She was tall—much taller than her lover—with yellow
ir and big bones, and George Louis fell promptly in love.
phie Dorothea was furious.

We must remember that the princess had her own set of
ues, which though they may not be ours, were important to
r. Although she did not love her husband, she was nevertheless
able of fierce and very painful jealousy over him. A discreet
ison between George Louis and some woman would not have

troubled her at all, even had she known all about it, but this was in full view of the whole court; that is what she could not bear. Jealousy, after all, is chiefly composed of pride and possession; very little of it is due to frustrated love. That is why the seventeenth-century royal system of infidelity was so cruel, so much more brutal than the modern way.

For George Louis followed his father's example. Not quite as conscienceless as Charles II, who insisted that his mistress serve his bride as one of her ladies-in-waiting, he was exhibitionistic enough to annoy any wife. At social gatherings, regardless of who might be watching, he paid his amorous attentions to the Schulenberg with the happy abandon of a goldfish. He set her up in luxury and saw to it that she moved in the same circles as did Sophie Dorothea. The princess naturally felt that he had degraded her own rank. She felt herself scorned, which was bad; laughed at, which was worse; and pitied, which was insupportable. Why, the woman wasn't even attractive! She was a great clumsy blond giantess. Little Sophie Dorothea complained bitterly about it.

She was no philosopher, and the reflection that other queens and princesses had to cope with similar problems did not soothe her. Her mother-in-law Sophia coped superbly, and was on good terms with her rival, but it was not in the princess's intellectual power thus to accept and ignore. She made childish scenes, which did not at all shake George Louis: after them he simply avoided her for a bit. Then she rushed off to Celle to wail to her parents and beg that they make representations. But George William, standing stanchly by his own sex, told her brusquely to go home to Hanover and do her duty. There, having obeyed him, she went into new fits of rage and grief. Again and again she followed the cycle, while the court gossiped and tittered and George Louis calmly spent the days and nights with his mistress.

Sophie Dorothea had quite got used to being unhappy by the time Philipp Christoph von Königsmark arrived.

During the six years that had elapsed since Karl Johann's escapade and consequent trial, Philipp had behaved much like any other young man of his family, wandering from country to country, taking an officer's commission now and then, and, when he tired of it, giving it up. He had returned several times to Dresden and there had become very friendly with Frederick Augustus, the Elector of Saxony who was later to fall in love with Philipp's sister. Like Karl, Philipp had had his successes at arms, but he had not been so spectacular a fighter as Karl, perhaps because the ladies ran after him and distracted his energy. A few months before he came to Hanover he had received the sad news of Karl's death, which had, of course, taken place on a battlefield, in a fight with the Turks.

Philipp inherited Karl's fortune, as well as his position as nominal head of the family. Strictly speaking, he should thus have been accountable for the behavior of his two sisters, one of whom, Amalie, had married a Count von Lewenhaupt. The other was the charming and notorious Aurora. All three young people, however, would have laughed heartily at the idea of restricting each other's movements. Anyone but a Königsmark, coming into so much money, would have gone home to Sweden immediately, and stayed there at least long enough to put his affairs in order. The question of Philipp's estates and property soon became even more complicated, because Uncle Otto Wilhelm died without issue, and his fortune too, a very considerable one, went to Philipp. But the young count was in no hurry to leave Germany, for he scented trouble and a great war in the offing.

It was 1688. James II of England was putting himself off the throne with as much energy as if he were aiming for that end instead of merely clinging to the Roman Church. Louis XIV's activities were stimulating Leopold to a burst of activity; the Emperor was busily collecting allies, preparing for the all-out war which was Louis's evident ambition. Among other rulers on the

Continent, Ernest Augustus had been approached with regard to his loyalties and those of his brother the Duke of Celle. So far, the Duke of Hanover had evaded the question and put off signing any treaty. As I have already said, Ernest Augustus was not compelled to support the Emperor. He could with impunity line up with France if he wished. Whether he would have been wise to make an ally of Louis XIV, considering that everyone else except Turkey was going to be on Leopold's side, was another matter. Ernest Augustus played for time and for more than time: he wanted to make a good bargain before he signed.

It is not quite clear just why Königsmark went to Hanover, but it was a natural enough thing to have done, for he was idle at the moment. He had made friends with Prince Charles, a younger brother of George Louis, at Dresden, and Charles no doubt suggested that he come home with him for a little hunting and gaiety; even, perhaps, to take a commission in his father's well-drilled army. That is how Count Königsmark came to meet his childhood sweetheart, Sophie Dorothea, for the second time.

The situation between George Louis and his wife had become fairly static. The prince was still in the first excitement of his infatuation with Ermengarda Melusina, and Sophie Dorothea was still kicking up an occasional row. There exists a book about Philipp's love story, supposedly written by Aurora, which is in the form of a novel, the characters denoted by initials and dashes. A passage in it describes one of these scenes:

"The Prince . . . not only avoided her Bed, but her Company, and for two whole months together, never exchang'd a Syllable with her, nor allow'd her a Moment's Opportunity to enquire the Cause of so sudden and undeserv'd an Alteration.

"Not being able, however, to digest the Affront any longer, as likewise believing it to be her Duty to solicite an Explanation, she one Day made a Shift to surprize him in his Closet alone, and, when able to speak (for Tears and Passion for a while held

er speechless) conjured him in the most urgent and affecting
[m]anner, to let her know wherein she had offended, and why he
industriously avoided her. For myself, said she, I am not con-
[sc]ious of a blameable Thought, nor can I attempt to justify my
[c]onduct, till I am informed in what I have had the Misfortune
[to] displease you. . . . I would fain make it my Glory to please
[yo]u, and should esteem it the highest Obligation you can confer
[on] me, if you would point out the Way.

"By leaving me to myself,—interrupted the Prince, with a
[vo]ice like Thunder, and a Look if possible, yet more killing; and
[withal], rush'd out of the Closet like a Fury, leaving the Princess
[in] Agonies not to be described."

Overcome, Sophie Dorothea rushed back in turn to her apart-
[m]ents, where Königsmark was waiting with Knesebeck to pay a
[c]eremonial call. The princess was crying, and in her excitement
[tol]d them all about it in a wild outburst. It seems quite in-
[ev]itable that Philipp should have been seized at that moment, if
[no]t before, with chivalrous love for Sophie Dorothea, and a
[de]termination to remain near her. Soon afterward he accepted a
[co]mmission as colonel in the Hanoverian Guards, and he also
[bo]ught an estate near Hamburg.

Correspondence which has survived shows that this gesture,
[far] from being a practical arrangement made between confirmed
[lov]ers, was purely romantic. The affaire did not yet exist. Philipp
[ma]y not even have intended, there at the beginning, to attempt
[to] seduce Sophie Dorothea. The danger of such a relationship
[wa]s great, as he fully realized, and the princess would have run
[a] far greater risk than his. There were some courts where the
[lad]ies of the reigning families were as dissolute as the men, but
[tho]se of the Brunswick-Lüneberg group were not among them.
[So], Philipp loved the princess, he probably told himself, in a
[dif]ferent way—a purer way; the way knights of chivalry were
[err]oneously supposed to love their ladies, at long distance. He
[wo]uld stay near her as long as he could, in order to protect her if

need be from that brute of a husband, but as for anything carnal
—no.

Still, for all these uplifted sentiments, Philipp was no Gala-
had. He had a deserved reputation for gallantry, so there were
plenty of interested spectators when he mooned about, looking
unutterable things at Sophie Dorothea. More than two years
before the pair became lovers, it was whispered, and believed,
that they were guilty.

This mischief-making was due in the main to Sophie Dorothea's enemy the Countess Platen. The story is that there was a
splendid ball held at Hanover, at which George Louis, as usual,
paid marked court to his fair giantess. Count Königsmark,
magnificently arrayed in pink and silver, danced with Sophie
Dorothea, who was dressed as Flora, all in white with a flower
wreath. Everyone regarded them with admiration. As a portrait
made of Philipp at the time shows, he was a good-looking man of
boyish appearance. Whether it was his pretty face and the pink
and silver, or the fact that he was supposed to belong to the princess, he had an electric effect that night on the Countess Platen,
and she invited him to come to her apartments after the ball was
over. Let Aurora continue:

"There was . . . a Mixture of Self-Conceit and Spleen to the
Princess, as well as Affection for K—k, in this forward step of the
Countess's; She had neither been accustomed to Neglect, nor
was of a Temper to bear it; much less could she suffer any Body
else to dispute the Pre-eminence with her, or rob her of the
Homage which she thought still due to her Charms, though now
in their Wane.

"Resolv'd then, to make a Convert of the Count at all Hazards,
and believing Advances on her Side to be the only Way; being,
likewise, of a Libertine-Turn, and thinking the Ceremonial in
Love-Affairs to be most of all impertinent, she had so disposed
herself on a magnificent Settee, as, at first Entrance of the Count,

ght prepare him for what was to follow; as might totally efface
ery other Image from his Heart, and fill it with hers only.

"It seems to be a Frailty entail'd upon Man, that Heaven at
stance does not attract us so forcibly, as a Fool's Paradise in
ght. K—k found himself a Son of *Adam* in this dangerous Inter-
-w. To see himself at once overwhelmed with the Caresses of
andsome, powerful Woman, melted down all his Constancy at
ce, and made him fit to receive what Impression she pleased.
"But let us here draw the Curtain. . . ."

Nothing of that sort ever remained secret at court, and Sophie
orothea heard of it almost immediately. She had as yet no
oprietary interest in the count; her emotions were chiefly those
a woman who feels she is being politically betrayed. The
untess was her enemy, and now it seemed that Königsmark as
·ll had gone over to the other side. She reproached him, not
olently, but enough to fill him with remorse. Henceforth, he
wed, the countess would spread her nets in vain, and he stuck
his promise. His neglect insulted and annoyed the countess,
d turned her more than ever against Sophie Dorothea.

The treaty with Leopold was still being bruited and still un-
ned. Ernest Augustus was holding out for the Emperor's
omise to raise him in rank to the dignity of elector; though the
nperor protested that he had already created his quota of elec-
·ates, the Duke of Hanover would not accept refusal. He was
led and abetted by his ever-ambitious wife Sophia, who also
nted assurance that she and George Louis were definitely in
e of succession to the English throne. Leopold's hesitation to
et the two dukes' terms worked in well with the sentiments of
éonore of Celle, who, as a Frenchwoman, urged her husband
side with Louis XIV. But Ernest Augustus waited, confident
at his armies and the geographical position of Hanover would
rry the day for him, and he was right. He was created elector,
d at the same time William of Orange, or rather William III
England, as he now was, gave his word that Protestant Han-

over should inherit the throne in time, for Popish James had fled and no Papist must rule England again. In the winter of 1690, therefore, and from then on for years there was war on the Continent. Königsmark found plenty to do in his capacity as officer in the Hanoverian Guards.

Had there been no war, and no intermittent absences of the count from court, and no anguished farewells and rapturous greetings and terrible suspense, his affair with the princess might never have begun at all. It really was a mad thing for them to have done. Security and secrecy were impossible; both knew it. But passion had its way, though there was a long struggle first against temptation. The princess and the count did not succumb until some time around the middle of 1691, three years after Philipp came to Hanover, and even then they quaked and took elaborate precautions, and hoped against all sane hope that they would get away with it.

We know all this in spite of the earnest endeavors of statesmen dead these three centuries to conceal it from our eyes. Long after the disgrace to the royal house of Hanover had been discovered and avenged, trusted clerks of George II were put to work erasing Philipp's name from the army records or anywhere else it could be found. For decades Sophie Dorothea was kept under wraps, a living corpse, while Philipp's body rotted under a lavatory floor. Every scrap of the lovers' letters which could be found was destroyed. But Ernest Augustus and his successors reckoned without Aurora.

This merry, reckless girl, during Philipp's liaison with Sophie Dorothea, was dividing her time between her sister's house at Celle, where her Swedish brother-in-law Count Lewenhaupt held a post with the Army, and her brother's two residences in Hanover and Hamburg. She was in Philipp's confidence, and doubtless heard from his own lips the details of the story which she later, in a furious, revengeful spirit, put into her novel. It was natural that she should act as go-between whenever she could,

working together with the Princess's companion Eléonore Knesebeck. The lovers spent a good deal of time on letters to each
other, partly because it was fashionable for lovers to do so, partly
as a relief to overcharged feelings when they could not meet.

To correspond at all was as dangerous as physical intimacy
itself. When Sophie Dorothea consented to exchange letters, a
few weeks before her final surrender, she must have known that
her mind was made up. Philipp's first few missives, written from
military camp, are pleading and ardent, but humble. Then there
is a proud burst of protestation: "Do not doubt my love; God be
my witness, I have never loved as I love you. . . . You may not
believe it, but on the word of a man of honour, I am often so
overcome that I am near swooning away; and yesterday evening,
when I was out walking, and thinking of the many days that I
must pass before seeing you, I became so agitated that it brought
on a palpitation of the heart, and I was obliged to return home.
I know not what would have happened had not my servant
brought me a cordial, and even then it was a long time before I
recovered. . . . I am ready to cast at your feet my life, my
honour, my future, my fortune. I have foresworn all other
women for you; if you doubt this, name any one you would like
me to abandon, and I will never speak to her again."
When he was away he complained; when he was in Hanover
he was in even more difficult a mood, accusing his mistress of
being too timid to take risks, or of being cold to him when they
met in public, or of being fond of her husband after all.
"With what grief I hear that you have been in other arms than
mine! I cannot express what I feel, but it must be so, I suppose;
at least, you suffer it with regret, and take care to tell me. . . . I
adore and love you to distraction, yet I must not see you! Are
there any torments like this in hell?"
"To convince you the better how I love you, how I worship
you, I sign this with my blood."
"I slept like a king, and I hope you did the same. What joy!

what rapture! what enchantment have I not tasted in your sweet arms! Ye gods! what a night I spent! The memory of it blots out all my troubles, and for the moment I count myself the happiest man on earth."

Sophie Dorothea's letters were equally ardent, but one understands the count's complaint of her timidity, for she was really terrified of the Countess Platen and suspected her of supernatural powers to discover the intrigue. Her letters are full of references to the countess; she blamed her for every setback, whether or not the theory was reasonable. She collected, avidly, every word that was said in gossip about herself and reported it to Philipp, searching it for dangerous hidden meanings, and wondering if the speaker were friend or foe. Wandering back and forth between Celle and Hanover, or Hanover and Herrenhausen, she was naturally preoccupied with getting the letters through safely. Everything depended upon the efficacy of the arrangements made by Aurora and Knesebeck. Everything depended upon the packets not going astray, where they might be read by some spy. The lovers used a code, but even so there was always danger.

The amazing thing about the affair is that Sophie Dorothea did persist in carrying on, timid-hearted as she was. Though many people, inevitably, were aware that something of the sort was going on, no crisis arose for many months. George Louis's indifference was responsible for this delayed judgment. He loved his wife so little that even his possessive jealousy was sluggish.

"It is agonising to think of your being perpetually exposed to danger," wrote Sophie Dorothea to Philipp. "Am I destined to sorrow all my life? Shall I never be able to taste quietly the joys of loving and being loved? I long for news of you on the morrow. I shall spend a sleepless night.

"My father and mother have just interrupted me. I was writing this letter and it was all I could do to hide it; it would have astonished them if they had seen it. . . ."

Sometimes they quarreled, accusing each other jealously.

Philipp scarcely dared attend any social function, especially when he was at Hanover and if Countess Platen might be present; it always made Sophie Dorothea angry. But his tyranny over the princess was worse than that. She had to write for his permission even to make the little trips which were her only amusement, to Celle or Herrenhausen. When on one occasion she had no time to write for his gracious consent before dashing off to Frankfort, he poured out his angry heart to her companion, Fräulein Knesebeck.

"It is not fair. Did she not say she hoped I would not go often to Brussels? That was sufficient. I only set foot there for four hours for a game of tennis; I did not even go to Ghent. The wealthy marriage they proposed for me I rejected from the first. I also refused to undertake the journey of which you know, though it was the only thing to save my property. Count Oxenstern assured me that if I had gone the King [of Sweden] would have made me an offer of a regiment with the title of general, and Marshal Hasbert also said that if I had attached myself to the service of the King I should at present be a general. Consider, dear friend, what I have sacrificed and what she is doing, and then say who is in the wrong."

Nerves exacerbated, they waited for their meetings sometimes for months at a time when he was away on campaign, sometimes only for several days when both were at court. But those periods of proximity were perhaps worse than the definite separations. They had to see each other every evening under the most exasperating circumstances; she must smile on other people, he must watch, or undergo the risk of being talked to by Countess Platen. The stolen love meetings could not have taken place at all if George Louis had not altogether stopped paying visits to his wife. Knesebeck would wait in her mistress's apartments until the attendants had gone to sleep, and then would unlock an outer door, confident that the count could find his way in the black darkness to the princess's room. The danger was chiefly in the chance that he would be seen slipping in or out of the door, and chased for a robber. Once this did happen as he came out; two menservants gave pursuit, but he got away.

There were countless quarrels by letter—a running argument about Sophie Dorothea's brother-in-law Prince Max kept them busy for weeks, and at one time she grew so bitterly jealous when he had gone to Countess Platen's for dinner that she threatened to take another lover. Then Philipp tried to stir her up by describing an evening he had spent with a lady he could not resist, she looked so like Sophie Dorothea. The storm might have broken then with terrible results, but the princess had been forewarned by someone else, and gleefully let him know she understood his joke and knew he had spent the evening concerned making card castles for her little daughter.

Difficulties and dangers not only kept passion bright; they increased it. A change came over the affair. If Sophie Dorothea had begun it merely to assuage her hurt vanity and revenge herself against her husband, if Philipp had laid siege because it would be a feather in his cap to have seduced a princess, the lovers forgot these trivialities now. Their whole lives were bent on finding some means by which they could be together openly and forever. They must elope, and for people of their rank this was not easy. They must find their way to some country not inimical to them, where the authorities would be willing to give them sanctuary and risk the displeasure of the Elector of Hanover, the Duke of Celle and all their clan.

This could not be done without money, and as things were, neither of the lovers had any. Sophie Dorothea's entire fortune was in the hands of her husband. She never had a penny of her own that was not doled out by him. Even in those days such a marriage settlement was unusual; a woman of the princess's rank usually had guardians wily enough to see that she possessed some claim to her own dowry, but George William had allowed himself to be diddled when the contract was drawn up. Philipp had exhausted the patience of his own King by lingering near Hanover, refusing to come home to look after his estates, and now his Swedish possessions were held by the Crown, pending some kind of settlement. His pay as a colonel was more an honorary gesture than an important source of income. All his other resources, any moneys he had with him in Germany, he lost at card play, like many another young blood. His debts of honor were enormous.

Nevertheless, he would have gone ahead with the elopement at any time if only the princess would consent. It was she who held back, probably from mixed motives of prudence, fear, and reluctance to leave her children (though she does not seem ever to have given them very much thought). For a long time she hoped she might persuade her parents to settle money on her in her own right. Eléonore was quite willing, but it was George William who had the money, and he was distracted by the expenses of the war and would not be coaxed. Sophie Dorothea didn't give up hope as long as he did not flatly refuse. Months were wasted while she hung around Celle, pleading with him.

Eléonore, sympathetic mother that she was, must have known about Sophie Dorothea's love affair, because so many other people knew, or suspected. But not even Eléonore had any idea that an elopement was being discussed. She would have been terrified of such treason, and not unreasonably so.

The popular version of the debacle is that Philipp brought it on by being a cad. I am impressed by the difference of attitude shown by various historians toward the behavior which I am about to describe. Aurora takes his caddishness very much for granted; it was reckless of him, she admits, to go about boasting of ladies' favors, but it was only natural. He ought to have held his liquor better, perhaps. The more idealistic Victorians, already horrified by the affair, imply that it was only to be expected; the fellow's whole behavior was extraordinary. And yet in his way, one must admit, he showed himself sincere. My own attitude, which is naturally of this generation, rather inclines to sympathy with Aurora's. People are what they are, and they do not seem to change very much in these respects through the generations. Certainly Königsmark should not have lost his head in his cups and boasted about his conquests, but he was a romantic and that is the way romantics behave. The gesture in a vacuum does not satisfy. There must be witnesses.

It is a short, ugly story. Königsmark was dining with fellow officers and local nobles in Dresden, and everyone got drunk. It was an occasion for drunkenness if ever there was one, for the Elector Frederick Augustus, Philipp's old friend, had just inherited Dresden. Königsmark had hopes that the elector would now be able to pay him a large sum which, for once, was owing to the count instead of the other way around. They were good friends and Philipp had full confidence that Augustus would pay if he possibly could; in the meantime, everyone made merry. As the evening wore on, the talk turned inevitably to The Ladies, and to scandal in general, and then somebody asked Philipp to give them the true story of the liaisons of the court of Hanover.

Königsmark willingly obliged. The floodgates were open. He was just drunk enough: in modern parlance, he really let down his hair. Nobody, save of course Sophie Dorothea, was spared—fat old Ernest Augustus and his domineering Platen, George Louis, ungainly Ermengarda Melusina with her parsimonious habits, and then the Countess Platen again. Philipp was especially amusing about the countess. He described her seduction of himself, her later attempts to continue the affair, his rebuff, and, as a *bonne bouche*, a suggestion she had recently made, that he marry her daughter. Of course, said the count virtuously, he couldn't have done that sort of thing—I mean to say, after having had the mother!

It must have been a brilliant performance; his audience was convulsed. But one of them at least was not too drunk to remember every word. Next day a long letter was sent off to the Countess Platen; perhaps other letters went to other addresses as well, for nothing travels so fast as slander.

The countess could hardly show the entire scurrilous story to her duke, but something had to be done, and quickly. She was livid with rage. There were other ways to get even. She hurried to the Schulenberg and told her what Philipp had said about her. Ermengarda Melusina was satisfactorily horrified and angry. She in turn went weeping to the electoral prince.

Then followed a scene which would do very well in modern French comedy, though an English audience might not like it. George Louis bumbled off to his wife and railed at her for what Königsmark had done. So this, this was the sort of fellow she loved! This villain was the man who was permitted to dishonor his couch! This scoundrel who dared to mock his Schulenberg!

It may be a platitude, but one must say, all the same, that real-life princes and princesses are not very much like the ones in fairy tales.

Incautiously, Sophie Dorothea answered back, defending Königsmark, and George Louis lost all restraint. For once his phlegm deserted him. He flew at his wife and beat her up, and attempted to strangle her. She screamed, attendants rushed to the rescue, everyone was scandalized, and the sobbing princess was carried back to Mother, by fast coach.

In Celle, history repeated itself, monotonously and discouragingly. The returning daughter was unwelcome. Eléonore, of course, was all loving sympathy, but George William held out in his stern, stupid way for discipline. Wives must not be encouraged to rush away from their husbands after every little quarrel. Sophie Dorothea embarrassed the duchy, running back like this; she must return to Hanover without delay.

The poor princess had only one recourse, to fall ill. She could not move from Celle, she insisted; she was feverish from shock, and bruised from her husband's brutal assault. She took to her

bed, and there she remained until she could be quite sure that
at least two of the hated electoral family were away—Sophia and
George Louis. Ernest Augustus was still at the *Schloss,* but she
was not afraid of him. Then, and not until then, did she go back
to Hanover. At the same time Königsmark abandoned discretion
and rushed back himself, from Dresden.

The lovers' indignation now transcended all fear. Sophie
Dorothea was at last just what Philipp had wanted her to be all
those years, reckless in her love and defiant of the world. They
had been writing to each other daily, ever since George Louis's
big scene, and had come to a momentous decision. Earlier there
had been a hazy plan of going to France, where they knew Louis
XIV would make them welcome if they renounced the Protestant
religion and embraced his, but now they rejected that idea. The
thought of committing treason did not deter them, but France
was too far and they had not enough money to bribe their way
into enemy territory. Sophie Dorothea had nearer friends, the
ducal family of Brunswick-Wolfenbüttel into which she had
once been destined to marry. If they were to go to Wolfenbüttel
they would be safe, for Duke Antony Ulrich hated the Lüneberg
faction and had always been fond of Eléonore and her daughter.
After Wolfenbüttel, Philipp said, he would go back to Sweden
and make his peace with the King, and regain his estates, and
take his love home where she belonged.

It was already agreed, before they met in Hanover, that the
flight was to take place on the second of July 1694.

The liaison was three years old. If it was not openly spoken of
by this time, the whispering was so near the surface that very
few people could have pretended to be unaware of it. Sophie
Dorothea and Philipp Königsmark were like actors on a bril-
liantly lit stage who cannot see their audience and who become
so absorbed in their roles that they actually forget they are
watched. Mechanically they still went through the customary
gestures of caution—the smuggled letter suggesting a rendezvous,

the eager lover awaiting his signal as he lurks near his beloved's window, the faithful handmaiden craftily letting him in, but that night, July 1, they were not afraid. They were so near their deliverance!

It is a question how carefully the Countess Platen had timed the moment to close in on her prey. Certainly she had planned her revenge ever since the news of Königsmark's loose talk came from Dresden, but one cannot be sure how much she knew of the elopement plans. That she should have sprung the trap on the very last night she could have caught her victims was either coincidence or a calculated cruelty that was fiendish. That night somebody watched the princess, and somebody else watched the count, so closely that their every movement was observed.

Königsmark walked straight to the garden outside the nearest entrance to the princess's apartments. He whistled a few bars of music and a light flashed briefly in the window. Then he went in the door, which opened at his touch. The man who had followed him hurried to report to his employer, Countess Platen.

She, in turn, hurried to the bedchamber of the elector, and told him excitedly what she had discovered. To say that Ernest Augustus was amazed and horrified would be to exaggerate, for like everyone else at court he had heard the whispers, and suspected as much as his son did about his daughter-in-law's long-standing *affaire*. He was not surprised, but he was very angry; he could not well be anything else. Now he was forced to face the truth, and with the furious countess waiting for his orders, he could not do what he was very likely tempted to do—roll over and go to sleep, pretending nobody had told him anything that might disturb his peace. Resignedly he said that he would go in person, immediately, and catch the impertinent Don Juan in the act, and defend the family honor.

No, no, said his mistress, that would never do. It would be beneath an elector's dignity, and would create a frightful scandal besides. She, the Countess Platen, would manage the matter with dignity and discretion; all the elector need do was provide her with a few armed men, and she guaranteed to capture Königsmark quietly, and bring him straight to Ernest Augustus for questioning. It was a very grave matter, which must be dealt with delicately.

The elector was an old man, ailing and depressed. After a lifetime of giving in to women, especially to this one, he felt no compunction in taking her advice in this crisis; besides, he was greatly relieved to be spared what was bound to be an unpleasant scene. Without much protest he gave the countess the direction she asked for to the commandant of the Palace Guard, to let her have four halberdiers who would obey her orders.

There is no doubt that the royal mistress was overexcited, or she would not have given these men the commands she did, to take Königsmark "dead or alive." She must have been trembling with a variety of strong emotions. Königsmark had humiliated her once too often. It had been appallingly bad mannered of him to have dropped her after that one night's enjoyment; that slight alone, in her estimation, should have been washed out in blood. But after that he had behaved as badly again. He had dared to fall seriously in love with the silly, doll-faced little princess from Celle, though the countess could not abide the creature; he had tricked the countess and deceived her with courtesy and friendly words; he had refused to marry her daughter, and as a final insult he had boasted openly of his earlier insults. She would show him! God, aided by spies, had delivered him into her hand.

The princess's apartments were approached by a long, wide corridor truncated at the other end by a great room, the Knight's Hall. Near this end was a small room of the sort which has various euphemistic names; in those days it was known as a House, or Room, of Ease. The countess disposed her four men-at-arms in a hiding place in the Knight's Hall, under the great jutting chimney piece; she herself hid behind the door of the Room of Ease.

All this traveling back and forth, to the elector's apartments

and the guard room, with a side journey to obtain refreshments
for the men, had used up a good deal of time. The halberdiers
had not long to wait before Philipp stepped out of the princess's
room and started down the corridor, walking softly, to the door
leading out of the Hall, through which he had entered.

The men under the chimney piece waited.

Königsmark tried to open the door. It was locked. He turned
back, still unsuspecting, to call Fräulein Knesebeck, and as he
stepped toward the princess's door the four men leaped at him.
The count was not prepared either in mood or weapon for an
assault; he was carrying only a small sword, but he fought
bravely and well, wounding two of his enemies before his sword
broke. Perhaps that is what angered them to murderous fury.
One of the unwounded men ran him through, the other hit him
in the head with a battle-ax, and Königsmark fell. It is said that
he was still conscious when the countess leaned over him with a
candle, eagerly peering, and that he cursed her with such a
stream of foul abuse that she stopped his mouth with her foot,
stamping on that pretty face she had so admired. Soon afterward,
he died.

It was over. Countess Platen had her revenge. But now, in
cooler blood, she grew apprehensive. Ernest Augustus had not
expected murder; even she knew that the consequences could
be very awkward. The countess began to rail at her halberdiers
for having been overzealous, but soon, realizing that she was
wasting time, she ran from the Hall, back to the elector, to report
the calamity. Just as she had feared, he flew into a rage, and all
his bellowing could not hide the fact that he too was afraid of
what might happen. Whatever had possessed her? He could not
understand how anyone could be so maladroit. Now there would
be the devil to pay. Königsmark's Swedish relatives would be bad
enough, but there were other people, nearer home . . . The
countess knew he was thinking of the Elector of Dresden. Then
he turned to the matter of Sophie Dorothea and she felt herself

on firmer ground. There at least Ernest Augustus would not be too timid to mete out justice.

They must have proof, he said suddenly. Had the count been carrying any papers, any documents they could use? Ernest Augustus dressed hastily, and with the countess and the crest-fallen halberdiers who had accompanied her he went down him-self to the Knight's Hall where lay the poor bloody corpse. No more time must be wasted. More members of the Guard were summoned, and very quietly, so that not even Sophie Dorothea or Knesebeck heard a sound, they did their work.

They searched the body for any line, scrap, or shred of in-criminating evidence, and when they found none, for his papers had all been left at home, they had no further need of the corpse. In the little room where the countess had maintained her vigil there was, of course, a hole in the floor. Seventeenth-century plumbing was crude. They thrust Count Philipp Christoph von Königsmark down this hole, covered him with quicklime, and filled in the aperture with masonry. As well as could be man-aged they cleaned up everything, though it was impossible to wash away quite all the blood. Before sunrise their work was finished.

Sophie Dorothea was raving mad for some months. She was so wild and intractable that it was exceedingly difficult for the grave ministers and other officials handling the case to deal with her at all. When she grew more coherent she was ready and eager to be divorced, she said over and over emphatically; she would do any-thing they asked, sign anything they liked, if only she need remain no longer in Hanover, and be spared for the rest of her miserable life the sight of any of George Louis's breed. She could hardly wait to affix her signature to the paper which consented to divorce, and incidentally gave the Hanovers their right to keep her confined and retain her dowry while doing so.

When she was sent into captivity, it was at first thought this was merely a temporary disposal of a princess who was a great but equally temporary embarrassment. A good deal of thought had gone into the matter, but nothing very satisfactory came out. The electoral princess had contemplated treason and betrayed her husband, but she could not be executed, like one of Henry the Eighth's wives, however much the family would have liked to do it; times were different now, and Hanover was not England. On the other hand, she must not be permitted to see anybody who wasn't owned by the Hanovers. If she were, she would most certainly talk in wild fashion, accuse everyone, and spread even further the whisperings which were going on already. Knesebeck had been locked up and held incommunicado; Sophie Dorothea must be dealt with in the same way, though it could not be quite so frank an incarceration.

They sent Sophie Dorothea to Ahlden, a lonely village and castle about twenty miles from Hanover. She was given the rank of Duchess of Ahlden, and placed under a guard camouflaged as attendants and military escort. She was permitted to go out, but when out of doors was always guarded by several men; she held no communication with any outsiders. She could wander in the castle yard but not in the village. She could be driven in her coach as far as a certain bridge, six miles from the castle, and that was all. During the first years she was allowed no visitors; later her mother came to see her. All communication with her children, of course, was cut off.

This attended to, Ernest Augustus and his worried family, wife and mistress and son, turned to the awkward task of replying to, or evading, the questions about Königsmark which kept pouring in. There could have been no real doubt as to his fate. The townspeople, for example, knew that the Electoral Palace Guard had gone through Königsmark's house and taken away all the papers they could find. There were whispers among the staff, too, about the blood on the floor of the Hall, and the closed hole in the room of necessity. However, nothing could be definitely

proved, and as long as Sophie Dorothea did not get out, there
was no one within the limits of Hanover and Celle who dared to
push the matter.

Inquiries arrived thick and fast, but they were from abroad
and could be parried. Many Swedish noblemen and the Swedish
court itself kept asking. Königsmark had friends all over Germany, and they too were exigent, especially the powerful Elector
Frederick Augustus, at whose elbow stood Aurora, urging him
to greater and greater efforts. She was almost convinced her
brother was dead, but there was still a faint hope that he languished in some dungeon. Amalie Lewenhaupt, who with her
husband had been sent away from Celle as soon as the discovery
took place, joined her sister at a safe distance from Hanover and
helped her keep things stirred up. Ernest Augustus mopped his
brow, took fresh counsel with his women, and went on fighting.
Secrecy, mystery, diplomacy were his only weapons, but in the
end they served.

Later, when the emergency had passed, there never seemed
a right moment to let the princess out. Eléonore d'Olbreuse kept
after everyone, but Ernest Augustus ruled his brother, the
Countess Platen ruled Ernest Augustus, and with each year the
countess's venom grew. Königsmark's friends were not confined to
foreign countries; many people at the court of Hanover liked him
too, and Sophie Dorothea had been loved and pitied. These
friends of the lovers could do nothing overtly, but they knew the
countess was to blame for whatever crime had taken place that
night, and they showed their sentiments. None of this gave her
any desire to relent toward Sophie Dorothea.

The days, the weeks, the months, the years went by. In 1714
soon after Sophia's death, George Louis mounted the throne of
England as George I, and nobody in his new country liked to
ask awkward questions about his wife. Was there or was there
not a Queen of England? What was the legal position of the
prisoner of Ahlden? Nobody knew. The King was accompanied

everywhere by two women, the thin Ermengarda Melusina, Duchess of Kendal, and the fat Madame Kielmansegge, Countess of Darlington. Was Kielmansegge, who was daughter of Countess Platen, the King's mistress? Was she, instead, his half sister? Was she both? The questions had a grisly sort of fascination at that strange court.

In the meantime, the Duchess of Ahlden spent the days of captivity in all their weary thousands, dressing carefully, putting diamonds in her hair, and driving up and down her allotted six miles. Sometimes she wrote letters to her mother, and, later, to her daughter the Queen of Prussia, who got into communication with Ahlden as soon as she was married and outside George I's jurisdiction. Various people cooked up plots now and then to get Sophie Dorothea out. The plots never came to anything; George I was not a type to soften with age, or to grow less apprehensive of political trouble.

Sophie Dorothea, wife and mother of kings of England, died in November 1726, having spent more than thirty-two years at Ahlden. On George I's orders they tried to bury her there and then in the castle grounds, but all the land was waterlogged and so the coffin was left lying about in a cellar for a while, and finally carted by night to Celle, where it was hastily shoved into the church vault.

George I was dead, and George II was reigning in England when some workmen in the *Schloss* at Hanover made an interesting discovery. Taking up the floor near the Knight's Hall, they came upon a skeleton. A few shreds of clothing still survived what had obviously been quicklime, and among the bones they found Königsmark's ring.

The Bearded Demoiselle

IN THE GOLDEN DAYS before most of us were born, we are told, people were nicer, and had codes of conduct which we moderns have lost. There must have been people who did the dirty work, but they lurked in government basements; they weren't people one met. In the dear old days before Hitler and Stalin, it is said, snoopers were kept out of everyday life. Somehow I cannot believe this. The fascination children feel for spy stories is not a purely modern phenomenon. The secret agent as a romantic conception has always had his admirers. The secret agent as a citizen in good standing has always found his place, and a comfortable one at that, in society. When I say this I am not thinking of Communist fifth columns, but of that eighteenth-century wonder of France and England, the Chevalier d'Eon.

Like most of the people we are discussing in this book, he was not a happy, contented creature living a good solid family life. Had he been, Burgundy would have kept one more vine-growing gentleman at home in Tonnerre, and London, St. Petersburg, and Paris would have missed a most titillating scandal—I had almost written *the* most titillating scandal of the century, until I remembered how rich that age is in gossip about the great.

D'Eon was not normal. Nobody is, if it comes to that, but d'Eon was doubly un-normal. Most outstanding figures of history had some mental quirk or bias, but not many of them, as far as we know, were hermaphrodites, whereas there is some reason to believe that our chevalier was. Not that the term explains much. The word "hermaphrodite" covers a variety of types, since the dictionary definition gives a lot of leeway: "A human being, or animal, in which parts characteristic of both sexes are combined." Well, perhaps that describes the chevalier. Outwardly, he must have looked like a man, though he had unusually full breasts. His parts were masculine and he grew a beard. But he had no love affairs. He seems to have had no ordinary sexual desire at all, unless his behavior regarding Beaumarchais, when he was nearly fifty, indicates anything more than an ability to pretend. He must have been able to imitate feminine characteristics, but for the most part his tastes were what used to be called manly—smoking, drinking, swaggering, dueling, and all the rest. There was certainly nothing of the delicate mama's boy about the young d'Eon.

Strangely enough, the mystery of his sex has remained stubbornly alive. In actual fact it should have been killed long ago, immediately after his own death, when plenty of responsible witnesses (who knew nothing about hermaphrodites) examined the corpse and announced that this difficult creature, after long years of pretense, was indubitably a male. That should have settled it, and would have, had the world wanted it settled. But the world did not. People *like* mystery. They follow the hard way from choice, not necessity. It excites them. There was a letdown when the flying saucers were explained; there are people who refuse to believe the explanation. Just so, when d'Eon was dead there were people who continued deliberately to argue the point against all proof; was he a woman, or was she a man?

Whatever they may decide, it seems a pity that this question of the chevalier's gender should overshadow the rest of his story.

He was in many other ways as well an extraordinary person. Not many people have succeeded in blackmailing a powerful king to the extent d'Eon blackmailed Louis XV. For many years he kept the court of France in a cold sweat.

Well, and if it comes to that, Louis himself was extraordinary. A faithful record of his complicated manipulations would make the most seasoned scholar dizzy. Even mystery-story addicts would lose track, sooner or later. Schemes, plots, secret papers, hidy holes—such a thriller needs no sex fillip, no "cheesecake," to hold the interest. Yet there is cheesecake thrown in for good measure wherever the chevalier enters the picture, as if the author of Louis's life story had determined not to miss one trick.

The child at birth was certainly considered to be a boy, and this, remember, for a human being is the *most* important moment for decisions as to sex. Never again will the question matter so much to so many people. Never again will the little creature's private organs be subjected to such publicity. Midwife's inspection, mother's first question, father's natural anxiety as to whether his offspring is to be an aid or a millstone—rare indeed would be the baby about whose gender any mistake could prevail. Moreover, in the Burgundian town of Tonnerre where he was born, on October 5, 1728, there seems to have been no gossip about d'Eon's early years. He was not isolated like a freak; he had a wet nurse, and she, like the midwife, never contradicted the report that he was a boy. He was baptized and registered at church as a boy, with the following staggering list of names: Charles Geneviève Louis Auguste André Timothée Déon de Beaumont. The family name was not spelled "d'Eon" until much later, when King Louis XV began to write it like that, thinking the latter version looked more swanky. Young Déon was called "Charles Geneviève" for short. The feminine "Geneviève" may look significant to English eyes, but many men in France have feminine names somewhere among their labels. They are called

"Anne" or "Marie" because these are saints' names: little Charles
Geneviève happened to be named after an aunt.

Charles Geneviève had one sister; his only other sibling, a
brother born before him, had died soon after birth. The family
was not a famous one, but they were noble and well enough off,
and the child was given a good sound gentlemanly education.
Though rather undersized, he was sturdy, good at games and
exercises, and an excellent fencer. He was apt at his studies, and
took a doctorate in law before his twentieth birthday. This did
not necessarily prove prodigious cleverness, but it was better than
average and must have called forth admiring comment in his
family's friends: most of his circle were not bookish. However,
he came by his talents naturally, they decided, for his father
wrote and published an occasional pamphlet.

It must not be supposed that books were Charles Geneviève's
only pleasure. That is one of the interesting things about him.
Had he been a delicate young man who hugged the hearth and
shrank from rough pursuits we might better understand those
later developments which astonished Tonnerre, but he was not.
Déon liked his bottle and his boon companions. He was a
normally dissipated young gentleman of his century, fond of a
glass and a game of cards. When he was called to the bar of
Parliament and went to Paris, he might have been any one of a
number of such young men.

The only generally popular pastime which he never went in
for, as his friends were to recall in later years, was chasing
women. But France did not in those days enjoy, or suffer, the
music-hall reputation she now bears for super-sexiness; young
Frenchmen, like young Germans and Englishmen and gentlemen in general, led vigorous lives conditioned by the complicated
continental wars of the time. Drinking, not wenching, was the
social obsession, until gambling took its place. Déon loved to
drink, but he also wanted to get on in the world. This desire for
advancement was probably considered the influence which kept

him steady. It would not be the first time ambition has crowded love from a man's mind. No doubt his early companions explained away his chastity, in so much as they worried about it at all, in some such fashion.

Charles Geneviève's father died in 1749, soon after finding a good post for his son as secretary to the Intendant de la Généralité de Paris. This job provided the young man with a groundwork of knowledge of government finance which he turned to account several years later when he wrote a book on national finance under Louis XV and the regency. A natural-born scribbler, he soon followed up the publication of this little volume, producing a few pamphlets on related subjects. As a result, he made friends with the journalist group of Paris. Then, all in the natural course of events, because of his appointment to the intendant, he held for a time a post as one of the royal censors of literature. What with all this writing and publishing, Charles Geneviève bade fair to settle down into middle age as an intellectual rather than a man of action. But politics soon changed all that.

France and England came to blows and started the Seven Years' War in 1754, when Déon was about twenty-six. We are apt nowadays to think of geography as a formidable obstacle to eighteenth-century statesmanship because communications were slow and difficult, but in a sense they were not so difficult as they are today. One is struck, reading the record of international negotiations, with the family atmosphere of the whole thing. European war as it was fought in those days seems almost cozy. Love may have been betrayed and murder done, to quote Rupert Brooke in another connection, but at least everything that happened to those monarchs seems to have happened within a tight little perimeter. And their methods seem much less violent; almost gentle. Their weapons cannot compare in killing potentiality with a simple modern peacetime motor bus. In two hundred years the thundering roar of their biggest cannon has died away into silence. So has the grief that followed. They killed, but the tragedies thus perpetrated do not live save between the lines of government archives. From which we may deduce that for all the coziness of royal relations, emphasis then as now was not on the individual.

Records are deceiving. The disputes between eighteenth-century European sovereigns sound, when we read of them, like ill-natured family squabbles rather than the battles of giant armies which they were, which left sorrowful heaps of dead bodies on the battlefield. Bodies rot and disappear; widows remarry; soldiers are forgotten. Only the querulous letters of diplomats remain. History has few traces of the families bereaved and despoiled by Louis XV's ambitions, but at least we do inherit a mass of gossip.

Louis XV was a strange man. His nature actually reveled in deceit. He played people off against each other with such zest that he told lies even where it would have been better policy, both in the short and the long view, to tell the truth. He had what it is only understatement to call a devouring passion for intrigue. It was he who perfected the institution of "intelligence" as we know it today, where espionage, diplomacy, and planning merge. A few of Louis's trusted courtiers spent all their time collecting bits and pieces of information about important persons of other nations. This material was regularly turned in to the King —very discreetly, for he never let his Foreign Office know what his secret service was doing, nor even that it existed—and he would pore over these reports, studying with relish the news his scavengers brought him about private habits, preferences, and intentions of people who for one reason or another interested him. Italian, Prussian, Swedish, Russian, British—all were included in Louis's dossier.

Gossip had it that Louis locked all these documents away, but that his mistress La Pompadour inevitably found access to them and spilled the secrets to her favorites. It may not always have been Pompadour who told. After all, Louis had to take more than a few people into his confidence, and the possibilities of leakage were great. But, whoever did it, the setup became so complicated and talk so wild that after a few years knowledge of Louis's knowledge began to find its way back to those whose behavior gave rise to the original reports. His own ministers played for power as cunningly as he did, and there were hidden currents and struggles without number.

On one occasion the King's secret weapon backfired in public. In 1744 his ambassador to Russia, Chatardie, had the most humiliating experience one can imagine: the Czarina Elizabeth kicked him out of the country. It seemed hardly playing the game, but *her* intelligence officers had spied on *him*. Those Russians! They had cleverly and dishonorably intercepted his private, unofficial letters to Louis, which as luck would have it happened to be packed full of unflattering descriptions of Her Imperial Majesty's morals. Elizabeth was furious.

Now in 1755, eleven years later, Louis's intelligence agents began to make efforts to repair the breach. These overtures were made secretly, since that was always Louis's way, but even using the most tactful methods did not get French messengers very far toward Petersburg. Two of them were captured and imprisoned as spies as soon as they entered Russian domain. Nevertheless, Louis continued to try. He had several good reasons to be interested in Russia's internal affairs, not that Louis ever *needed* a reason to be nosy. He was acutely curious about Sir Charles Hanbury Williams, the English ambassador to Petersburg, for he had information that Elizabeth was negotiating to lend Russian troops to England.

All of this is important if we want to understand Déon's career. His friend, the Chevalier Douglas, who got into Russia at last, was a strange character, through whom Déon's dainty, plump feet were ultimately to be set on the road to eminence. Mackenzie, not Douglas, was his real name. He was an ex-Jesuit, an exile, who served for some years as tutor in the house of the Intendant de la Généralité de Paris, the employer, we recall, of Déon.

Renegade Scot, renegade priest as Douglas was, he took well to the life of a spy. It must have been a great relief to get out of the schoolroom. He did better than his predecessors and evaded the watchdogs at the Russian border. Safely arrived in St. Petersburg, he achieved meetings with Elizabeth. She was so encouraging to his overtures that he hastened back to Versailles to report that the King might safely send a proper mission to Petersburg, someone empowered to sign a treaty with the Czarina on behalf of France.

This was good news for Louis. Douglas himself, he declared, should have the honor of bearing formal credentials as the French envoy back to the Russian capital. He was to correspond openly with the Foreign Office during negotiations, and secretly with the intelligence service, in the person of its head, Tercier, who was also, incidentally, chief clerk at the Foreign Office. For his secretary on the mission the new ambassador selected Déon de Beaumont.

Thus our hero found himself translated from humdrum work in the civil service to an adventurous, exciting job. In Paris they thought of Russia as a barbarous, romantic country, and no doubt they were right. Déon must have been thrilled by the prospect. The only drawback was that nobody gave him any money for his expenses. It was often that way when people embarked on these semi-official secret-service missions; everything was so very hush-hush that the agent's salary too remained mysterious and invisible. The Chevalier Douglas had already departed, leaving cryptic directions: Déon was to follow and join him. Nobody else knew anything about expense money. The few people he dared ask kept passing the buck. Déon finally borrowed the impressive sum of ten thousand livres—one wonders how—and set off.

It was easier now for Frenchmen to get to St. Petersburg, and at court the atmosphere was much better than it had been before. Hanbury Williams was out of favor. Douglas found it beautifully simple to formulate a Franco-Russian treaty. In fact, Elizabeth was easier to manage than his own King, for during the negotiations Louis turned awkward. In the emergencies which resulted it was Déon who came forward and smoothed matters over, with tact and charm persuading the Czarina to give in to the French demands. He must have had great talent for this work, for he came out of it still friendly even with Douglas.

In truth he made a good impression wherever he went. The Russians liked Déon. He was a good mixer, a ready spender, and he had a strong head for drink, thanks no doubt to the Burgundy wine on which he had been brought up. He was a remarkably good fencer and horseman. There was only one thing lacking, in the opinion of the courtiers, to make him a perfect specimen of nobleman: he was no womanizer. Gallantry was a favorite indoor sport at St. Petersburg, but Déon was notoriously backward at it. This, it was evident, was no fault of the court ladies. Several did their best to encourage him, and they redoubled their efforts when he proved unresponsive. Had he played his cards cleverly he could have made a wealthy marriage. His well-wishers hoped he would do so, for he had lost his father's money and had no private means, but oddly enough he showed no mercenary tendencies of this sort, though he was frankly ambitious in other ways. His manners toward the ladies were beyond reproach. He waited on them, paid them pretty compliments, hung about them, but made no amorous advances.

This indifference amused the court and caused comment. His boon companions teased him roughly. "You're not a man at all," they declared. "It's our considered opinion that you're a girl in disguise."

Gleefully they embroidered on the idea. The more one thought of it the more reasonable it appeared. Why, Déon even looked like a girl. Look at his plump chest and his delicate hands and feet! He was small; his waist was slender, even supple. Then there was his soft skin and effeminate voice. . . . "You could pass for a girl anywhere," said the Russian counts and barons.

Déon laughed good-naturedly at this badinage, but his laughter was not hearty and he turned the topic elsewhere whenever he saw a chance. He was always the same when people twitted him about his appearance and his austere disregard for sex. The subject seemed to displease him, as naturally it might; what he-man would enjoy such teasing?

Thus after dinner the gentlemen of St. Petersburg drank their wine and amused themselves with masculine jests, while the ladies in the drawing room strummed the harpsichord and idly twittered.

A visit to Paris indicated with what swiftness Déon was making his way. He had been honored by the Czarina on his departure; now Louis greeted him with kind words of praise, and valuable gifts. The King also began to refer to him in writing as "d'Eon," a distinction difficult to describe in English save by saying that it implied he belonged to a high caste.

For all his success, he was not keen on going back to St. Petersburg, of which he was tired. But he could not refuse in light of the King's insistence. Someone of his caliber was needed there, as Douglas had been recalled. The regular ambassador who took Douglas's place, the Marquis de l'Hôpital, was not a member of the inner circle of intelligence agents. It was d'Eon's task, and d'Eon's only, to further the *rapport* between the Czarina and Louis, to arrange a private correspondence between them, and as a side line to sympathize with Elizabeth in her troubles.

What with the Czarina's favor and that of his King, d'Eon enjoyed great power and responsibility for a man who was officially only secretary of the legation. Even when Breteuil, his titular head in secret service, arrived from France, d'Eon was given his own way to pursue their common aims. The two agents had a ticklish task to perform. The end of the weary war was in sight. England and Hanover had lost ground on the Continent, this being due in part to the recent excellent showing of Russia's army, but English ships were meeting with such success that even Louis realized a general peace settlement was in order. His peculiarly twisted mind leaped straight ahead of the cessation of hostilities to the chances of double-crossing his allies as soon as the treaty should come up for consideration. He felt that he must at all events prevent his dear Russia from making too good a showing. With this laudable aim in mind, he directed Breteuil to retard Russian military operations in any way he possibly could.

It would be pleasant if we could find any evidence that d'Eon was shocked and disgusted by this example of Louis's perfidy, but there is none. He had been one of the King's ardent workers in the vineyard for a long 'time; many of his tasks had been of a sort hardly calculated to foster noble sentiments; presumably, like many other diplomats, he was past being shocked. He was, however, more than ever bored with Russia and the job. The war phase was drawing to an end and soon his special talents would not be needed there. He was not for a moment tempted when Elizabeth offered him a permanent position in her service. He knew she was sincerely fond of him, but he was homesick. Besides, life with the tempestuous Russians was notoriously chancy. As he wrote to a colleague at home in reference to the offer, his maxim was to keep his back turned on Siberia. In a letter to Tercier he said, "I will never leave the service of France for all the Emperors and Empresses in the world. I prefer to live from hand to mouth in France to being in the enjoyment of an income of 100,000 livres in fear and bondage."

He was thirty-two, still young, with a very creditable career already on the record. Unlike others in his profession, he had as yet made no bitter enemies. He was attractive, though of late, like

many small men, he had shown an inclination to dumpiness. His
fencing and horsemanship were as good as ever, and he was
eager to take up what he considered his rightful profession of
arms before the war should be quite finished. This keenness was
all the more intense because Louis had recently promoted him to
the rank of captain of dragoons.

One would have said he was a typical specimen of his time and
class—a gentleman in the diplomatic service, well equipped by
nature and training for his work, likable and intelligent; in short,
just another bright young man. Only that one idiosyncrasy
marked him out: he still showed no slightest tendency to marry
and settle down.

D'Eon was happy when he was at last allowed to see active
service in Germany. It is true that he did not serve in an ordinary
capacity for very long, but that was not his fault. Besides, as a
staff officer he was to encounter quite as much action as he
would have, probably, as a regular captain.

From Versailles came orders: he was to be posted as A.D.C. to
the Broglie brothers. The Comte de Broglie had met d'Eon in
Poland when he was on his way to Russia. Broglie was himself in
Louis's inner circle and had remembered the clever young man;
they would now be able to work together for the King. The
count's brother, the duke, who like his father was a marshal, was
for his part pleased with d'Eon. While d'Eon, though at first
dismayed to find he could not rid himself of intelligence work,
was appeased to discover that he was genuinely in the Army
anyway.

Soon after he joined the corps, in 1761, he found himself involved in controversy. The Marshal de Broglie and the Marshal
de Soubise, presumably united in battle at Villinghausen against
the Anglo-Hanoverian army under Prince Ferdinand, fell out.
Soubise, jealous of Broglie's better showing, failed to respond in
time to the other marshal's appeal for help, and as a result the

whole battle was lost. D'Eon was of course furiously indignant at
this betrayal of his chief, and his loyalty was later to cost him
dear.

Nor was Villinghausen his only experience with that phenomenon of military life now denoted as Snafu. One day on the
banks of the Weser the marshal sent him to escort a load of
powder and cartridges across the water, under enemy fire. Broglie's orders were to find one Lieutenant General Comte de
Guerchy when d'Eon had made the dangerous crossing, and deliver to him the marshal's written instructions with regard to the
distribution of this ammunition to the troops.

Guerchy, as it happened, was distantly related to d'Eon. But
until that day they had never met, and when they did it was
hardly the moment to figure out whose aunt had married whose
uncle back in Burgundy. Cannonballs were whistling around
them; shot and shell continued without surcease. Hastily d'Eon
handed over the orders.

One hesitates to say that a lieutenant general could possibly
have been afraid. There is no doubt, however, that Guerchy behaved in a manner which indicated he was at least cautious. Instead of following Broglie's orders, he simply turned horse and
galloped off the field, shouting over his shoulder as he disappeared, "If you've got any ammunition, take it half a league
downriver!"

Naturally, d'Eon was annoyed with Cousin Guerchy. Rally-
ing the other's officers, he distributed the cartridges himself.

Before the war came to an end he had been wounded twice,
and was commended in dispatches by both the count and the
marshal for general bravery in action. It was a distinct letdown,
when the campaign was over, to return to Paris and find the
Broglies in trouble over the Villinghausen controversy. He threw
himself into the affair, as one would expect him to do, but politics
are never as satisfactorily direct as open battle. All the efforts of
d'Eon and the other Broglie supporters could not prevail against

La Pompadour, who was on the side of Soubise, and the wrong man won. Louis was feebly noncommittal, as he always was when it came to open defiance of his tyrannical mistress. The Broglies had to retire to their country estates in disgrace. Loyal servants of the Crown, they remained faithful to Louis though he had let them down, and the count, despite the difficulties of distance, continued to act as head of the intelligence corps.

Apart from his superior officers' troubles, d'Eon had worries of his own. It was the age-old question of the soldier home from the wars: what to do next? For one thing, he was broke. His pay both as legation secretary and as army officer was in arrears, and he had never completely settled that enormous debt incurred when he first went to Russia. True, he was not the only man in the country who found himself in this position; the whole aristocracy of Europe, I sometimes think, must have lived on tick. But though he was in good company, the problem remained pressing until another job came along and saved him, temporarily, from his impatient creditors.

England and France were beginning their preliminary peace talks. In those easygoing days, once a war was over there does not seem to have been any hangover of resentment between nations recently locked in bitter struggle. The Duc de Nivernais went to London, and the Duke of Bedford came to Versailles, to resume diplomatic relations and work out a treaty. D'Eon went with Nivernais as first secretary of the Embassy.

Everyone in England, as I have said, was polite, and there was no hangover from the war, but that does not mean that the haggling over the treaty was not sharp. Every item was fought over, while the British watched the process with cynical eyes. The people hated Lord Bute to begin with. Now they were quick to believe that he was being bribed by Nivernais to give the French the best of every argument. Many other ministers too were accused of corruption, of making their fortunes by selling England's overseas possessions.

If English ministers were not bribed, it was not for want of Nivernais trying. When d'Eon published his so-called memoirs some years later, he made no allegations to this effect, but he did retail an interesting anecdote of successful trickery on the part of the French, during the course of the negotiations. According to him, the settlement by which Spain recovered Havana from England, swapping Florida for it, was accomplished thus: Nivernais and d'Eon plied the British Undersecretary of State with Tonnerre wine; then, while he slept, d'Eon copied the papers about the Havana affair which the Englishman was carrying in his portfolio. Sent posthaste to France, the papers forewarned the ministers there, and they then found it easy to push the deal through with the Duke of Bedford. Whatever Florida may be worth today, it was not a fair exchange for Havana in 1763, so d'Eon had good reason to boast of his triumph.

Once more he found himself making friends and influencing people everywhere he went. The British court liked him, and the French made much of him when he brought messages from Nivernais to Versailles. Praslin, French Minister for Foreign Affairs, had no real reason to love d'Eon, being an anti-Broglie man himself, but he commended him nevertheless, and actually gave him three thousand livres in hard cash. Louis was even more generous. He rewarded the secretary with a six months' warrant of protection against his creditors, a gesture which pleased everyone but the creditors, its chief beauty being that it cost the donor nothing. But even this splendid gift was insignificant compared with the Cross of St. Louis which the King bestowed on d'Eon. This presentation marked the Burgundian's proudest hour; he returned to London a chevalier.

He had reached, I repeat, his proudest hour. Crisis is close upon him. Before it overtakes him, knowing in advance as we do in what form it comes, a summary seems to be indicated. Ladies and gentlemen, here is the Chevalier d'Eon, firmly installed in favor on both sides of the Channel. A man among men. An astute statesman, a loyal subject, a discreet intelligencer, a level-headed drinker, a good fellow. He is a famous swordsman. Tried under fire, he has come through with an excellent record, under superior officers whose word cannot be doubted.

In the face of all this, how could there have been any possibility that he wasn't really a man? I mention the matter at this point deliberately. Later the canvas gets so crowded that certain small things might easily be lost to sight in the picture. I do not at all mean to say that a woman could not have been just as astute as a man, just as courteous, discreet, good at drinking and fencing and all the rest of it; I refer to less spiritual matters. Sooner or later, if the chevalier had been a woman, somebody was bound to see her body and reveal the masquerade. It would have been awkward enough always to manage to undress in privacy, though it could be done. But there were other considerations. Remember the habits of eighteenth-century gentlemen, for only one example, at dinner parties. At these it was the custom for the ladies to take their leave of the table when the long meal had come to an end, and retire to the drawing room. Today a remnant of the custom remains, but in our time the gentlemen do not as a general rule dally for hours over their port; sooner or later they have got to rejoin the ladies. In d'Eon's time there was none of this nonsense about rejoining the ladies; the gentlemen settled down quite simply and frankly to get stinking drunk together. Bottles were brought in, the fire was repaired, and there you were. You didn't even have to leave the room to go to the gentleman's room. There were chamber pots provided; they were kept in that left-hand aperture of the buffet which was made on purpose to hold them handy for the company.

Well, under these circumstances, how could d'Eon possibly . . .

And another thing. He was twice wounded in battle: it's on the record. The most redoubtable of male impersonators, if they join the Army, usually get caught out when that happens. One of his wounds was in the thigh. But after all, I need not draw diagrams. My point is that the public, later, must have been more credulous than even Barnum gave it credit for.

The treaty was ratified: Nivernais's mission was at an end, and he was recalled. To assume the post of peacetime ambassador, the court at Versailles named the Comte de Guerchy, d'Eon's distant relation, the poltroon of the ammunition incident in Germany. The chevalier would have had reason had he declared bitterly on hearing the news that it is a small world after all. Almost certainly he did say it, and attempted to get himself transferred to some other post rather than work under a man he held in such contempt. But he was advised by his superiors to stay. Once more, as in Petersburg, his peculiar talents were in demand. Once again the King of France, having signed a treaty, was now brooding about the terms and casting about for some way of going back on his word. For this he needed expert help, and he was used to D'Eon's methods. The chevalier had to remain. He could solace himself if he liked with the reflection that Versailles was not a healthy place for a man committed, as he was, to the support of the Broglies. And in another way the change did him good, for Nivernais insisted that Praslin name d'Eon, during the absence of any other responsible diplomat, French resident in London. On general principles Praslin objected, but at last he gave in.

Louis's latest project, held secret as usual from his own Foreign Office, was dynamite. The peace had just been signed, and Nivernais's London bed was not yet cold before the King of France began plotting to invade England. Regrettable as the fact may be, d'Eon threw himself with enthusiasm into the plan when he found out that his chief, the Comte de Broglie, had conceived the original idea. The chevalier's part of the work was especially important, for he constituted the nucleus of the French cell on the isle of Britain. He was to carry on with the usual

routine duties of resident, but his real duty was more complicated.

For one thing, he entertained and aided a certain French
officer, the Marquis Carlet de la Rozière, who came to England
ostensibly on a visit, but actually to survey the coast and select a
good landing place for Louis's troops. (La Rozière was related
to d'Eon.) D'Eon acted as clearing agent for the necessary correspondence between La Rozière and Broglie. A cipher code was
selected in order to confound the not-yet-arrived Guerchy, if by
any chance the envoy upon arrival should suspect the plot and
attempt to discover it. As a final precaution against publicity, a
certain young lieutenant named Charles Maurice d'Eon de
Moulize stood by in order to receive The Papers and keep them
out of Guerchy's hands, just in case anything like illness or
sudden death should happen to the chevalier. Moulize, like La
Rozière and Guerchy, was related to d'Eon, and the entire affair
began to assume the appearance of a family reunion.

In France, Guerchy was not too busy with his packing to collect general information about the world he would soon enter.
He was not quite happy with the reports he received about the
French resident. D'Eon sounded much too popular with the English to please his cousin, who was not a Broglie man. The King
and Queen liked the chevalier, the English aristocracy liked the
chevalier; everyone, it seemed, liked the chevalier, which was all
wrong, since his own chief, Praslin, did *not* like the chevalier.
Would Guerchy be able to take the spotlight away from this
pretty upstart, this temporary resident? Like d'Eon, he had not
forgotten their first encounter, and he resented the man who had
seen him behave badly. The chevalier could not possibly have
been on Guerchy's mind in those days as much as Guerchy was
on the chevalier's, but whenever d'Eon did happen to come onto
the scene, Guerchy was irked.

Then, even before he set sail for England, the tiresome under-
ling began to make trouble for him, though d'Eon would have

put it another way. Once more the chevalier was running into financial difficulties. His six months' grace had expired, and though he was out of the country creditors were again snapping at his heels. It wasn't only the old ones, but a host of new, and d'Eon felt, aggrievedly, that the debts for which they claimed settlement were not his to pay. The old debts could have been paid if only the arrears owing him from the Government and Army had been settled; while as for the new, they had been incurred by the entire Embassy in London. True, he had been promoted to minister plenipotentiary, but that did not mean he was personally responsible for embassy expenses. Rather, the Embassy should have been responsible for him.

Plaintively at first he wrote to Nivernais, to Praslin and to Guerchy in turn as his difficulties increased. The replies were never satisfactory. In time-honored bureaucratic style each man handed him on to the next. The chevalier was harried, and as his resentment grew it seemed to center on one figure alone, out of the number who had incurred it. Guerchy was the man he blamed; Guerchy was the man he suddenly, surprisingly, amazingly attacked. Without warning, and without any obvious cause —for, after all, debts had been a chronic complaint with d'Eon for many years—he seems to have gone mad.

Mere loss of temper might have accounted for one or two of the letters he wrote. Even diplomats sometimes behave in undiplomatic fashion, and he had ample provocation. He wrote angrily to Praslin, which was unwise, and to Guerchy, which was equally unwise, both men being his superiors. Yet if he had stopped there, all might have been smoothed over, but he did not stop. Their replies were naturally angry in turn, and the reprimands stung him to greater fury. His next letters were too extreme to be ignored even had the recipients wished him well to begin with.

It was altogether strange. Until this crisis one would have said that coolness and balance were d'Eon's outstanding qualities.

Without them he would never have succeeded as he did with the Czarina. He must have possessed calm judgment, too, when he dealt with such an important matter of state as the peace treaty recently concluded between France and England. No one at the court of George III had ever accused him of lacking tact. It was Guerchy, evidently, and Guerchy alone who could drive the chevalier to such wild fury that he lost all his ordinary self-control.

On the other hand, the Guerchy affair may have been merely coincidental with some sort of general nerve collapse on his part. The chevalier had risen to dizzy heights, after several years of intense effort to do his job. He had been saddled of late with responsibility of a peculiarly grave kind. He had shouldered similar burdens before, but this time even Louis's tortuous mentality had outdone itself. At the behest of his royal master, d'Eon was finding it necessary to double-cross in a particularly unpleasant way not only his hosts the English but his own superior officers. Plot was piled upon plot, and now, as if this were not enough, they, conspirators and uninformed together, were pressing him for money, and refusing to pay him his rightful salary, and accusing him of graft. . . . The world was against him; he felt he had just learned it. Had he no other cause for hysterics, these would have been sufficient.

Remember that the chevalier was not normal. Whether at this time he began to consider himself a woman, or only knew dimly, as he must have known for years, that he wasn't like other men, there must have been considerable accumulated strain on his nervous system, like a blight which worked inwards in the dark under a veneer of self-control.

Latins, Italians, southern French and Spanish alike take their honor seriously and often use it as an excuse to blow up in the scenes their stormy natures crave. D'Eon the Burgundian now luxuriated in self-abandonment. He continued to write letters which no diplomat should ever send to his own chief no matter what happens. At Versailles, Praslin furiously complained to La Pompadour, and the correspondence with him, as well as equally uncontrolled missives to Broglie and Tercier, was all turned over to Louis. Dear, dear, said Louis to himself; it was evidently necessary to recall this man. He wrote to Tercier:

"D'Eon's office as Minister Plenipotentiary appears to have turned his head." When Guerchy arrived in London, in October 1763, he brought orders from Louis that d'Eon was to turn the embassy business over to the envoy, return immediately to Paris, and—a final insult—*not* present himself at court until summoned.

From that moment on, if not before, genuine madness seems to have taken possession of the unfortunate chevalier. He ignored his orders to go to France. As to the embassy business, he gave a portion of the ordinary aboveboard correspondence to Guerchy, but he retained the remainder, as well as all documents which had to do with the invasion plan and which, naturally, he was not expected to give Guerchy in any case. Tercier and Broglie had intended to take those over, after d'Eon's return to Paris. Both of them, friends of his though they were, were worried about his behavior and had come to the obviously correct conclusion that he was out of his head. But d'Eon wouldn't come home.

It was, to say the least, a very awkward situation for Louis's secret service. All their most private, shameful plans were in the hands of a lunatic who was where they could not get at him, and who in defense of his honor or what-not might quite easily tell all, to everyone concerned. They felt like animal trainers whose prize gorilla has got loose and is romping about with a gun. Perhaps they felt even worse. After all, animal trainers presumably expect accidents, but Louis was not a zoo keeper; he was a king. It was worse for him, because as King he should not have had guns lying about.

An odd state of affairs now obtained in London's diplomatic circles. Guerchy had to put a good face on the matter. However much he may have wanted to choke d'Eon's stiff neck he must not do so, nor even administer to him so much as a public snub. The English were not to know anything about this civil war among France's distinguished representatives. A Frenchman who had refused to obey orders and was holding his sovereign's property as an instrument of blackmail must nevertheless be allowed to come and go in the French Embassy as he liked, and continue to be received everywhere as minister plenipotentiary, though he had been officially demoted and recalled. Whatever next?

In our unhappy times renegade diplomats usually ask protection from the governments where they are resident, and then call in the press. Kidnapings are feared; indeed, kidnapings sometimes actually take place. The methods of totalitarians in our unhappy times are not always quite original. D'Eon feared some similar retaliation, but he was not yet ready to ask protection from the British. Anyway, it is unlikely he would have received it without making a full confession of Louis's plans, and this he did not— as yet—think of doing. He did not blame Louis, but Guerchy. Guerchy was the man who was after him, Guerchy and the traitor Praslin. Anyone who sided with Guerchy joined the sinister mob against him, but Louis, of course, would side with himself. At all costs d'Eon must defend himself against the abominable Guerchy.

The first move was that "they" tried to trick d'Eon into fighting a duel. He tells the story in his confessions. A suspicious character named Vergy had recently arrived from France and was usually to be found hanging about the Embassy. One night when the chevalier was dining there, Vergy picked a quarrel with him, or vice versa, and a few days later called on him to deliver a challenge. D'Eon was not at home, but when he returned he found the message. (It all sounds most unlike our usual ideas of dueling. Until I read this account I always assumed for some reason that a man was invariably at home to receive such a challenge. On second thought, I don't see why this must always be true.) D'Eon, at any rate, got the message, rather as if he had read it on a telephone pad, and then he changed his clothes and went out to a dinner the Foreign Secretary, Lord Halifax, was giving for Guerchy.

Most people in the duels I have read about also keep quiet when they intend to fight. After all, it *is* usually against the law. But this impending affair of honor was probably on the poor chevalier's mind, and he began to talk about it in full company. He could scarcely have picked a group more likely to be startled by the information. Halifax suggested, tactfully at first, that he give up the whole idea. D'Eon refused, and Halifax said that in that case he had no choice but to give his guest in charge. A confused and somewhat drunken scene ensued, at the end of which the fiery Burgundian was actually placed under guard, where he remained until he signed a declaration that he would not disturb the peace without first communicating with Lords Sandwich and Halifax.

Poor d'Eon. After that evening he began to suspect all manner of other plots against him. Guerchy one evening doped his wine with opium, he declared, with the object of kidnaping him once he had fallen asleep. "They" kept spies on him, too, day and night. They supplied a new lock for his door when he attempted to change the one he had, but he was too clever for them: he knew what they were about. By far the most fiendish thing they did was to hire a chimney sweep to drive him mad by tapping on the walls all night. Had he gone mad as they wished, said the chevalier, they could with impunity have carried him off for a lunatic.

Again the chevalier was too smart for his enemies. He moved. He went to stay with La Rozière, and fortified the house. The whole ground floor was mined. Furthermore, "He kept a lamp burning throughout the night, and had a red-hot poker at his side during the day. His arsenal included four brace of pistols, two guns, and eight sabres. The garrison consisted of several dragoons of his old regiment, for whom he had sent, and some deserters whom he picked up in London. . . ."*

After the embarrassing affair of the duel and the declaration in Lord Halifax's house, the French Foreign Office decided that as one of the cats was out of the bag in any case it was no use to go on pretending nothing was wrong between d'Eon and his Government. With the reluctant permission of Louis, who was thinking of The Papers, Praslin directed Guerchy to apply for extradition of their fugitive minister plenipotentiary. Louis added a personal letter, saying that the ambassador was to hold himself ready as soon as extradition was granted to seize all papers which d'Eon had in his possession, and bring them back *in person* to France, there to hand them over to Louis himself. We can well imagine what a coil the monarch was in, and how he worried and said to himself, as soon as these letters were dispatched, "Yes, but what if Guerchy grows suspicious of my marked interest in this matter? What if he takes a little peep at the papers I have mentioned? Of course he will. I was a fool to have made such a point of it. I must take more precautions yet."

So he sat down again, and wrote to the chevalier, and warned him about the request for extradition. "If you cannot make your escape, save at least your papers, and do not trust M. Monin [an assistant to d'Eon's secret intelligence work, who had come over with Guerchy]. . . . He is betraying you." If trying to follow Louis's mental processes makes us dizzy, how much more confusing the effort must have been for the chevalier's already puzzled brains!

For no one knows exactly what reason, d'Eon now sent his kinsman and host, La Rozière, to France with a selection of innocuous embassy papers. At his first glance at these Louis was overjoyed with relief, thinking they were the whole lot. He

---

The True Story of the Chevalier d'Eon, by Vizetelly (Tylston and Edwards, 1895).

hastily decided he did not need the chevalier's good will any more, and gave orders to increase pressure on him in London. Until then the English had refused extradition; but with Louis himself backing up the demand, they permitted word to go out that d'Eon, having been pronounced guilty of high treason, was henceforth forbidden to attend court and was formally divested of diplomatic status, with all his arrears forfeit to the Crown of France. Then, after thus abandoning his hitherto faithful servant, Louis discovered that he did not, after all, hold the most dangerous of The Papers safe in his hand. The chevalier had tricked him.

Like a wicked producer in an American novel about Hollywood, Louis hastened to make up to d'Eon again and repair the damage. But he kept tripping over his own former behavior. How was he to placate the man without stimulating suspicion in the Foreign Office? There was Broglie nagging at him to do something to reassure d'Eon, reminding him that France could not possibly face war as yet, and Louis knew very well that England might attack if the story of the invasion conspiracy should come out. But Praslin was determined to punish the impertinent creature, and Louis had already slipped the leash on Praslin; he dared not control his Foreign Minister again on the d'Eon question.

The King simply could not cope, and for a long time nothing at all was done. Vainly waiting in London for some secret reassurance, penniless and disgraced, the chevalier at last began to behave exactly as Broglie had feared he would do. He published.

He broke all the rules of diplomacy (he was not the first nor the last disgruntled diplomat to do that) and told, if not all, at least very much too much. The essence of his secret work he held back; England was not yet to know, evidently, of Louis's perfidy. D'Eon kept the faith on that. But for the rest he took the world into his confidence. He blasted away at Guerchy, jeering at the envoy for his ignorance of writing, which as a matter of cruel truth did come very close to illiteracy. He published any amount of private correspondence from the embassy archives. Some of this—quite a lot of it—related to his own grievances, but there was a portion which had nothing whatever to do with the case of d'Eon *vs.* Guerchy. It was put into the volume of *Lettres, Mémoires et Négotiations du Chevalier d'Eon* only to confound and embarrass the unfortunate ambassador and those who dared to support him. *And* he promised a second installment soon. More than ever, the situation was uncomfortable for Louis. It might be described as The Monarch's Nightmare.

They absolutely loved the book in London. Horace Walpole, especially, enjoyed it, and became a prominent d'Eon fan. It was more than mere amusing scandal, however, to the higher-ups, who pricked up their ears. The chevalier was soon able to write to Tercier that the opposition had offered him any money he might require for the rest of the papers.

"You must feel how repugnant such an expedient must be to me," he said artlessly, "and yet if I am forsaken what would you have me do?" What indeed? The chevalier's mind was fixed on Guerchy as the author of all his misfortunes; even more than his own future, his enemy's punishment preoccupied him. "If I am entirely forsaken, and if between now and Easter Sunday" (it was nearing the end of March 1764, when he wrote) "I do not receive a promise, signed by the King or by Comte de Broglie, to the effect that reparation will be made to me for all the ills that I have endured at the hands of M. de Guerchy, then I declare to you formally I shall lose all hope; and in forcing me to embrace the cause of the King of England . . . you must make up your mind to a war at no distant period. . . ."

Threats of blackmail, hasty messengers from Broglie, more messengers from the French Foreign Office, secret offers to buy The Papers, kidnaping plots—none of these had the effect either Louis or Praslin wanted, for d'Eon remained uncaptured and unrepentant, and grew more and more violent and paranoiac. He went about London heavily armed, even to the theater, and boasted wildly to the world of what he would do if anyone tried to take him prisoner.

The attitude of the British public toward all this was a strange one. Society observed developments with a cold amusement which leads one to wonder if the English would have been so horrified by a revelation of the invasion plans after all. Perhaps nothing would have shocked these people, who had few illusions at the best of times. Everyone seemed quite sure that the chevalier's ravings were not without foundation, and they were perfectly right. The whole thing, one gathers, was merely what Londoners would have expected; they watched the drama with an interest unmarred by any trace of partisan indignation or sympathy. Would France get the chevalier at last, or would he outwit the Foreign Office and save himself? Languidly, gentlemen laid bets on the question.

Then their sport was spoiled. D'Eon, sued for libel by Guerchy on account of his memoirs, was found guilty, but his trial was held *in absentia*. The chevalier had gone underground.

It is reasonably safe to suppose that nobody ever before escaped a libel suit or evaded a judicial sentence in quite the same manner as that employed by our hero. He did not conceal himself in an unimaginative manner by staying indoors. His method was much simpler. All the chevalier found it necessary to do was to step into female clothing and move to a house far from his former haunts, a house of the sort qualified by the phrase "ill fame," run by a Frenchwoman, Madame Dufour. Heaven knows how d'Eon happened to know of Madame or her house, but there he was, safely incognito, for as long as he found the masquerade convenient. Certainly he was better fitted than most men of his acquaintance to play such a part. In woman's dress the chevalier, as long as he was careful to shave, was remarkably convincing. He moved about the streets of London quite freely.

Also, he was able without interruption to carry on his one-man war against the French ambassador from the call house. He sent a challenge to Guerchy, but the envoy declined the honor, retorting that since their military ranks were so widely disparate, such a duel would not be proper.

Then d'Eon joined forces with Vergy and brought suit against Guerchy in the English court, alleging attempts to drug, murder, kidnap or otherwise do away with him. Guerchy was actually indicted on Vergy's evidence, but d'Eon never followed up the matter, to the great relief of the British authorities, who were not sure just how far they would be able to proceed with such grave charges against a foreign ambassador.

In the meantime, in France, Louis's ministers had nearly caught on to the plans which he had until now so carefully concealed from them. Something definite would have to be done, and quickly; Louis's own safety was not involved, but that of the Broglies and many others was, and the King could not afford such a loss of his following as discovery would involve. At last the Comte de Broglie prevailed upon Louis to make overtures of peace to the recalcitrant and fugitive chevalier. The first offer, which was ambiguous, d'Eon flatly refused. Haggling continued, until at last the ante was raised to what the chevalier considered a respectable level. He was to have a pension of twelve thousand livres a year, guaranteed by Broglie's own property; there would be no reprisals, and he would carry on as before with his work as intelligence agent in England. Gratified and reassured—had he not won his battles all along the line?—the chevalier stepped out of hiding, once more in breeches, and appeared in public. He also resumed his secret reporting. A man in better mental condition would have realized that his King would never again trust him, nor rest until he was silenced, but d'Eon had no qualms. That is, he had no qualms concerning his safety as long as he held onto the mass of incriminating documents. To all suggestions that he give them up the chevalier turned an absent ear.

One letter only he exchanged, for a written promise from Louis respecting his pension. He went on living in London, writing for his own amusement and spying out of long habit.

The whisper first started as a joke, perhaps, like the jokes the Russians had made years before, during jovial parties in St. Petersburg. Then it was reinforced from an unexpected source. Madame Dufour on a visit to her native land blabbed to someone, in the hope of getting a reward from Louis for the information, that the Chevalier d'Eon had once found refuge with her and had dressed as a woman for a long stretch of time, fooling everybody. Or were they fooled? Was it not, perhaps, the other way about, that the chevalier was in reality a chevalière, who spent the greater part of her life in masquerade?

Nobody paid Madame Dufour for her little bit of scandal, but the story spread. Or, rather, it seeped. It took years to get a grip on the British public; it moved slowly, collecting inference as it went, until in time the inference, from being so often repeated, began to sound like evidence. *Was* the chevalier a woman? To be sure, he had a beard, but bearded women were not unknown. Could any female step forward and swear, from personal experience, that he was a man? Whether anyone could is a mystery; at any rate, no female did. Tittering, whispering, the world continued to speculate—to speculate in a genuine sense: people began to bet on it.

D'Eon himself acted in a manner strangely coy. The wagering reached enormous proportions before he would make any official statement whatever on the subject, although privately, among friends, he was willing enough to talk about how disgraceful and ridiculous the whole question was. When there seemed real danger of his being kidnaped, stripped, and examined by force, he disappeared from town and went on a journey. Coming back to a much quieter atmosphere, when he deemed himself safe from outrage, he announced that he would never permit himself to be examined. Naturally, such a statement did nothing to stop the talk.

In 1771 when the uncertainty was raging at its highest pitch of excitement, Broglie asked d'Eon outright, by letter, to tell him once and for all what he was. The chevalier replied with what was evidently perfect frankness. He was, he said, a man, but a man without sex urges. Sexless men are apt to cause that sort of talk, he explained. Broglie and Louis believed this, until a year later when one of their agents—a trusted one, not a pensioned menace like the chevalier himself—brought from London what he swore was positive proof that d'Eon was a female. This convinced them.

However, there did not seem to be anything to do about it. D'Eon, no matter which sex he was, remained, as far as Versailles was concerned, what he had been for many years, a nuisance who must be kept quiet at a price. Recently he had shown fresh signs of restlessness, wanting to come home, but Louis would not consider granting this request. D'Eon with The Papers had become so accepted a danger that he was almost a myth in France, and the situation might have continued indefinitely had the rest of the Continent's politics remained static. Unfortunately for d'Eon, politics don't stay fixed and kings are mortal. Louis XV died.

He discovered just before he died that his secret service was not so awfully secret after all. Other monarchs as well as himself knew how to bribe, trick, and snoop, and the Black Cabinet of Vienna possessed accurate copies of his most carefully cherished documents. What might have happened to his secret service if Louis had continued to live is a moot point. It would seem to have outlived its usefulness, but it had become an ingrained habit with the King; could he have done without it? The point was settled in any case by death, for when Louis XVI heard what an unsavory organization he had inherited, he lost no time in dispersing the agents and pensioning them off. Thus the matter of the chevalier was again reviewed, and again the court began sending messengers to bargain with him.

The intervening years had reduced the value of the secrets the chevalier was holding onto, but he did not realize it. He made enormous demands. He asked so much, to begin with, that Louis XVI nearly withdrew all offers. After all, it was not his own name he was protecting, and it seemed rather farfetched to suppose England would now go to war over an outdated plan of his predecessor. Still, many living people were involved; it would be better to hush it all up. So he continued to send messengers to d'Eon, trying to make him see reason and abate his desires.

No one succeeded until, quite by accident at first, Caron de Beaumarchais blundered into the affair. Beaumarchais, now remembered chiefly because he wrote the story of *The Barber of Seville*, was a man of many talents, but was not overburdened with nicety of conscience. In his way as great an adventurer as the chevalier himself, he scented a possible advantage in d'Eon's quandary.

D'Eon appealed to him for help when the latest of the King's men had lost patience and gone back to France. Could not Beaumarchais resolve this problem, he asked, and make the court see reason? If so, the author would himself profit by it; the chevalier would divide with him.

Beaumarchais hung back. The chance of making his fortune was tempting, but he probably felt that a man as tricky as the chevalier would cheat him after the settlement had been made. He was still hesitating when d'Eon played his trump card. He would hold nothing back, said the chevalier; the time had come to confess. Beaumarchais had doubtless heard the rumor that he was a woman? Yes, said Beaumarchais, everyone had heard it. Well, said d'Eon, shyly hanging his head, it was true. . . .

We will never know, now, just why d'Eon did this. He may have thought it out coolly and carefully, blurting as he did merely in order to push through the bargain with Beaumarchais, but even so it was an extraordinary idea, just as it had been extraordinary to disguise himself as he had done *chez* Madame Dufour. Admittedly there are many transvestites and other inverts to whom such a role would appeal, but d'Eon had never until now behaved at all like an invert. Perhaps, however, he didn't know why he did it. Did he feel attraction for Beaumarchais? Possibly.

Beaumarchais for his part was later to declare that he had been tricked, lured into a lot of trouble by his fatal kindness of heart. Here was a poor old maid in the devil of a fix, begging him to help her out. How could any normally chivalrous man refuse? Moreover, she gave him to understand that she loved him. She led him on. He fell in love with her, said Caron de Beaumarchais.

It has been suggested that what motivated him was not charity so much as greed. He was confident d'Eon would get a large sum of money out of Louis XVI sooner or later. If Beaumarchais married the chevalier, beard and all, he would be sure to reap the benefits of the payment, whereas if he merely trusted in a gentleman's agreement, he would get left. That is what Caron's enemies said, and of course that theory, too, is quite plausible.

The subsequent antics of the two rascals would make an excellent comedy, quite as good as "The Barber" itself, were it not that transvestitism is such a difficult theme. They worked together for a while in perfect amity, and then, inevitably, they quarreled, and broke off their engagement. However, progress was made in the affair d'Eon versus the Crown. Little by little, the chevalier let go some of his cherished documents. Little by little, a satisfactory agreement was drawn up. D'Eon was to get a pension. He was to come home to France, as he wished, and live there, but he must relinquish his way of living, adopt feminine clothing, and give up all his masculine wardrobe. One uniform of dragoons he would be allowed to keep (but not to wear) for sentimental reasons.

Through all the negotiations Beaumarchais busily played the market, preparing to make a killing among the many people of

London who were again wildly laying bets on the sex of the chevalier. It is almost certain that d'Eon himself had some money on it; perhaps that was one of the things they quarreled about afterward.

Louis's insistence that d'Eon renounce his manhood and make public the fact that he was a woman was thoroughly consistent, for the King was a good Catholic, and the alleged lifelong masquerade of the demoiselle d'Eon deeply shocked him. But he had another more practical reason for laying down this law. D'Eon's return to France in the ordinary way would cause trouble in the Guerchy family, and the late ambassador's son would almost certainly call d'Eon out. However, as the chevalier was really a woman after all, young Guerchy's hands would be tied. Everyone's hands would be tied, even d'Eon's. Peace would be maintained.

At last the agreement was settled, signed, and sealed. The chevalier was a chevalier no longer, but a demoiselle; it was time for him to become her, and go home to France like a perfect lady.

Understandably, the demoiselle at the last moment had a change of heart. He reflected sadly that he hated skirts. Was there no way out? Could he not trick the King? Reason replied that he could of course back down, but in that case he would sacrifice his pension. And, as usual, he was broke and in debt.

With a deep sigh, in August 1777, the chevalier became the demoiselle. She held a sort of dress rehearsal for a week at her house in Brewer Street, and friends and acquaintances thronged to see her holding court in black silk, with diamonds, her face carefully shaved and powdered. She *did* look like a woman, they said, marveling. Why had they never been sure before? That fair skin and plumpness above her bodice, that matronly figure!

In the meantime the bottom dropped out of the d'Eon betting market.

Came dawn of the day she was to set sail for France. A large crowd waited in the streets to see her off, and to see. But the demoiselle always had an eye for the dramatic. When she stepped out to the coach, a sigh of disappointment went up from the crowd, for she was the demoiselle no longer. Brave in green and gold, the chevalier appeared in his forbidden uniform, a captain of dragoons.

The rest of it is a sad story. Tied by her agreement, her legs hampered by petticoats, the Demoiselle Charlotte Geneviève Louisa Augusta Andrew Timothy d'Eon found her new existence very tedious. For a time she lived in Paris, and she was presented at court, upon which occasion she wore her Cross of St. Louis and performed a remarkably awkward curtsy. "She is not yet accustomed to the usual ceremonials established between the sexes," wrote a correspondent to the *Gentleman's Magazine,* "or rather it is obvious that having always, in her former state of life, shown great attention to the ladies, she finds it difficult to restrain it; at table when she sits near them she is always ready to fill their glasses; at coffee, no sooner has a lady emptied her cup, than d'Eon springs from her chair to hand it to the table."

Her appearances in public attracted so much notoriety, and she was so annoyed by curious sight-seers, that she gave up Paris at last and retired for some years to her family home in Tonnerre. There she had leisure to write the pamphlets and quarrelsome letters which she enjoyed composing, and there she was free of Paul Prys. The town barber came up to the house every two days to shave her. He, at least, never believed for a moment that she was a woman, and most of Tonnerre agreed with him.

From time to time the unfortunate creature tried to escape. Once she wrote to the archbishop begging for permission, on the grounds of health, to wear men's clothing on ordinary days. She promised she would always wear petticoats when she went to church or made journeys, but the archbishop refused her request. When France became embroiled in the American War of

Independence, d'Eon tried to join up, and was promptly thrown into jail for wearing the forbidden uniform.

There came a break in the monotony at last. In 1785 d'Eon got permission to go again to England, in order to look after the books and other possessions she had left there, and to try to collect money she declared was owing to her. According to d'Eon, somebody always owed her money, and probably most of the time this was true. She had no success at her collecting, but in an odd way she hit on a new and original method of eking out income. One day, while acting as one of the judges at a fencing exhibition, held by special request of the Prince of Wales, the old Adam rose up in the demoiselle: she engaged an exhibition fencer in a bout, or, as it was called, an assault. The novelty of the sight much impressed the audience, and when d'Eon actually touched her adversary, a famous French fencer named the Chevalier de Saint-Georges, they grew wildly enthusiastic. So did Saint-Georges. This encounter led to others, until Mademoiselle was traveling all over England with the other chevalier, giving fencing exhibitions in all the main cities.

She earned money in this way, but when did d'Eon ever have enough? Times grew harder. The French Revolution cut off her pension. She sold her bits and pieces of property. She went on fencing—no mean feat, considering she was nearly sixty when she began the exhibitions—until a wound put a stop to that.

At the age of eighty she had to take to her bed. By that time she was accustomed to living on charity; the Prince of Wales once gave her money, and various noblemen sometimes remembered to send her something. She had lodged for years with another old woman, Mrs. Cole, who now waited on her, as the demoiselle was quite helpless.

Charles Geneviève died at the age of eighty-two. The comedy was finished; concealment was no longer possible. When the undertaker's men discovered that he was a man, after all, most of his contemporaries were already dead and gone. It hardly mattered, by that time, to anyone. Only Mrs. Cole, poor old thing, was terribly shocked. It is a shame that no one in 1810 knew enough to come forward and explain things to her.

For that matter, it is a shame that no one was ever able to explain the chevalier to himself. At times during his long life he must have been pitifully bewildered.

The Innocent Admiral

THE NELSON STORY is surprising in several respects. Perhaps the most surprising thing about it is that it should have happened to Nelson, of all people. That such an out-and-out ship's man should have found himself mixed up with the diplomatic crowd was an accident which does happen now and again, but not often. He himself often complained that diplomacy wasn't his long suit. I don't suppose he believed it; like most of us, he probably thought he was pretty good at most things when he put his mind to it, but the fact is, he wasn't a born diplomatist. He was too honest, too unsuspicious, and far, far too much of a specialist. Nelson was the Navy itself, the first genuine John Bull seaman. He made the pattern. He was not bluff, but he was terse; not swaggering but thoroughly self-respecting; not reckless, but fearless.

It's no use going on with the list, I realize; it's too easy and inconclusive. Nelson made the British Navy. If we accept the popular theory that courage is simply lack of imagination, then we can't believe Nelson existed, for his genius lay in imagination and courage together. It seems inconsistent to add of this complicated character that he was simple as well, but he was.

Sir William Hamilton, on whose life he was to have such an effect, was the opposite of the admiral in many respects. His background, his work, and his world were not conducive to Nelson's kind of brave originality. Methods may have changed since the eighteenth century, but Foreign Offices do not lightly give up their traditions, and envoys are still a race apart. British envoys then as now were generally incorruptible in more than one sense. Against tremendous odds, most of them won their battle to remain exactly the same, regardless of where they were posted or how long they stayed there. A really good British ambassador ought not to be adaptable. Diplomacy is no career for a chameleon. British envoys go on being British. French diplomats, Americans—even Germans may sometimes amuse themselves by bending just a little, absorbing the spirit of some foreign land, joining in with the native life of whatever community they're quartered upon, but you seldom find an Englishman behaving in such fashion if he holds an important diplomatic post abroad. It was the same in the eighteenth century.

Sir William, though he had been so long in Naples, remained an Englishman. I do not claim he was conventional, because he was not; he was an eccentric. But he was eccentric in a thoroughly English way, and at a time when such eccentrics were, if I may be allowed to scramble a phrase, very much the normal thing. Had he been less extreme as a specimen of the type he represented, Nelson's fate would have been different. Had Sir William been a family man, Nelson might not have been a father at all. But Nelson—and no doubt Sir William as well— had happier lives the way things turned out, and the common cause of all this was Emma Hamilton. Sir William would have hated having a child. Lady Nelson might have kept her husband had it not been for Emma, but the admiral would have missed his chances of paternity, and very likely he would not have become quite so good a friend, either, of the Queen of Naples. His daughter Horatia meant a good deal more to Nelson than Maria

Carolina of the Two Sicilies did, but it is Maria Carolina rather than Horatia who seems at this distance in time to stand out. Gossip, piqued at not having known from the beginning about Horatia, turned attention to the Queen instead. It is a dubious compliment to accuse a Queen of a hole-and-corner affair, even with Nelson. Fortunately for the peace of whatever ghost Maria Carolina may have left on the earth, it is now obvious that not a word of the story was true.

Emma Hamilton, blacksmith's daughter, who was known before her marriage as Emmy Lyon, and also as Amyly or Emyly Hart, had a beauty no generation would deny. The record is full and clear, for she was painted many times by Romney; she was his favorite professional model.

Like the Princess Talleyrand, another study of ours, Emmy lost her reputation as soon as she grew up. About her morals in that early youth, versions differ. Considering everything, one could hardly say that Emmy was ruined, exactly. It depends on what you call ruin. Like many another poor girl she found herself better off when she began selling sex instead of domestic labor. In her class virtue wasn't a talisman against ruin, nor was there a prejudice against a woman when she lost it.

Emmy's first adventure with sex seems to have taken place soon after she went out, at the age of fourteen, to work as a nursemaid. Her employers moved to London, taking Emmy with them, and she promptly started a baby. Naturally, the employers, belonging as they did to a wealthier social group, did not approve of the baby; they had prejudices which Emmy's mother, fortunately for the girl, could not afford to possess. Emmy lost her job, but her people rallied round and helped. The baby, a girl, was pushed out of sight, as illegitimate babies usually were, and grew up in the country. Emmy remained in London, where Romney picked her up, recognized her beauty, and painted her again and again—as a bacchante, as Circe, as herself.

From eminence in a studio to eminence as a kept woman was not much of a journey. Emmy Lyon inevitably became sophisticated, and assumed the more grown-up name of Emma Hart. She met men of fashion who dropped in on Romney to get a thrill out of bohemian life and to watch the lovely girl he had found. Some one of them took her on as mistress, and when the first gave her up there must have been another eager and waiting, as there always is for a woman who becomes the vogue. The life suited her and she suited it. If one comes to think of it, being kept in the way Emma was is a good, solid means of livelihood. It never goes out of fashion; mechanization cannot reduce its appeal to clients. Without education or training in any trade, Emmy Lyon had made good, and found security not only for herself but her mother, Mrs. Cadogan, as well as various relations who seem to have clung through life to the chariot of the erstwhile nurse-maid. Emma Hamilton's is a success story, but it was not one of your sudden, flashy successes. She moved slowly and carefully at first.

I do not understand why so many writers persist in calling her an adventuress. There was nothing adventurous about Emma Hamilton. She was a good, solid type, domestically inclined. She was, indeed, very like her mother, except that she was amazingly beautiful and Mrs. Cadogan evidently wasn't. She was so little adventurous that she never cut the silver cord; she and her mother remained inseparable through life, just two simple, good-hearted women getting along as best they could. Admittedly they made silly remarks when they were out of their intellectual depth; who doesn't? But as for being adventuresses—no, decidedly not. The Lyons were every bit as conventional in their way as Nelson's wife was in hers.

Of course one cannot say that Emma never caused her mother a moment's uneasiness. She did make a few mistakes at the beginning. She cheated on one important protector; at least he was sure she did, and he threw her out for it, but any girl might have done the same before she learned policy and principle. Fortunately, Emma landed on her feet after this mishap. She became Mr. Charles Greville's girl.

Greville educated Emma. He thought her beauty worth accompanying graces like music and dancing and conversation, and as he had little to do otherwise, he set himself seriously to work on this Galatea. Emma learned music from professors he employed; she learned to play the harp and the pianoforte, and to sing. That is, her admirers say that she learned to sing; her detractors say she didn't. She learned to walk and to act. She had already learned to pose, in Romney's studio. And she reacted well to all this encouragement. She did not become pretentious: she remained, to a surprising degree, unaffected. Her conversation had never been inhibited and Greville seems to have been wise enough not to suppress it. Emma chattered gaily, verbally and on paper, never pausing too long in order to correct a slip in grammar or the spelling of a word.

Was the young woman in love with Greville? It seems very likely that she was; her letters indicate it. At any rate she respected him: she worked hard for his approval, and thought that they were good friends. In Emma's position it is more important than love, perhaps, to feel friendliness and confidence in one's protector and teacher. Unwittingly, Greville taught her something apart from music and deportment. The fact that he worked so hard at his task seems to have given Miss Lyon a new idea—a justified one too, everything considered—of her own importance and worth. Then something happened which administered a severe jolt to her recently acquired complacency.

We are not sure why Greville behaved as he did, but we can give a good guess. He was no doubt merely tired of his lady. What really mystifies us is how any gentleman could so coldly and openly behave like a pimp. However, codes change and we should try to understand that. Today it is not a pretty story, but then, in 1785 when Emma was about twenty-one, it was probably a reasonably ordinary thing to have done. Greville handed Emma over to his uncle. It was a more complicated procedure than it sounds as I describe it, but that was his intention and his deed.

The uncle, Sir William Hamilton, lived in Naples and had been His Majesty's ambassador there for some years. Ambassadors for unimportant posts like this one were selected from the ranks of moneyed gentlemen who wanted such appointments and could afford them. If they found themselves well suited, the authorities left them there indefinitely. Sir William, a childless widower, loved Naples. He was a dilettante and antiquary in an era when gentlefolk were making a great fuss about marbles from Italy; he collected vases and coins and statuary, lived in a palace in the country, and had things in general his own way in Naples. Greville was his heir. Nephew wrote to aesthete uncle about Emma, describing her, much as an ancient Roman might have done about some rarely beautiful slave he intended to bestow on a kinsman. She was making great progress, he said, in her music, and the two men agreed that it might look better if Sir William told Naples society he was importing the girl as a protégée, to finish her training under Italy's artistically sunny sky, rather than that he was taking his nephew's castoff mistress on approval.

Emma didn't know she was being dumped. Settled in at Naples with her mother, she waited for Greville, who did not come. When Sir William began making passes, she wrote anxiously to her erstwhile owner, begging him to hurry and extricate her from a position which grew hourly more embarrassing, and she was angry when she realized, at last, what had happened, that the men had agreed on a transfer of property. At least she claimed to be angry, and I really do not see why she shouldn't have been sincere in this reaction. If Greville did not keep his promise to join her, she wrote, she would have her revenge; she would marry the older man.

Sure of his inheritance, knowing Sir William could never cut him out, Greville told her to go ahead. He even advised her as to the best way to go about persuading Sir William to marry again at the age of fifty-six. Emma began to take the possibility seriously. She stopped merely threatening Greville, and got down to work. She polished her manners as her faithless master had taught her to do; she practiced her singing; she made up to the Neapolitans, who were not so strait-laced a crowd as the English would have been, until they forgave that past which most of them had already divined. Above all, she made herself thoroughly agreeable to Sir William. Mrs. Cadogan probably clinched the deal merely by being herself, the perfect, self-effacing housekeeper. Naples did not chatter overmuch: there had already been five years in which the world accustomed itself to the arrangement.

So far, save for the rather lurid light cast on the exchange of a mistress by our twentieth-century code, this is not an out-of-the-way narrative. It was Maria Carolina, Queen of the Two Sicilies, who gave the proceedings that something special which made Nelson's love story extraordinary. She would have made friends, no doubt, with any woman Sir William married; love of England was her idiosyncrasy. But any other ambassadress than Lady Hamilton, any woman who had been with her husband from the first in the ruthless career most diplomats undergo, might not have gone overboard, as Emma did, on the friendship. A woman of Sir William's own class would have been held back by her training: Emma was a better ambassadress in that Latin country.

Maria Carolina was Marie Antoinette's sister. She looked like the Queen of France, but Marie Antoinette was a gentle soul, whereas Maria Carolina was of a strong, dominant nature, with ideas about how a country should be run. In the earlier days of her marriage to Ferdinand, who was no firebrand himself, the Queen of Naples had fancied herself as a social reformer, and made an experiment in founding a model community. Somehow, perhaps from her mother, she had acquired a passion for England and English ideas, and though she never learned to speak the language, she retained this prejudice for many years. The Prime Minister, Sir John Acton, was English. When Sir William married his beautiful young musician, the Queen began showing special favor to Lady Hamilton. By 1793 Emma was an intimate of the royal palace.

Fellow diplomatists and British envoys to neighboring countries tittered and twittered over Sir William's misalliance, but they could not deny that Lady Hamilton in her warmhearted way was a great help to him. She was as much at home with the Queen as was any Italian member of the court. Indeed, she was more so, for Maria Carolina, like many another sovereign, found it safer to confide in someone who like Emma was not a compatriot. The plot was thickening, not only at the court of Naples but in most countries of the Continent, now that the nobles of France were overthrown. Republicanism was spreading like any plague; at least that is how it seemed to European princes. Queen Maria Carolina, who had longed ardently in the past to liberalize her government, thought of her sister in prison, awaiting trial and execution, and in self-defense and fear became a violent reactionary.

England, she felt, was her only hope. England was at war with republican France, and so the Anglophile Queen redoubled her favors to England's envoy at her court, and to his wife. When she was not sending word-of-mouth messages about this to Sir William through Emma, or interviewing him in person, she wrote letters to her dear, dear Lady Hamilton, relieving her feelings and passing on useful information at the same time. The ladies' friendship became animated, warm, and frenetic, as female friendships have a way of doing in southern countries, but the foundation of it all was policy. A few of the Queen's most violent enemies were later to declare that she was actually in love with Emma, and that the women maintained a Lesbian relationship, but the story is manifestly false; just the sort of thing a diplomat dreams up when he needs a vacation. The suspect letters, when we read them today, do not sound in the least like passion. On the contrary, they are rather stately and stuffy, like that which Maria Carolina wrote to Lady Hamilton on the occasion of Louis XVI's death:

> *Ma chère Miledy,*
>   *J'ai été bien touché de l'interet que vous prenez à l'execrable catastrofe dont ce sont souillés les infames françois. . . . Je compte le plus sur votre Genereuse Nation, . . . et pardonez a mon cœur dechire ses sentimens.*
>   *Votre attachee amie,*
>
>   *Charlotte.*

King and Queen more than ever inclined to Anglophilia when they heard that Toulon, which the French had recaptured, was again in English hands. It seemed that a British captain, one Horatio Nelson, had been sent to Naples on a mission: he was on his way to collect as many soldiers as he could borrow from Their Majesties. The royal couple determined to give Nelson the red carpet treatment, and like the conscientious envoy he was, Sir William Hamilton too went to great lengths to render Nelson's stay pleasant. The captain stayed at the Hamiltons' house; the Hamiltons assisted the captain with supplies when he entertained his royal hosts aboard ship; Lady Hamilton and her housekeeper mother did all they could to make the guest comfortable. Nelson liked Lady Hamilton. He said so when he wrote to his wife.

Had Horatio Nelson been another sort of man, we might safely suppose that he began even in those early days to covet Emma Hamilton. But Nelson was dedicated to his work. He lived for ships, he dreamed of ships, he thought constantly of ships. Some years before, when he found himself being distracted from ships by falling in love with one girl after another, he did what, according to his lights, should have settled all that: he fell in love with someone who was conveniently near him at the time, and married her between voyages. She was a widow named Mrs. Nisbet, and she was not a good choice, though when Nelson first met Emma Hamilton it is most unlikely that he was so much as whispering this criticism to himself. The fact was, Mrs. Nelson was a moaner; she was hopelessly self-centered, thin, nervous, and complaining. One gets the impression that she was anemic, but whatever her state of health, she was definitely not an ideal helpmeet for a sailor. A sailor like Nelson doesn't need a wife at all most of the time, but when he's got one he wants a comfortable, admiring creature who sees to his food and lodging in a practical manner. Mrs. Nelson did not answer to that description.

Nevertheless and notwithstanding, she was Mrs. Nelson, and that was that. The captain was not a man to brood upon such matters. If he did think wistfully sometimes, after sailing away from Naples, about that comfortable, dazzlingly beautiful woman at the Embassy, the friend of the Queen, who kept such a lavish house—if he did reflect that Emma Hamilton probably saw to it that her husband's linen was in excellent order, he did not realize he was making odious comparisons. Nelson was a thoroughly honorable gentleman.

They were leisurely times. Transport and travel were slow. A woman in Naples might easily wait five years before again encountering a chance acquaintance she had met in the way of a hostess's duty. Five years did pass, and Nelson rose like a rocket, in the Navy and the world. They heard about his fame in Naples. He was now Sir Horatio and an admiral. In five years of unremitting war with a changing France he had lost an eye and an arm in honorable battle, and his popularity transcended everything one could imagine. The breath of scandal never smirched it; he was, according to hearsay, a perfect gentleman, whose devotion to his wife (on the rare occasions when he came to England and saw her) was beautiful to witness.

Now he was again in the vicinity of Naples, preparing for an important battle with Napoleon's fleet, if only he could find it. As soon as he could send messages, Sir Horatio wrote affectionately to his old friends the Hamiltons. Maria Carolina, all alert and eager to continue being chummy with England, penned one of her effusions to Emma for his benefit, and Emma forwarded it to the battered hero while he was yet at sea and approaching.

> *Dear Sir, I send a letter I have this moment received from the Queen. Kiss it, and send it back by Bowen, as I am bound not to give any of her letters.*
> *Ever yours,*
> *Emma.*

Some British admirals might have thought that note somewhat gushing, but not Sir Horatio. Nothing Lady Hamilton said could possibly be silly. He had always admired her, from the first moment he met her. He made no secret of his admiration, and often spoke to his wife about the remarkable woman in Naples who had so improved herself after a pitiful start in life. Someday, he promised Lady Nelson, he hoped to introduce her to the paragon.

Emma must have known she was in love with Nelson long before he did. It may have troubled her, for she had not indulged in falling in love since Sir William had made an honest woman of her. The fate of her love for Greville may have discouraged her softer sentiments; good fortune in marriage probably made her cautious too, unwilling to jeopardize her position. At any rate, since that triumph her behavior had been exemplary. Until now, when Nelson's name sent her into ecstasies of hero worship that was bound to spill over somehow, she had been contented and happy, and very proud of her friendship with Maria Carolina.

Maturity and content together contributed, incidentally, to a worsening of her figure; Lady Hamilton was getting fat. But it was nothing to worry about; most people didn't object to fat in those days. The world continued to admire her features, which were perfect and beautifully animated.

So there it was. Excited because Nelson was soon to arrive, and bubbling over with importance at being used by the Queen as a diplomat, Emma Hamilton told the admiral to kiss the Queen's letter. The admiral did as he was told, and sent it back to her.

When the news of the Battle of the Nile reached Naples, the Hamiltons in all the rejoicing city were proudest and happiest. Sir William was stirred up, as befitted his country's ambassador, but his wife's excitement was so intense it surpassed even his. Emma had developed a great volatility since coming to Naples; she had acquired a Neapolitan sense of the dramatic. She had caught the Queen's style of behavior; the incident of kissing the letter was a case in point. Now she outdid the Queen. Maria Carolina at news of the Nile victory wept and laughed and had hysterics all over the palace, but Lady Hamilton did better than that. Palpitating, she went out to the *Vanguard* to greet her hero in the ambassador's barge, accompanied by Sir William and a band of musicians. Nelson wrote to his wife about it afterward.

"The scene in the boat was terribly affecting; up flew her ladyship, and exclaiming, 'Oh God, is it possible?' she fell into my arm more dead than alive."

To receive the full effect of this scene we ought to remember that Sir Horatio was a slight, short man, whereas Lady Hamilton was neither slight nor short. It did not matter; the admiral loved her style. He may have reeled from the impact, but he was immensely flattered just the same. And that, no doubt, is how it all began.

The other day at a Dorset lunch party this writer mentioned Nelson. Someone at the table had just visited the nearby monument to "Kiss-me" Hardy, a tall gray chimney-looking affair which towers hideously over his village of Portisham.

"Nelson was a man whose private life had no effect, fortunately, upon his career," said the writer.

"No effect?" repeated one of the men in horror. "No effect? Why, that woman ruined him! Nelson would have been a great and good man if it hadn't been for Lady Hamilton."

The writer felt a trifle cowed, but muttered defiantly into her pudding spoon that he was a great and good man regardless. There was a pause. Emboldened, she added, "Don't you think he was?"

"After all," said the man. "I mean to say. Great, perhaps. But after all, Lady Hamilton was a *married woman*."

There was no denying it, and the writer allowed the conversation to wander off in another direction. But surely, she wanted to protest, there were circumstances which this dictum did not cover. The circumstances under which Emma married Sir William, for instance, and the later circumstance that he did not seem to resent her affair with Nelson. Were it not for the fact that the writer is prejudiced in Emma's favor on general feminist principles, she might defend Nelson by making the obvious conjecture that Lady Hamilton threw herself at him.

Oh, never mind, she decided at last. Nelson has never asked anybody to defend him, so why should I trouble to do so? Nelson seems to have had no qualms about it. We know he was, in the ordinary way, fantastically conscientious. He was honorable not only in his capacity as a sailor; he did more than his duty toward his father and siblings, for one example. If Nelson felt all right about his relations with Sir William, I do think it's not our place to carp.

Nelson gave in to his own feelings and Lady Hamilton's, very likely soon after the fainting scene in the boat, during the tremendous celebration of his birthday which Naples offered him as a well-earned honor. It is possible that for a little while before the seduction he simply didn't know what had hit him. He and his officers were treated like the greatest heroes of history, and the leader of all the festivity, the most assiduous adorer, was Emma Hamilton. Nelson probably fell then, but he would not have called it falling; he was uplifted.

One imagines Sir William, aging and tired, watching the situation with shrewd eyes. He knew his Emma. Approaching age had intensified his already strong selfishness. He wanted to retain his good name, naturally, but he also wanted peace and quiet in which to pursue his beloved antiquarian studies. As long as there was no open scandal, Sir William, I feel, could not have cared less about Emma and Lord Nelson.

But Gossip will not have it like that. Gossip always seeks a chance to feel righteously indignant. Not only did she fly to Sir William's defense, righteously indignant on his behalf since he would not trouble to be that way on his own, but she made up other accusations to hurl at Nelson when the original one grew stale. One affair for Nelson, Gossip felt, was not enough. In fact, none of it was enough for anybody; all the actors must be dragged in and accused of more sins. There had been Greville and all those other lovers for Emma, and there was already the salacious hint about the Queen and Lady Hamilton; why not finish the circle by pairing off Maria Carolina and the admiral? Busily, Gossip set to work.

She did not have much to go on. There was that footnote of Emma's about kissing the letter; there was Nelson's reply and a few similar scraps of writing. There was Nelson's private interview with the Queen. Certainly not much, one would say, but it was enough for Gossip. It was sufficient to start a rumor a generation later that Horatia Nelson, the child of Emma and the admiral, was not Emma's child at all, but the Queen's. Faithful Lady Hamilton, said Gossip, had promised to keep the secret forever, and so raised the child as her own.

Nothing discourages this sort of thing, least of all unromantic

Fact. Actually, the Queen was probably incapable by that time of bearing children at all—she had already borne eighteen—and Nelson would certainly have been incapable in any case of indulging in such a fantastic intrigue. Even had he not been absorbed in his staggering affair with Emma it could not have happened. He did admire Maria Carolina, with all the fervor of his simple soul. She was a tragic figure, like her poor dead sister Marie Antoinette, and his heart would have gone out to her even if Emma Hamilton had not shared with her lover her own loyalty to the Queen, though of course the ambassadress's dramatic urging just at that tender time had a tremendous effect on him. But as for an affair with that Queen, or any queen, one can only sigh wonderingly at Gossip's greed. It was strange enough that Nelson did what he did. Surely the true story should have satisfied the most inveterate snooper and babbler.

Nelson was undergoing a transformation; the sailor's heart burst its bounds. He was madly in love with Emma Hamilton, a fact which, apart from its effect on him, made for confusion in high places generally. And not that alone; on the face of it the honorable admiral had suddenly become dishonorable indeed. On the face of it, his behavior was shocking. He cuckolded his good friend Sir William, he outran his orders regarding the court of Naples and the Two Sicilies, and he took great liberties with his position.

He might with justice have protested far more indignantly than he did that he hadn't joined the Navy to become embroiled in the politics of a foreign court anyway. However, there was really no one else at that confused time to represent his country— no one save Sir William, that is to say, and Sir William was not so much in touch with home as was Nelson, in those telegraphless, radioless days. Briefly, the situation was this: England wanted the rulers of Naples to attack France. The King of Naples wanted first to be assured of the Emperor of Austria's support. The Queen, far more headstrong and courageous than

her husband, did not wish to hesitate. She vehemently declared
that such action was their only chance against republicanism, but
her influence was small, and Ferdinand was reluctant to take a
definite step, especially as the Emperor kept putting off his decision. At last, however, he allowed himself to give the order to
march against Rome, with the aim of unifying the lower part of
Italy and thus strengthening himself against France.

The Neapolitans had a brief success at Rome, but the tide soon
turned and they were routed. Panic seized Naples. The royal
family and court fled from the mainland, in Nelson's ships, to
Palermo, and the Hamiltons went with them.

So far, from the point of view of the British admiralty, Nelson
had behaved in exemplary fashion, doing only what he was told
to do. It was after the Sicilian interlude that his trouble really
began and he incurred violent criticism. The Neapolitan panic
subsided, the King's forces got the upper hand, and Maria Carolina's party, still accompanied by the Hamiltons, still most
obviously supported by the English fleet, returned to Naples.
The Queen's passionate nature, already soured by months of
terror and of brooding over her sister's fate, demanded revenge,
or, as she termed it, justice. Those of Ferdinand's courtiers and
officers who were suspected of treason were rounded up, and one
who was held to have behaved particularly badly was executed
out of hand.

Nelson, naturally, did not disapprove of this action. His reaction was quite simple; the fellow was a mutineer and of course
must be dispatched. Nelson would have done exactly the same
had he been in the Queen's place. But his critics did not see it
in that light. Nelson had no right, they said, to be helping in a
foreign court of justice. Maria Carolina had been bloodthirsty
and cruel, which was bad enough considering she was under the
protection of the British, but what made it much worse was that
Nelson was the lover of Lady Hamilton, the Queen's confidential
friend. The three of them together had been bloodthirsty and

cruel. People who behaved like that would not stop short of sexual excesses and wickedness of all kinds. . . .

All of this was said in England later, and it was said loudly because the way was paved for such criticism by what Nelson did next.

The Italian war, reflecting the general turmoil in Europe, now swung round again in favor of republicanism. Ferdinand refused to come back to the mainland at all. Maria Carolina refused to return to Palermo. But she could not remain in Naples, and so it was decided that she should make her way overland to take refuge in Vienna. The British Embassy must close down, of course, so Sir William and Lady Hamilton would travel with her and continue on their way to England. That was all quite in the order of the day, and might almost be called a conventional arrangement, if arrangements during wartime are ever conventional. But the fourth main member of the party was a rather surprising addition. Why should Nelson, an admiral, feel called upon to leave his ship and travel on land in such strangely selected company?

Nelson at least thought it quite a reasonable thing to do. If he had any misgivings about his course of action, he must have argued them into silence without taking anyone into his confidence. He felt he was answering the call of Honor itself in supporting Maria Carolina through his support of Lady Hamilton.

In his eyes Emma was a heroine, one of England's saviors. Her efforts with the Queen on his behalf, he felt, had been as much patriotic as loving; he was more than Nelson; he represented England's Navy. In all the excitement of evacuating the royal family from Naples, when he had taken them to safety at Palermo through a terrible storm and they had all lain helplessly ill in the tossing ship, Emma was just as cheerful, strong, practical, and helpful as one would expect her (or her mother) to be. The little son of Maria Carolina had died aboard ship, in her arms. She was maid, nurse, virtually doctor as well. In the emotion of that emergency she never faltered or showed weakness. Anyone would have admired her then, and Nelson's natural passion, that of an innocent man for an accomplished charmer, became more than ever fervent: it approached a pitch of idolatry. Passion alone would not have been permitted by a man like Nelson to shape his life, but this, he would have insisted, was a great deal more than passion. Emma, the beautiful big creature who resembled one of the more opulent of Grecian goddesses, was truly a goddess to Nelson.

As for Nelson's guilt in cuckolding Sir William, I do not for a moment doubt how he condoned that. Emma assured her lover that she had long been a wife in name only, and that Sir William was not only impotent but complacent as long as her affairs were not forced upon his attention. Moreover, I don't think she lied in saying so.

She was not always strictly truthful, however. She told Nelson it was her great sorrow that she had no children. "Love Sir William and myself," she once wrote, "for we love you dearly. He is the best husband, friend, I wish I could say father allso; but I should have been too happy if I had the blessing of having children, so must be content." Actually she *had* the blessing; somewhere in England, she knew, there was living an unattractive narrow-browed sulky young woman, also named Emma, who was maintained by a kind of family committee and who had no idea she was Lady Hamilton's daughter. But Emma the elder never told Nelson about the girl. Quite possibly she really forgot about the matter herself most of the time.

Regardless of Nelson's own state of mind, however, it was not a pretty story which reached England ahead of the party. Lady Hamilton and the Queen were painted as bloodthirsty creatures, Gorgons who slaughtered from sheer love of power, and Nelson was alleged to be their tool. After all, said the critics, the insurrection of Naples had not been directly aimed at Britain. The

Italian army had proved worse than useless; as allies Ferdinand and his Queen were a dead loss and there was no diplomatic necessity for Nelson to have committed himself so deeply. It was shamefully obvious that he had been dazzled by the Queen and/or Lady Hamilton, women who did not scruple to take turns as his mistress.

It was a savage, grotesque version of events, which was not to endure with the public for long, at any rate in such extreme form. But there is no doubt that the continental tour worsened matters for Nelson, especially in the minds of the admiralty. His reason for behaving so very unlike a seaman may have been sufficient to himself, and tenable, but Gossip was enabled to put a very different construction on the proceedings. What the world of London would have done had it known the worst, that Emma was pregnant by her lover at the time they arrived home, I shudder to think. Fortunately for Nelson, Lady Hamilton was a match for Gossip. The trip across Europe had been a long one, but not too long. She was in time.

It seems incredible that a woman so much in the public eye as Lady Hamilton could have concealed her state, but she was aided by several factors. She had always affected Greek draperies and a flowing style of dress, ever since the days of Romney and the studio; Sir William, the antiquary, had encouraged her to continue the style after they married. A sudden change to a "concealing" type of costume might have drawn attention to the necessity of concealment, but she avoided that. To all intents and purposes, Emma Hamilton *always* wore maternity dresses.

Then, too, she had gained weight steadily in the past few years, and had become what Lord Minto ungallantly described as immense. Possibly Minto, who disliked her, exaggerated out of malice; possibly Emma was merely Junoesque. But it is quite easy for a Junoesque lady in Greek draperies to hide her pregnancy, as Emma did. And we must also remember the important point that she had her mother to help her through this awkward adventure. Mrs. Cadogan was resourceful, knowledgeable, and trustworthy to the highest degree.

So it came about that Lady Hamilton, unknown to the world and Sir William, managed to be safely delivered of Nelson's daughter. It was quite easy, considering. Lady Hamilton was indisposed for several days, and then she was seen in public again, and Gossip knew nothing whatever about it. I don't know how the rest of the modern world may feel about Emma, but I for one admire her, if only for this outwitting of society's snoopers.

She was not always admirable. It is difficult thoroughly to admire a silly person, and Emma, I fear, was very silly. Admittedly it was a rather endearing silliness. She loved her hero to distraction, and was always telling him in a hundred ways how wonderful he was. When, after Lady Nelson left him, Nelson bought Merton Place and Emma furnished it, she put portraits of the master everywhere, in paint and marble and plaster and black and white; she hung up souvenirs of his glory and made of the house a museum in his honor. Nelson didn't seem to mind. On the contrary, simple sailorly soul that he was, he loved it. The thicker the butter was spread the more avidly he swallowed it, but as self-confidence seems never to have spoiled his admiral's technique, we must not be too hard on him. Besides, he paid Emma back in her own coin, and told her as often as he had a chance what an absolutely perfectly wonderful woman she was. He told everyone else the same thing. There must have been many awkward pauses in the conversations of London during that period, whenever Lord Nelson was at the party.

He did not quite lose his head; he continued to observe the conventions of the day, but we must be excused if we feel that the spirit of his observance, if not the letter, was somewhat lacking. Take for example the case of Lady Nelson. We have no way of knowing what went on between the pair in private, but it seems that Nelson did not confess his infidelity in so many words. Instead he behaved as if his wife would (and ought to) accept the state of affairs without being so crude as to speak of it, ignoring the evidence and continuing to go everywhere with him in company with the Hamiltons. Why he should have thought such an arrangement humanly possible is a mystery, but then he was an uncomplicated soul, and he was a man besides. Men often go on the assumption that these problems, if severely ignored, cease to exist.

For poor Lady Nelson, however, the problem was very much there. She hardly knew what to do. She was never a keen-witted woman. There were one or two scenes in public and a fainting fit at the theater; we can only guess at the endless quarrels and nagging and wretchedness that went on in private, until she took the last desperate course and left her husband. It is a pitiable story which her many faults as a wife do nothing to make less painful. Yet so strong are the forces of convention that the Hamiltons continued to be seen everywhere with Lord Nelson, as if they felt it their duty to do so and thus contradict the inevitable rumors.

Lady Nelson did not bring suit for divorce, as a woman in her position would almost certainly do today. It was not a thing people did in her day. Had she been able to manage events, she would have taken her husband back and saved appearances, but this was beyond her power.

The Hamiltons spent most of their time at Merton Place, Sir William showing no resentment whatever. Once he found it necessary to remonstrate with his wife because she rushed him about too much, more than he felt was right for a man his age. He did not like being pushed around, and he said so. But there is no written word of his recording a single accusation against his wife on account of her misconduct with Nelson. He had taken his stand and he maintained it. Every reference he made to the admiral was in a spirit of affection. When he died—in

1803, not quite three years after the return from Naples—he left in his will a legacy to Nelson, "the most virtuous, loyal, and truly brave character I ever met with, God bless him, and shame fall on those who do not say 'Amen.'"

The legacy was a portrait of Emma.

Still the conventions retained their grip. Lord Nelson could not marry Lady Hamilton, because Lady Nelson was not dead. There the situation was, and there it remained. Lady Hamilton could not live outright in his house, and he could not live with her in her London house, either. It was a little inconvenient. Otherwise, there was no difficulty; Emma had long since won the good will of his people, and there was always a sister or someone else suitable to chaperon them.

Two other complications were not so easily dismissed. The baby girl Horatia had been put out to nurse, and nobody knew about her, but now as she grew older her father wanted to see more of her during his periods of shore leave. How to account for the child? Emma and Nelson gave it out that she was the daughter of an old friend who had died. More and more often she was brought to Merton, and at last Nelson adopted her legally. But Lady Hamilton never told anyone, as far as is known, that she had any claim whatever to the little girl. Her contacts with Horatia were just what they would have been had she actually been the great and good friend of Horatia's adopted daddy, and nothing more.

The other complication was that more common one, shortage of money. Sir William had left Emma an income which in most hands would have been adequate. Emma, however, was hopeless about money. Nelson let her have all he could, but that wasn't enough, and anyway he had the unusual delicacy to see that she would prefer to be able to pay her own bills. A heroine like his wonderful Emma should not have to go in need. The nation owed her a pension, Lord Nelson felt, and he began working on the question as soon as Sir William's estate was settled. He besieged his acquaintance among the peerage, stoutly declaring that her rights should be observed, and asking them to use their influence.

Unfortunately the peers remained strangely obtuse. They were cross with Lady Hamilton; cross and embarrassed. No one save Nelson felt inclined to consider her a heroine or to give her rewards. On the contrary, they would have liked to punish her. Nelson would have been such a splendid fellow had it not been for that woman! But where she was concerned he was evidently blind, and the admiralty was forced to pretend blindness of another sort and condone the relationship just as Nelson's own family condoned it, by ignoring it and not snubbing Emma. It was far more awkward for the admiralty, of course, than for the Nelsons, for the latter genuinely liked Emma, as most people did when they knew her.

Nelson's emotions about Horatia, happily for him, were not complicated by such practical details, and they were full-flowering. To him, the baby was pure romance. She seemed an exquisite, almost mythical being, the personification of his and Emma's love. The little niggling details, the legal quibbles, the roundabout way Emma and her mother had to go to change Horatia's name to that of her "godfather," and explain her occasional appearances at Merton Place—such things did not trouble the romantic sailor who spent much of his time at sea. His not to fret in an atmosphere of hot milk and sour nappies. He was a hero; his life was consistently sheltered from everything but danger.

The question of Horatia's future, however, did trouble him. He was always short of money to keep Merton up in the style Emma was used to, but nevertheless he set aside a certain lump sum for Horatia, and through many financial worries he left it untouched, and often lectured Emma on the subject, telling her she must do likewise. His property, like his titles, would go to the brother who was his legal heir. That was the convention; that was his duty. But Horatia had her little income.

As for Emma—oh, Emma was a great problem, the most worrying of all. It is untrue that she wasted whatever Sir William left her at gambling. It has been proved that she was no card player, as her enemies have alleged, but she had no practical sense. She didn't use up money on any one thing; she was one of those people who merely disperse it somehow and never have much to show for it afterward. Pondering this truth, which even a hero like Nelson could not avoid facing, the admiral appealed to the generosity of his old friend the Queen of Naples, who was now reinstated, when on one of his voyages he found himself back in Italy. Surely Maria Carolina would think kindly of Emma, her faithful intimate of the past! Several times in writing to the Queen he repeated his urgings.

But Maria Carolina, like the peers of Britain, was slow to catch on to Nelson's meaning. She was warmly kind in referring to himself, but she never said anything about Lady Hamilton— nothing at all, not even a polite reference, let alone an offer of help. Nelson gave up in disillusioned disgust. He did not like the Queen, he decided. So much for the rumor of their affair, cooked up long afterward by defrauded Gossip.

Altogether, Gossip has been badly beaten by the Nelson romance. She never managed to break it up, nor even to spoil it for the admiral. One feels that Emma Hamilton, in spite of the dingy death awaiting her, emerged triumphant from that adventure. Not Gossip, but Lord Nelson's death and the loss of her mother sealed her own fate; without her love and her mainstay she was lost. She went down to ruin. All Nelson's family, all their affectionate care, couldn't save the bereaved, confused, defeated creature. There was no question of Horatia's proving her salvation, for Emma was not a strongly maternal woman. Because of the circumstances and her own deficiency, she had never been a true mother to the baby.

Only one thing was left: drink. She had always been fond of wine; now she depended on it. With a puzzled Horatia in her wake, she went to the Continent and wandered about, drinking more and more. She was miserably unhappy, and it must have been an ordeal for the girl as well. Horatia knew only that she was Nelson's daughter by some unknown, and that her aunts and uncles wished her to stay with Lady Hamilton, or at least did not object to her being with Lady Hamilton.

The situation came to an end at last. Poor Emma died in squalor. Yet when one thinks of her it is with a sense of her achievements.

It was surely no small feat, we must admit when we sum up her life, to have borne Horatia discreetly enough to have avoided Society's bloodhounds. In spite of the world's croaking, she made the hero happy, which Lady Nelson had never succeeded in doing. Moreover, to the end Emma kept the faith in her own way. Until the last few drunken months she even avoided dipping into Horatia's money, but that was not her greatest self-denial. Emma was a gushing woman, much given to "attitudes," not only the charade-like poses for which she was famous, but everyday indulgences in melodrama. She must have been tempted a thousand times to burst out with the truth to the fastidious, ladylike girl who accompanied her in her wanderings. However, she refrained. She never burdened Horatia with the true story of her origin, which would have much distressed the child. I think Emma deserves honor for that: Nelson's daughter never knew.

"He was treated with coldness by his wife . . ." wrote Horatia primly, long after Emma's death. "Had Lady Hamilton's character in early youth been irreproachable, I question much if Lord Nelson would have incurred the suspicions under which he labored."

Thus innocent Horatia, who married a reverend, and sometimes wondered with a delicious thrill if she might not after all be a queen's daughter.

Two
Ladies of Calcutta

IT IS A FAR CRY from Portuguese Angola to British India, from the early seventeenth century to the late nineteenth, from Nzinga to the Princess Talleyrand or Mrs. Warren Hastings. It is a farther cry still from Nzinga's Church to the Established Church of England, or whatever faith the princess may have belonged to in Chandernagore. Perhaps it would be simplest to sum it up in a phrase: British colonials were different.

Save for the very occasional religious fanatic, you saw no proselytizing in the early East India Company settlements of Madras and Calcutta. Unlike the Portuguese, the British were not interested in native souls. The Indians in all their numbers, with their bewilderingly many religions and castes, were too much to tackle, and so the British left them to stew in their own juice, interfering in gingerly fashion only when it came to the rites of Sati. The attitude of John Company's employees toward the mysterious East has been well expressed by a lady of my acquaintance: "Too many goddesses with too many arms."

This policy of live and let live, believe-as-you-like-only-don't-bother-me-about-it, and all the rest, led to an inevitable aloofness between the races. The British kept themselves to themselves, lived as they had always done, built their houses as if they were settling down in Twickenham or King's Lynn, and altogether maintained themselves in an amazingly uncomfortable manner. Even in love, as we shall see, they tried to keep it English, but this was difficult. There were not enough European ladies to go around. There were always plenty of bachelors who lost out in the eternal shuffle which took place whenever a new boat came in, and these gentlemen solaced themselves with Indian girls, but only a few hardy souls, determined, shameless reprobates such as William Hickey, made no attempt to cover up such liaisons.

The others, those lucky ones who captured girls from home, were theoretically free, after the honeymoon, to forget their courting pains and carry on with John Company's business. Actually it doesn't seem to have worked out that way. Marriage no doubt should have settled people, and at home in England it did. But out in India, somehow, it didn't make all that difference.

Gentlemen continued to pursue married ladies, quite regardless. Even more remarkably, husbands continued to pursue their own wives. Everybody behaved in an extraordinary manner which would never have done in London.

It wasn't only sex. People let go out East, in anger as in love. A man's emotions seemed to mean much more to him, and his career meant less, in India than in any part of Europe. What impresses us above all when reading the non-colonial archives of French and British and German diplomacy just before the French Revolution is the cold calm balance of these gentlemen. A man like Macartney, one of Fox's circle and a career diplomat, strikes ice to the soul as long as one reads the letters he wrote from Germany—or Russia—or Ireland. He was always correct, always deliberate, never impulsive. For the best of monetary reasons he made a loveless, boring marriage, and we gather that he never regretted it—in Europe. But as soon as he was sent to Madras he lost his temper.

Was it merely because they all felt themselves far from home, and thus could relax and be themselves? Or was it rather because they knew most of them would not survive more than a few years in that climate?

We don't know. We must keep in mind, though, that there are forces in the world which defeat the most adventurous. History in faroff places like India or Africa isn't carved out by conquerors. It isn't made. It just happens.

1. PEARLS AND KITTENS

THERE WAS ONCE A GIRL who went to a home for unmarried mothers and had a baby. A year later she returned, obviously again in need of temporary shelter. Although the authorities were somewhat taken aback, they let her in. On the third occasion of the sort, the matron felt it was time to make some kind of constructive criticism. Accordingly she said,

"Why don't you marry this man?"

"I don't like him," said the girl.

This old yet very modern anecdote may seem to have little in common with eighteenth-century colonial life and loves, but it is not completely irrelevant. They had a similar common-sense attitude toward love-making in those days, behind their façades of stately rhetoric. At least they did in India, where human nature has a way of becoming even more human than usual. Do not be misled by the literary style of the period. The colonists may have talked like people constantly involved in a minuet, but they didn't behave that way. The weather was hot in Madras and Calcutta, clothes were painfully stuffy, there were no ice cubes, no electric fans, and no air-conditioning. People grew passionate under the tropic moon, and when they were not being passionately sexy they were being passionately angry. Practically any epithet, if hurled in a tone offensive enough, was snatched at as fair provocation for a duel.

Into this electric atmosphere, in 1769, sailed Warren Hastings, who already knew India, and his new friends the Baron and Baroness Imhoff, who did not.

Like that unmarried mother of the twentieth century, the baroness, nee Chapuset, never liked the father of her children very much. Unlike the other girl, however, she married him, quite properly. Sixteen-year-old maidens in Germany were not encouraged to indulge their emotions, and when Anna Maria Appolonia was spoken for by Imhoff, it is doubtful if anyone, including herself, inquired as to whether she was madly attracted by her suitor. She was the barracks-born daughter of a sergeant, whereas Karl von Imhoff was a captain. To be sure, he was penniless, but sergeants' daughters cannot expect to have everything, and Imhoff was of noble blood. Anna Maria's father was of noble blood himself. He was descended, socially as well as genealogically speaking, from a Huguenot baron. The young Imhoffs may have been chronically broke, but they were wellborn, which has always counted for a good deal in Germany.

The title of baron is not rare on the Continent. There, every child of a baron inherits the right to use his handle, a custom which often leads to a plenitude of barons and not enough money to go round. Karl, younger son of a younger son, had no hopes of inheriting any family money, and his officer's pay was never enough, especially as Anna Maria, or Marian as she was called, promptly began to produce children. However, Karl had a talent for painting portraits; he preferred such work to military exercise. He also had connections with important people, including, fortunately, a claim on the interest of one of Queen Charlotte of England's attendants. That is why, after Marian had borne two sons and lost one, the Imhoffs went to London.

Their patron was Mrs. Schwellenberg, who had accompanied the dull, unhandsome Charlotte to England when the princess married George III. Mrs. Schwellenberg has been called various names by historians, none of them flattering. Fanny Burney's references are the best known. But Fanny wasn't to encounter her Cerbera for another two decades. Perhaps Mrs. Schwellenberg in younger days was not so formidable as she later became. At any rate she was very decent to the little Baroness Imhoff and her family. No doubt Mrs. S. felt gratified by the situation, and sentimentally moved; the pretty little wife of young Karl von Imhoff, who had married unwisely but so romantically, was a dependent who flattered the older woman's sense of power.

Karl didn't rise immediately to the top of his new profession in England, though Germans were presumably well liked at such a preponderantly German court. He might have done well enough, nevertheless. He probably moved on as soon as he did merely because he liked variety and adventure for their own sakes. Whatever the cause, instead of settling down, he used Mrs. Schwellenberg's influence to obtain an appointment as military cadet with the East India Company. Many young men were aspiring to such positions. Indian nabobs, coming home with their money, were giving a lot of people ideas; it was believed that one had only to go to India, risking the perils of the unhealthy climate, to reap a vast fortune. It was not a completely wild belief. But Karl hadn't the temperament that makes fortunes in such a manner. He was not a businessman, he was not a military man, he was an artist. His appointment was unusual, too, because he was not a bachelor, but a family man, and more than twenty-two years old, which was supposed to be the age limit for military cadets in the company.

Still, his hopes and Mrs. Schwellenberg's influence conquered these obstacles, and the Imhoffs set off for India with their three-year-old son, leaving another younger baby at nurse in England. They set sail in the Indiaman *Duke of Grafton*, occupying an expensive portion of the "great cabin," and taking with them two English maidservants. It was an impressive entourage for impecunious young people, but the Imhoffs always did things in the grand manner.

This may have been due to Marian's influence. There *was* something grand about her, something which belied the facts that her father was a sergeant, that her husband had no money, and that they had dropped their German title now that Karl was employed by a British company. Marian liked importance and she behaved like a woman who had a right to it. She wasn't unwisely haughty, but she had self-confidence, no doubt because of her beauty.

That beauty! A study of her portraits gives us no idea of it, but only makes us reflect on the mutability of taste. Yet Marian was generally considered pretty, and portraits are often misleading. She was tall, graceful, and slender. She was fair and blue-eyed, and had a long nose and a small pointed chin. Her great mass of hair was of a beautiful red-gold. European women go unbecomingly pale in hot climates, but Marian must have learned to use whatever cosmetic aids ladies permitted themselves in London's fashionable circles.

She was intelligent, though no bluestocking. Her vivacity contrasted well with the more phlegmatic manners of English ladies, who may have permitted themselves to gush on occasion but who never bubbled naturally, as Marian did. She talked English with a strong accent, and that too was fascinating.

Someone was sure to fall in love with Marian aboard the *Duke of Grafton*. A passage of four months was considered very speedy and, as it happened, this voyage took much longer. Marian was one of the only two ladies aboard. Men always fell in love en route for India, if there was anyone to fall in love with. If Hastings hadn't been an important man we would have heard no more about the voyage, perhaps: Marian would probably have ignored lesser admirers. But she did not ignore Hastings.

Had she indulged in extramarital flirtations before? It is possible, though her maternal duties must have kept her steady in

London, and Marian never behaved like a cheap woman. She did not flirt even now. What happened was much more discreet, slow moving, and serious in its effects.

At thirty-six Warren Hastings was making his second assault on fortune. He was a quiet little man, a bit smaller than the tall Mrs. Imhoff, with a hairline which would have led *Time Magazine* to call him "balding." He had first gone to India at seventeen, a poor, studious boy who harbored one ambition—to obtain the Manor of Daylesford in Worcestershire and restore his family there, because Daylesford had belonged to the Hastings before the Restoration. It was a romantic ambition. Hastings, though he seemed prosaic, was a tenaciously romantic man.

He did well in India, showing industry, a keen, unusual interest in local ethnology and excellent judgment. After exciting days in Bengal, after having been married and a widower, a father who lost his children, a rich man who gave away all his money, here he was, again on his way out East as a member of council for Madras.

He fell in love with Marian Imhoff, and he took it hard. The Englishmen of India tended to be solemn in their love affairs, especially when the objects were European women. Ordinary sex in India was cold-blooded and clinical; native women were plentiful, and accustomed to being treated casually, as conveniences, even by their own men. But the Westerner had been brought up to want more than undecorated sex in his love relationships. A man had his native mistress or he played the field, but he sighed nevertheless for the ideal white-skinned woman who might remind him of his mother.

Warren Hastings, having been in India before, of course had malaria in his system, and he got a bad attack of fever on the voyage out. Marian nursed him. He had already found her attractive; this accident settled matters. She was sweet, she was gentle, she had nursed him. Above all, she belonged to someone else. What romantic could resist the combination?

By the time the *Duke of Grafton* anchored off Madras, Hastings must have run the customary gamut of emotions. Round and round went his thoughts. First, no doubt, he resolved never to divulge his guilty secret, which seemed guilty indeed to a man of eighteenth-century England, still churchbound. He may have told himself that he must not disturb a happy marriage. Or had Marian allowed him to guess that it wasn't such a happy marriage after all? Very likely she had. One can imagine his reflections:

"I am a miserable worm. That excellent fellow Imhoff considers himself my friend. Yet, on second thought, is he really an excellent fellow? Is he not selfish? Is he worthy of such a peerless woman? Not that anyone could be, of course—but is he aware of his unworthiness, as I should be in his place? There goes a woman in a thousand. Yet he treats her as if she were quite an ordinary creature. God, if only I—— She needs someone who understands her nature. After all, a difference of fourteen years isn't so very much. . . . But it is impossible and I am a fool for hoping. What was it she told me yesterday about the divorce laws in Germany? Did she mean anything by it? What a miserable worm I am."

So musing, he disembarked to take up his new duties, as did Imhoff and his wife.

That is simply and quickly said. Actually, the din and excitement of landing at Madras must have vastly excited Marian and Karl, to whom it was all new. They had to go a dangerous long way from ship to shore, through the surf in a little boat; they were mobbed as soon as they stepped ashore by what are invariably called "India's teeming millions." Deafened, bewildered, half frightened by the clamoring natives, who were wild to get jobs with the glamorous Europeans, Marian must have clung to her admirer and observed with approval that he knew just what to do. The strong man, the great man, he ignored this Indian, pushed aside that one, made way for Marian wherever he walked, and strode purposefully toward the council members who had come to meet him. Karl could only trot humbly in his footsteps. Marian walked proudly with him, reflecting his glory, enjoying every minute of it.

Hastings was so kind to them! Without him they would have been quite helpless and ignorant, facing the enormous problem of acquiring a house and a full lot of servants, with all the necessary appurtenances. Hastings with one courteous action saved them all such headaches and financial responsibility: he simply took them in to live with him. Under his wing they quickly met everybody worth knowing. Otherwise they might have been ignored for months.

"A letter of introduction was the wedding garment of early Anglo-Indian society," says Spear in *The Nabobs*, "a *sine qua non* of entry into the polite world; once presented, the adventurer had a warm and generous welcome, but if he possessed none, or had lost them on the voyage out, . . . or found the recipients departed up-country, as might easily happen, he had no entry into society, no invitations to public or private breakfasts or dinners for an indefinite period. . . . The Anglo-Madrasis were lavish but exclusive."

So we can visualize Marian plunged straightway into colonial society, queening it over a bewildering number of servants in a big house which glittered white in its lime wash. I say "queening it" because European ladies lived royally in Madras no matter how humble their husbands' jobs might be. Marian duly paid calls in her carriage—or rather Hastings's carriage—and received calls from other ladies. She told them of the fashions in England and asked their advice on housekeeping matters. Though too well bred to say so, she must have found these ladies strangely languid. The newcomer to India, full of vitality, does not realize how slowly but certainly the climate saps European strength.

Always distrustful of innovations, the Anglo-Indians in 1765 were only beginning to understand and accept those devices which make a great difference to one's comfort in a hot climate. Take punkahs, for example. For centuries Indians had used large fans which, suspended free from the ceiling, could be swung back and forth over the entire room. But the British in India didn't get around to using punkahs until the nineteenth century. Merely to think of those wretched souls at Madras gatherings, in church or at parties, dressed to the nines in European clothing without some kind of ventilation in the rooms is enough to make one's brains boil in sympathy. In the worst of the hot season they would retire to bed, call periodically for changes of bedclothing, and keep wet cloths on their foreheads.

A few open-minded housekeepers did pick up hints here and there. They learned to hang wet mats in doorways and to leave doors open for drafts, while keeping windows closed to sunlight. They knew enough to keep their rooms rather bare, and certainly the houses themselves, covered with dazzling white lime plaster, were lovely. Many of them still stand in Madras, surrounded by their English-style gardens.

As a charmer Marian did not meet with much competition. By contemporary standards, Madras was a large city, but most of the population was Indian, Portuguese, or half-caste, and the English and other company Europeans did not mix with these people socially. They kept themselves to themselves, as they were to do for years afterward, for they were not primarily interested in society. John Company's officials were there purely and simply to make fortunes as quickly as they could. The novices among them usually started out with great industry, though in time, through a combination of overeating, overdrinking and laziness, they lost their singleness of purpose.

Such women as had accompanied them from Europe must have stared when Marian established her family in the newly arrived council member's house, but they knew better than to signify disapproval. There were in any case more than enough men to go around. India was the great marriage market of their world.

Single girls who could not be disposed of advantageously in England were shipped East in a steady trickle. If Hastings was not available, well, there were others.

However, the fact that Karl lived on the Choutry Plain rather than in the fort may have given rise to a certain amount of jealous muttering. As a cadet, he should have been quartered in the fort, but it would have been awkward to put him into a mess complete with wife and baby, and no one seems to have insisted on the technicality. He was not overworked. A European in Madras began his day at eight, dined at two or three, and went to bed until five-o'clock tea. The serious social life of the day began after that, when everyone went for a drive on St. Thomas's Road. As the sudden dark fell on the city, the ladies and gentlemen paid calls, and then the ladies went home to receive their own callers, and to sup at ten. The amount of wine they all drank daily, merely as a matter of routine, is incredible.

In this social round Marian quickly learned her way. She was no raw girl; she had served her apprenticeship in London on the fringes of the court. She knew the rules. To be safe, a woman must be liked by other women. Besides, she was well aware that the Imhoffs had to make themselves agreeable if Karl was to paint a lot of portraits, as was his avowed intention. Hastings does not seem to have been a stern taskmaster. Another company official might have frowned on Karl's ambitions and reminded the younger man that he had accepted his appointment and his passage money as a military cadet, not a free-lance miniaturist, but Hastings, on the contrary, helped Imhoff to get commissions. This is not so strange as it might sound. India was a long way from England; communications, even reprimands, were slow, and many other men took their home commitments as lightly as did Imhoff. The smaller the group in a foreign country, the more tolerant it must be if it wishes to survive at all. Undoubtedly the other colonists talked and gossiped; equally undoubtedly they did not overtly condemn Karl for neglecting his duties.

As for Hastings's passion for Marian, I am sure people suspected it and commented upon it, because of the Imhoffs' stay in Hastings's house. I am equally sure they suspected him of passion for various other ladies in the community as well. The main idea was to have an item of gossip; likely or unlikely made no difference. Colony gossip is catholic. Nobody escapes. The truth is told sometimes, but that is simply by the law of averages. The ladies tittered and whispered about Marian to their hearts' content, but they were courteous to her, and probably felt no real indignation.

Nor could Marian have worried very much about it, because Hastings was obviously a good man to have captivated. He would not let her down, and he was marked out for power and success. Imhoff's wife may not have been infatuated with the little scanty-haired fellow, but she felt genuine satisfaction in having acquired such valuable property.

In India a year is not a long time; yet not a year went by before Karl von Imhoff grew discontented with Madras. We can speculate if we wish on why he determined to go alone to Bengal to further his fortunes. Perhaps he was convinced that his wife preferred Hastings to himself. Brokenhearted, he may have gone away to lick his wounds, though as Marian rejoined him later, according to plan, this seems doubtful. Perhaps Hastings quite cynically paid him to go, and Karl as cynically agreed, but this too is doubtful, for the same reason: Marian rejoined him. It seems more likely that he was a restless soul, who became quite simply fed up with Madras and sought further adventure elsewhere. Perhaps he wasn't fond enough of his wife to take her along; his wife and child aren't every man's chosen companions for adventure. Judging from a letter of introduction to a friend in Calcutta which Hastings gave him when he set out for Madras, Marian's two men were on good terms, and Hastings was not reputedly a hypocrite, no matter what else his enemies called him.

"In my last I desired you to take the trouble to enquire for a lodging for a Mr. Imhoff, who proposes to try his fortune as a miniature painter in Bengal. Mr. Imhoff is a shipmate of mine, an officer of some rank in the German service, sent hither with great expectations as a cadet with a family, and must have starved had he not, happily, been qualified to seek a livelihood in a more profitable employment. He has had some success here, having taken off the heads of half the settlement, but he must soon be aground."

So Baron Karl von Imhoff went to Calcutta and Marian stayed behind. It looked to the gossips like an open-and-shut case, a game which Hastings had won. But they could not be sure. Marian may have been brazening it out, but she did not behave like a guilty woman. Imhoff, from all reports, was not behaving like a wronged husband. On the contrary, from Calcutta he actually sent Hastings a miniature portrait of Marian, which the council member had commissioned him to paint. Could such blandly peaceful behavior betoken a scandal and a quarrel? Not in 1771, when outraged husbands were prone to fight duels.

Still, the talk went on, a flood of lightly venomous chitchat which did small harm, for there were then no gossip columns in India (though one was to be launched ten years later). Who in Britain cared about the morals of a German lady in Madras?

Even Anglo-Indian tongues were stilled, or at least slowed down, when Marian after ten months calmly packed her effects and with her small son set off to rejoin Karl in Calcutta. Such a move was a major operation; people did not travel lightly in eighteenth-century India. It meant that the Imhoff marriage was not, after all, on the rocks. It meant a definite farewell to Hastings. And at this stage of the leisurely game it also meant that Marian's reputation was still intact. Very likely that is why it was done; very likely she and Warren Hastings renounced each other for what they decided was their own good. Or perhaps there was as yet no love affair to renounce, though such a supposition borders closely on the romantically unreal. We can rest assured that the Madras gossips who had driven Marian away gave them no benefit of the doubt.

Hastings, if not Marian herself, must have suffered deeply when she went. It is a pity Marian has left no letters or journal to give us a hint of her state of mind. Was she distressed by her position? We cannot but wonder. During the year Imhoff was away did she fancy she was being snubbed whenever she went out for her evening drive? Did she imagine that this lady or that had not bowed to her with her customary warmth? If so, she gave no hint of her feelings; Hastings's devotion helped her to face the world with calm. Her cool composure convinced the onlookers that Imhoff was a complacent husband.

The mental processes of lovers run to type. "It can't be wrong. Not a feeling like mine." When difficulties are vanquished by what the world calls chance, lovers hail their luck as a special manifestation of Providence's intentions for them as favored individuals. In London the company's directors may have thought they were being mere practical men of business when they appointed Hastings Governor of Bengal and told him to move forthwith to Calcutta. But Hastings, sorrowful and lonely in Madras, must have taken his appointment as the benevolent work of his fate and Marian's together. They had fought against it, they had tried to be good according to their lights, but it was no use. In spite of Imhoff, Marian was meant by Fate to be his. "It can't be wrong. Not a feeling like this."

So Hastings went to Calcutta.

He found Imhoff under difficulties, as he always seemed to be when no protector stood ready to shoulder his financial burdens. Life in Calcutta was much like that in Madras, but it cost more, and the people of Imhoff's circle were fond of gaming. Like the Imhoffs, Hastings took up residence in the suburb of Alipore, and though his young German friends did not move in with him lock, stock, and barrel as they had done in Madras, he began helping with the rent and other expenses of their house as a matter of course.

Word quickly spread that Marian bore a special relationship to the governor. Here as in Madras nobody snubbed her because of it, at least not openly. Calcutta was tolerant, and hers was not by any means the only bit of scandal in the town.

A few months after Hastings arrived there came a letter from London which must have gone a long way to confirm his belief, if it had needed confirming, that Destiny was shaping his ends just as he wanted them shaped. For Imhoff, in so cavalierly quitting his cadetship, had displeased the company directors and they were out for his blood.

Every so often they had to grow tough with young men who, like the baron, took jobs and got themselves sent to India at company expense, only to break the contract as soon as it suited them. In a general roundup the directors now wrote sharply to Hastings about Imhoff and other company men as well.

"You ought to have sent them home immediately. And, as we are determined wholly to discountenance this practice, we do hereby direct that if Messrs. Imhoff and Dupuy do still refuse to serve in the Military, that you do send them home by the first ship. . . ."

Neither Hastings nor Imhoff could have been staggered with surprise by this letter. They probably understood each other and had realized earlier that the directors might very well take this attitude. But letters took so long to come and go that Imhoff had already had two years' grace, enough to have given him a trial in Calcutta, enough for a volatile man to grow tired of the place.

He refused, of course, to serve in the military. He would return to Germany. This time there was no suggestion whatever that Marian go back with him. When the public substitution of her male protectors should take place was by now an academic question. She was Hastings's, and as soon as the law made it possible they would be married.

Had the baroness been English, this arrangement could not have been made without difficulty. Fortunately for appearances—though appearances under the circumstances were the last things the trio could afford to worry about—German divorce laws were much easier than British. A British divorce could only be got if one party to the marriage was unfaithful. A German divorce was very much an opposite thing; it was awarded without trouble and fuss if both parties agreed they were temperamentally unsuited. Marian had only to make it clear to the court in Franconia, Imhoff's native district, that she and her husband were not living together and had no intention of again living together, and she would be declared not so much divorced as unmarried, for the marriage would be annulled. Imhoff was to take home her statement of refusal to cohabit with him and turn it in to the court.

The little boy Charles went with his father. It was not necessarily that Marian wanted to get rid of this reminder of her marriage, but it has always been the custom in India to send children of his age home to Europe, out of the dangers of climate and disease.

All these details were arranged between husband and lover. They left no written record of their decisions, but we know that Hastings took on the financial responsibility of the children, and did well by them. It is very likely that he gave Imhoff money with which to start out afresh in Germany. Rumor says ten thousand pounds, but rumor is monotonously fond of that round sum when speaking of Hastings's payments to relatives and dependents. We don't know how much money was given, or when, or where. And we must also, however regretfully, discard the scandalously attractive story that Marian was won from her husband as a wager at cards, one of the wilder theories bruited about during Hastings's impeachment, years later.

The Imhoff divorce sounds an altogether modern arrangement,

but some of its factors fell short of modernity. There was no Reno where Marian could repair for six weeks to finish the job tidily. She was out in India, thousands of miles away from her home or Hastings's, and the decree was years in coming through. She had to go on living, ostensibly alone, until then.

If Marian had been a heroine in a novel, her position would have been piteous and dramatic. People would have spat at her in the Calcutta streets, or at the very least refused to allow their children to associate with her. In real life, nothing of the sort occurred. In public everyone pretended the conventions were being observed, and if in private they found titillation in the scandal for a while, the thrill ultimately wore out, which is what usually happens to scandals in high places and small communities. That Marian was the governor's girl friend was undeniable. But she was also a lady, living in her own house. She observed appearances. Everyone had already met her before her husband went away; they could hardly drop her now. Besides, what was one to do with a woman in a constricted place like Calcutta if one didn't accept her presence at parties?

A good deal of fuss has been made over a few words one of Hastings's associates wrote, referring to Marian. He was talking, as it happened, not about Hastings's private life, but about Nuncomar (Nanda Kumar), a Brahman rajah who had been convicted of forgery and publicly executed in accordance with the severe English law of the day. Feeling ran very high over this execution; later it was one of the most telling points made by the prosecutors in Hastings's trial at home.

Hastings's correspondent warned him that his food might be poisoned by some Indian in revenge. He must take precautions: ". . . let your fair female friend or some trustworthy European oversee everything you eat while in the cooking room."

Difficult as it may be for us to credit, it was the phrase "fair female friend" which set Victorian writers by the ears; they said it was offensive and that Hastings should have resented it. Hastings, representative of a more hearty age, would have stared at the suggestion, as do we. We may object on different grounds; it sounds, perhaps, too arch. But neither Marian nor Hastings, as far as we know, took exception to it.

I don't mean to imply that there was never any criticism of Mrs. Imhoff, or that a few cats did not scratch. Lady Impey did. She was wife to Sir Elijah Impey of the Supreme Council, a body sent out by company headquarters to check up on some of Hastings's actions, which were being reported on, adversely, at home. The case of Nuncomar was one of those under examination. (As it turned out later, Impey became one of Hastings's most valuable supporters.) Because of her husband's position, Lady Impey was one of the few women in the settlement who would dare to criticize Hastings's fair female friend. Another voice which sometimes made itself heard, though more slyly, was Philip Francis's; Francis was secretary to the Supreme Council, and, like the Impeys, was privileged. But nearly everyone else in the town depended either directly or by relationship on the governor general, and so, in spite of Mrs. Grundy, Marian was in a strong position.

Moreover, she did not flounce about in an irritatingly conspicuous manner during those months of uncertainty. She was intelligent enough to wait in patience for her triumph. Conscious of insecurity, she minded her manners. As poor little Mrs. Imhoff, the governor's mistress, she was more popular among the other European women than she was ever again to be when she was Mrs. Hastings the governor's wife. In her equivocal situation she maintained a measure of humility which was later lost.

The divorce decree was slow in coming through the Franconia courts; even after it was granted, news of the event did not arrive in Calcutta for two more years. However, all was settled and everyone was duly notified at last, in 1777, and then Hastings was legally united with his beloved Marian. The wedding interested everyone in the colony, of course, but one cannot suppose they were unduly excited by it after all that time. Lady Impey was not pleased, if we believe Philip Francis's journal, which goes as follows:

July 9: News of Imhoff's divorce, and hopes of her marriage with Hastings.

July 12: The Chief Justice very low. His lady enraged at the match and distressed about the future visits.
N.B. The dames for a long time were bosom friends.

July 24: An entertainment made on purpose this night at the Governor's to effect a reconciliation between Lady Impey and Madame Chapusettin; the former sends an excuse. A mortal disappointment.

July 26: Sup at Impeys'. Her ladyship swears stoutly that Madame Imhoff shall pay her the first visit—an idea which I don't fail to encourage.

July 29: Mrs. Imhoff sups at Lady Impey's by way of submission.

We have mentioned Francis, and we must go on with the subject. Nor will we be able to dismiss him after the first explanation, for Philip Francis even now, though he has been dead more than a century, cannot be ignored. Warren Hastings could bear rueful witness that he always made his mark.

Since his day it has been all but proved that he was "Junius," that brilliant secret figure who set London by the ears with his anonymous letters in print. Whatever political figure Junius attacked had reason to regret it, but he seems never to have discovered a foe worthy of his serious efforts until he gave up his appointment in the War Office, joined the East India Company, and came out to Calcutta with the Supreme Council. In India, Francis seems to have felt that he found his life's work at last. Hastings was his natural prey. Hastings aroused his rage, which he thought was righteous indignation, and his jealousy, which he would have called crusading fervor. One scarcely knows exactly why the two men were so antipathetic. It could not have been a case of hate at first sight; Philip Francis had made up his mind well in advance of first sight that Hastings must be got rid of. Admittedly, all members of the Supreme Council approached their host the governor general in Calcutta with a certain amount of cautious reserve; had they not come out to investigate certain allegations against him? But it was Francis above all who seemed to have ready prepared in his soul a great accretion of gall. On the subject of the execution of Nuncomar, Francis had espoused the cause of the dead Brahman before he read any of the reports on the spot. His was a complicated character, not easy to understand. I hesitate to say flatly that all he really wanted was to oust Hastings and take his place. Other things came into the matter. Francis's excellent opinion of his own capabilities played an important part in the war which he waged within the company. He would never have reasoned simply thus: "Room for ME; make way for ME." His was a more roundabout approach: "This man Hastings is unworthy. I, on the other hand, am very worthy indeed. It is not selfishness that urges me on to compass his destruction. I am Fate. I am Detachment. I am Genius. I am water finding its own level. Hastings must drown, for the good of humanity."

Junius would have argued that Hastings was a monster ready-made. His later reports to Burke and others, when he returned to England more than ever envenomed by having been checked in his ambitions, said exactly that. But nowadays we get a different picture from our place in the audience. We see a tempestuous, brilliant but malicious man pitting himself out of pure ambition against a sober, solider fellow who is at first surprised by the attack and then by degrees rendered formidable in his resistance. Francis never achieved what he wanted, but from the very beginning he called attention to himself by virtue of the attempt. There are more ways than one of becoming prominent. In every council discussion, on every possible occasion, Francis attacked and obstructed Hastings. It was war, civil war. Those who fell into line with the secretary became known, inevitably, as "Franciscans."

The reader must not suppose that any of these official struggles carried over into social life. People were formal in those days, and kept their worlds separate. Hastings and Francis met each other a dozen times a week at this dinner and that ball; they entertained each other regularly in their own homes. They had to maintain appearances. Had they and their associates behaved otherwise in Calcutta, life would have been insupportable. Hastings's marriage took place, as it happened, close upon the heels of a particularly lively set-to in council, during which Francis had entertained reasonable hopes of turning the governor-general out of office. The fact that he was disappointed would not have made Junius's temper any sweeter, but he proffered his congratulations in a handsome way nevertheless. Characters and morals may have deteriorated swiftly in Calcutta's heat, but for the most part manners remained.

It was September 20, 1777, and Francis recorded in his journal, "Lady Impey sits up with Mrs. Hastings; *vulgo*—toad-eating."

Mrs. Hastings was sitting pretty. She was the highest lady in the land, and she had an adoring husband. She would not have been normal had she not now felt her power. Malicious eyes, which kept close watch, observed that her dress, always her chief preoccupation, became more and more elaborate and individual in style. Never a slave to convention, Marian did not recognize the petty rules of fashion which governed Calcutta's lesser lights. After all, who had a better right than the governor's wife to set the styles?

Moreover, as the former consort of an artist she had every claim to knowledge and taste when it came to costume. And since she was not English, why need she arrange herself like an English-woman? Undoubtedly she had strong ideas about the typical

English toilette, and these unflattering opinions, forcefully expressed in her very German accent, must at times have made Hastings laugh immoderately.

Other ladies powdered their hair and wore it in stiff, towering edifices, but Marian refused to disguise her chief beauty. She kept it its own red-gold, and wore it in a natural-looking coiffure with ringlets clustered carelessly about the brow. In her Zoffany portrait her hair hangs about her neck. To our eyes it looks uncombed and messy, but it couldn't have been as messy as the conventional headdress of the day, held together as it was with some sticky concoction or other and redone only once a fortnight at the most.

Other ladies attempted to follow whatever fashion was decreed by the latest female arrival from England. Marian would not thus follow. She thought up her own fashions, more brilliant, gorgeous, and generally noisy than English creations.

Other ladies were presumably fond of jewels, but in deference to their husbands' resources they controlled their fondness within reasonable limits. Marian seems not to have controlled herself at all. Hastings made a far bigger salary than anyone else in the company, and he grudged her nothing. The native rulers loved jewels and bedecked themselves and their women like Christmas trees. But Marian outblazed the Indians, and it must be admitted the Indians themselves made it all too easy for her to do this.

Here we should remind ourselves that bribery in India was a long-established custom, accepted by everyone in high or low circles before Europeans ever arrived in the country. Rajahs and their nobles all exacted tribute; so did judges. The English who first arrived on behalf of John Company seem to have taken enthusiastically to these notions, which were after all not quite strange to contemporary England either. Bribes passed back and forth openly until Hastings's time. Hastings deprecated the practice and attempted to reform it, on the common-sense principle that it was not good for business or government, but he did not consider an occasional exaction of tribute on his own part—for example, from some recalcitrant native ruler—as a heinous crime, nor could we expect him to share our open-and-shut attitude toward such matters. The fact that he applied any funds he gained by this method to the public interest, instead of putting them in his privy purse, shows that he was morally head and shoulders above his colleagues, at that. He was above Marian, among others.

He forbade his wife to accept lavish gifts when they were obviously intended to prejudice him. But there were many border-line cases when he was either too busy to oversee what she did, or preferred to let her have her way, just to save time: he was always overworked. Doubtless Marian also received many presents she didn't tell him about at all. Word went around among the native millionaires, moneylenders, and petty princes that the governor's lady's favor could be won by pretty gifts, and most of them promptly assumed that the governor as well smiled on such compliments and was impressed thereby. Indian potentates were not dewy-eyed, and they never gave other people credit for high principles which they themselves lacked. And so Marian collected a surprisingly large lot of costly ornaments. A description of her possessions when she had to pass through the customs in England sounds like a hashish dream. There was one riding habit encrusted with pearls which gave her quite a lot of trouble there.

Life in Calcutta when she reigned was incredibly elaborate and luxurious. Comfortable it was not and never could be in that climate, where cesspools abounded and dead bodies sometimes remained in the streets for days, but the European residents carried on as best they could with their droves of servants and their lashings of food and drink. The general stately progress of the day's social doings was much like that of Madras. During the evening calls which followed the ceremonial outings at dusk, gentlemen retained their hats and held them stiffly as they sat in some lady's drawing room. If the hostess asked a caller to put down his hat, that was a tacit invitation to supper. If she didn't, the gentleman went on holding it, that was all. A lady named Mrs. Fay, an original, lively character who wrote long letters and reported her adventures in detail, described the effect of this point of etiquette; many a gentleman she had seen in a lady's house, she said, forlornly dangling his hat in the air, waiting in vain for permission to put it down.

It is Mrs. Fay who gives us several revealing glimpses of Mrs. Hastings, whom she did not like. Mrs. Fay, admittedly, must have been rather tiresome. She had suffered through several unusual adventures and naturally she liked to talk about them. She had been captured by Hyder Ali in company with her husband and the entire passenger list of their ship, along with the crew and the captain; they were held prisoner for a long time, and lost all their possessions before they got free. Arrived in Calcutta, she lived for a time with her husband, but he kept an Indian mistress, so Mrs. Fay at last left him and set up in business for herself. She was, one gathers, energetic and egocentric, a Brave Little Woman. Obviously she irritated Marian. Soon after arriving, when she paid her duty call on the governor's wife and began to moan about her bad luck, Marian choked her off with a levity Mrs. Fay thought was in bad taste.

"Come, come, my good woman," said Mrs. Hastings in effect, "you asked for it, deliberately setting out on perilous adventures the way you did. It was your curiosity which got you into trouble."

Not much womanly sympathy *there,* said Mrs. Fay, bristling. Of course she herself was lower than the dust compared with such a *great lady,* but nevertheless one would have expected a little more respectful attention to an unfortunate story. And when the sufferer was a member of her own sex too! One wonders if Mrs. Fay and Mr. Francis ever had a heart-to-heart talk. It is unlikely they would have met at intimate parties; as Mrs. Fay truly observed, she was not the social equal of such highly placed officials. But there were plenty of large routs to which everyone was invited.

At Christmas, for example, the governor and his lady were expected to invite everyone in the colony to festivities which went on all day. Francis felt called upon to give breakfast parties in his bachelor establishment, twice a week, to thirty people. Everyone entertained. There were masque balls and receptions and the inevitable amateur theatricals, and above all, card parties. When we read that it was customary for each guest at a dinner party to bring his private personal servant, who stood behind his chair and tried to grab the best piece on every serving platter for his sahib, we feel a rush of admiration for Marian, who broke down that particular piece of chi-chi by precept and example. To *her* parties one was requested to bring only his *hookahburdar,* no other servant being necessary.

And what, you may ask, was a hookahburdar? Why, he was the man who took care of your hookah, that snakelike hubble-bubble, that water pipe which men puffed at during supper parties, card parties, theater parties, and even hairdressings. The ladies sometimes smoked them too. The ladies would prettily beg for a puff, and the gentlemen would indulgently and obligingly fit on new mouthpieces for the ladies, and everyone would laugh merrily at the faces the ladies made. A hookah needs a lot of attention at the business end, which is a long way off from the smoker. The man about town simply had to be accompanied by his hookahburdar. Marian would scarcely dare try to reform such a firmly rooted custom as that; the best she could do was to dispense with the man behind the chair.

The common-sense economy she showed in this cutting down of fuss and expense was characteristic of the governor's lady. She was no spendthrift; she was not carelessly generous like Hastings. She loved material possessions, whereas he really had no interest in money for itself. It was characteristic of him that he should have given away everything he owned during his early retirement to England; needy relatives and friends had never to apply to him in vain. Many a time Marian must have bewailed that wicked waste. Nor did he hesitate, in harness, to dig into his own pocket when he should have used company funds. The company was often short of cash; if Hastings himself happened to have money during a company emergency, he supplied it, and was not always overcareful to pay himself back. He was the despair of his thrifty German wife. It was the one point on which they quarreled seriously.

Soon after they married she tried to introduce strict economy into his housekeeping. Everyone knows how ruinous it is for a bachelor to keep house, but he was a bachelor no longer and she, Marian, would change all that. Alas for her plans. At their first large dinner party her cheese-paring was so embarrassingly evident that Hastings was furious and actually rebuked his adored Marian before all the company.

This taught her a lesson. Thenceforth she practiced her little economies in a less public manner. She took to hoarding, like a jackdaw or like a spendthrift's wife. Jewels were a great help in her secret campaign; after all, they are investments, and she loved them anyway. She collected more and more jewels and other costly things: enormous diamonds, emeralds, sapphires, pearls by the hundred with which she embroidered her clothes; carved ivory furniture, those lovely Mughul enamel bibelots, and countless Indian gauzes and brocades heavy with gold and silver.

Oh, Marian enjoyed her life as the governor's lady. She exacted everything she could from it; not only jewels and brocades, but a more shadowy kind of tribute as well. Mrs. Fay again comes forward to tell us how Mrs. Hastings comported herself. She ". . . expects to be treated with the most profound respect and deference. . . ." At a party one evening Mrs. Fay's companion asked her if she had paid her respects as yet to the Lady Governess, who was present. "I answered in the negative, having had no opportunity, as she had not chanced to look towards me when

I was prepared to do so. 'Oh,' replied the kind old lady, 'you must fix your eyes on her and never take them off till she notices you; Miss C—— has done this, and so have I: it is absolutely necessary to avoid giving offence.' I followed her prudent advice, and was soon honoured with a complacent glance, which I returned, as became me, by a most respectful bend. Not long after she walked over to our side, and conversed very affably with me."

During this time Philip Francis was pursuing his way vigorously, never losing sight of his twin objects of getting ahead and bedeviling Hastings. He was making good progress in both, and he never missed a trick. It is very likely that he was not quite unknown to the man Hicky—James Augustus, not to be confused with the ebullient William Hickey—who began publishing a newspaper in Calcutta in 1780. This paper, the Bengal *Gazette,* was lively. Its editor indulged in scandalmongering to a degree which takes away the breath of a reader conditioned to our less lusty age, in which awkward libel laws abound. No such laws constricted Mr. Hicky. Many of the hapless victims of his wit have been forgotten along with their resentment, but it is significant that he seldom slipped up on a chance to sideswipe the Hastings couple, especially the lady. He shared Mr. Francis's sentiments, too, about Chief Justice Impey, who had recently incurred the wrath of Junius by finding for the plaintiff in a case we will discuss in the next chapter, when Francis was sued for damages.

For example, there was the *Gazette's* skit on the "Pul-bandi" contract which had been given to a cousin of Impey's, to keep the bridges and embankments of Burdwan in repair. As long as two years before, Junius had noted, "Poolbundy of Burdwan given for two years to Mr. Frazer; one lakh and twenty thousand the first and eighty thousand the second; job, job. . . . The present shameless contract is a clear £15,000 in the contractor's pocket. . . ."

Junius never forgot anything he could use. Perhaps by coincidence the *Gazette,* printed, in 1780, a satirical piece in which a "displaced civilian," looking for work, was advised: "Pay your constant devoirs to Marian Allypore" (Alipore being the district where the Hastings lived), "or sell yourself soul and body to Poolbundy."

Though no one else was sacred to him, Hicky never attacked Francis. It looks very much as if Junius was at it again, using the press for all it was worth. There is evidence, too, picked up with loving, scholarly care by Mr. Busteed, that the council's stormy petrel was in constant communication with Edmund Burke at home, either directly or through friends. When all this plotting came to fruition in Westminster Hall, Burke sounded at times as if he were acting as Francis's mouthpiece. He was fully informed of many small scandals which only Francis could have retailed, and the language in which he was informed sometimes slipped through in his oratory like echoes of Francis's Calcutta journal.

However, all this is anticipating. For the moment Francis was doing as he liked and wanted. Like Marian, he was riding high. He had survived the scandal of the damage suit, he was a senior member of council, and he was needling Hastings with great success. Then he overreached himself, in the matter of the duel.

It was one of the seasonal illnesses from which he was suffering which pushed Francis off balance. His temper was always fiery, as we know, but his judgment for the most part was cool. During the heat of that summer, however, he overstepped the bounds and got into a position where he simply had to challenge the governor general.

As soon as the thing was said, both Hastings and Francis must have been astonished that they had let themselves in for such a violent means of settling their long-standing differences. Neither was the dueling type. It was precipitated because Francis obstructed a military move which Hastings considered vitally necessary; this, too, after he had given his word to keep the peace in council, and not to interfere in Hastings's conduct of the current war against the Mahrattas. Hastings wrote a hostile minute which Junius felt in honor bound to challenge, and there it was.

The affair was some weeks in the boiling up. Before the encounter took place, Hastings, without telling Marian what was happening, took her up-river to Chinsura, and left her there, ostensibly because she needed a holiday from the oppressive Calcutta weather. His letter to her after the event was calm and correct, like all his behavior:

> *Calcutta, Thursday morning.*
>
> *My dearest Marian,*
> *I have desired Sir John Day to inform you that I have had a meeting this morning with Mr. Francis, who has received a wound in his side, but I hope not dangerous. I shall know the state of it presently and will write to you again. He is at Belvedere, and Drs. Campbell and Francis are both gone to attend to him there. I am well and unhurt. But you must be content to hear this good from me: you cannot see me. I cannot leave Calcutta while Mr. Francis is in any danger. But I wish you to stay at Chinsura. I hope in a few days to have ye pleasure of meeting you there. Make my compts. to Mr. Rose, but do not mention what has passed. My Marian, you have occupied all my thoughts for these two days past and unremittedly.*
>
> *Yours ever, my most beloved,*
> *W.H.*

As duels go, it had been a grave affair, the more so as neither of the chief actors in it had ever fought in this way before. It must have been very tense, but the proceedings could hardly be called efficient. "When the pistols were delivered by the seconds," wrote Colonel Pearse, Hastings's second, "Mr. Francis said he was quite unacquainted with these matters, and had never fired a pistol in his life, and Mr. Hastings told him he believed he had no advantage in that respect, as he could not recollect that he had ever fired a pistol above once or twice." The gentlemen stood fourteen paces apart and "presented" arms, but Francis twice had to signal that he wasn't ready, and on the third attempt Hastings courteously waited, since Francis's powder was not dry enough to fire, until substitute powder could be provided. Then they rearranged themselves, and Francis got in his shot first. It went wide. Hastings took aim more deliberately—he would, of course—and his shot went home.

"Mr. Francis staggered, and, in attempting to sit down, he fell and said he was a dead man. Mr. Hastings hearing this, cried out, 'Good God. I hope not,' and immediately went up to him. . . ."

Well, Francis wasn't dead, but as far as Calcutta went he was finished. As soon as he could wind up his affairs and travel, he went back to England. There he burrowed away assiduously, and there at last he had the satisfaction of seeing his enemy impeached. There, too, Marian's thrift may have atoned for the sins which helped to ruin her husband.

But again we anticipate. Let us leave Marian for the moment at the height of her glory, the acknowledged queen of Calcutta. Let us look at her, languishing at ease in her boudoir, playing a strange game. None of us, I venture to say, would have the imagination to invent it, even if we had the material. She has filled a bowl with pearls and then placed two kittens on top of them. That is what I said—pearls and kittens.

The kittens find the pearls difficult to stand on. They flounder about, unable to get clawhold either on the slippery globes or the equally slippery inside of the bowl. Marian laughs delightedly and claps her hands.

It was a childish amusement, perhaps, but one must admit it was an original idea.

2. *THE PRINCESS*

NOW LET US LOOK at another Calcutta lady who flourished about the same time. It does not seem to have struck contemporary chroniclers that her early career was parallel in its outlines to that of Marian. Yet it was. Perhaps the coincidences were obscured by the wide discrepancy which existed between the women's social standings, as well as their ages. Moreover, nothing could have been less similar than their ultimate fates, and it is usually man's conclusion one notices, rather than his beginning.

Marian Imhoff, though still young when she married the second time, was twice as old as Catherine Noël Worlée, who was wedded in the same year, before her fifteenth birthday. Mademoiselle Worlée, though her people were (it is believed) French, was born in the Danish colony of Tranquebar, on the coast of Coromandel. Later the Worlée family moved to Chandernagore, the French colony near Calcutta, and there she grew up in her father's house, no doubt sighing for the great world, until George François Grand came from Calcutta and married her and took her back to his own place. Even for the eighteenth century fourteen seems a shockingly young age at which a European girl should have married. But life in tropical countries ripens women early, and all the records about her indicate that Mrs. Grand looked and behaved like a full-grown woman when she came to Calcutta with her bridegroom.

All this took place, as I have said, about the time of the Hastings-Imhoff wedding, but Catherine's ceremony must have been, in comparison, a humble affair which attracted little attention in the settlement. Her husband George Grand was a Swiss who had English connections and who had, through them, obtained the chance so much sought after by young men on the Continent,

to come East in John Company's employ. All his experience
among the British had never perfected his English, which if we
judge from his memoirs was to remain through his life rather
Gallic in style.

Grand was a big, strapping fellow, inclined to put on weight.
Like Karl von Imhoff he had come out to India originally as a
military cadet, and again like Imhoff he had left the military as
soon as he could. But he did not desert the company: he became
a writer in their civil service. Barwell, Hastings's colleague,
seems to have been his special patron. When Grand wanted to
marry, Barwell got him a good appointment on the Salt Committee, so it would be hardly fair to call him an office boy, but
among the company officials he was still small fry. He was probably noticed in Calcutta, if at all, because of his wife's remarkable beauty.

Catherine was truly striking; of good height, with delicate,
perfect features, and a great mass of yellow hair, which unlike
Marian's was dutifully powdered and controlled. (Catherine
usually observed the little conventions of dress, though not always the big ones of morals.) She had one of those innocent
sweet faces and a lovely childish smile. Before the debacle, everyone seems to have agreed that she and her husband were happy
together.

Now enters that villain Philip Francis, the scourge of Hastings. It would be difficult to find a man whose appearance and
temperament better suited the role of seducer. Junius was not
only alert in politics and a brilliant writer; he was also good-
looking and something of a dandy. At the dangerous age of
thirty-eight he was living alone in Calcutta: his wife remained in
England, minding the five children and rightly suspecting the
worst of his morals. He wrote long affectionate letters to her at
first, but after a couple of years the correspondence flagged somewhat, for he was a busy man, what with his campaign against
Hastings and his card playing. He took cards seriously, and there

was good reason for that; he made a fortune out of gambling in Calcutta. In fact he made much more that way than he did out of the company, though he was one of their better-paid men.

Busy as he was, however, he was not too busy for love. Junius's linen and ruffles were snowy, his figure tall and imposing in the tight breeches of the period, his dark eyes compelling, and his conceit unbounded. He had a droll, mocking, flattering, Irish way with women. Poison he may have been to the governor general, but he was just the man to sweep a child bride off her feet.

Something about India is very aphrodisiac. Perhaps it's the climate, as some aver, or it may be the highly spiced food, or the ever-present examples of Hindu religious art with their sex motifs, or the heavy scent of night flowers, or all these things together. Whatever it is, even the British in India often behave in most un-British fashion, and Catherine Grand was not British to begin with.

Francis must have decided to seduce the pretty creature as soon as he set eyes on her. Nor could he have been the only man in Calcutta to entertain the idea. It was a notorious fact that unattached men in India were apt to make passes at practically every lady, married or single, they came across, and then Mrs. Grand was so very attractive! Most ladies soon learned from experience how to parry these sudden attacks, or if they did not parry them they were discreet in their acceptance, and usually succeeded in not being caught out. Mrs. Grand was an exception. Either she was too young to manage properly the feat of rejecting Francis, or—a more likely alternative—she wanted to be ruined by him. He was very important. He was considered a desirable figure by most women, and he must have fairly shone in comparison with Grand. Perhaps it was not much fun anyway, being married to Grand.

Catherine appears for the first time in Junius's journal only a little while before the crisis. Writing of a ball he had given the night before, which everyone in Calcutta attended (including the Hastings couple), he quoted the simple Latin tag, *"Omnia vincit amor."*

Immediately thereafter he added the unrelated and unromantic words, "Job for Wood, the salt agent," which somewhat spoils the sinister quality of the Latin, but there it is for what it is worth. Whether you admire him or not, Francis was always a practical man: love for him never conquered politics.

A fortnight later he had something really interesting to put in his journal. It is a pity that he didn't go into more detail, though God knows the whole affair was detailed to the last tiny item in court and in public before it was settled. One would like to have more of it in his own words. "At night the *diable à quatre* at the house of G. F. Grand, Esq.," wrote Philip Francis, and that was all. It is from other sources that we learn what he meant. He had been caught poaching in that house, and there was the devil, not to mention Grand, to pay.

This is how it all happened. That evening Grand went out without his wife, as was his custom once a fortnight, to play cards at the house of a Mr. Le Gallais. Fully to understand and to imagine the subsequent occurrences one must remember how badly lit, according to our standards, were the houses of those days. As for the highways, they were not illuminated at all. The roads and the countryside, even between residences, were pitch dark.

At Mr. Le Gallais's house the evening's gambling went on like every other card party until the gentlemen called a halt for supper. They were just sitting down to it when an Indian, recognized by the surprised Mr. Grand as one of his own servants, came running in and breathlessly demanded his master. He blurted out as much as he knew.

Sahib *must* come home quickly, he said. Sahib's upper servant, or *jemadar,* had captured Mr. Philip Francis skulking about the house, and was even then hanging onto him with the greatest difficulty.

Times have changed in India, and today a Calcutta domestic would know better than thus tactlessly to proclaim that his master was a cuckold. It is to be doubted, too, if a servant of today would dare to apprehend his mistress's lover. He would understand that northern Europeans are not like Indians. He would realize that, in their strange code, the tomcat on the tiles, even the pussy he is after have their rights of privacy. Grand's servants, being less sophisticated than ours, behaved as though their sahib were another Oriental. However, in their defense it must be stated that Grand reacted just as the servants would expect a right-minded Bengali of property to do.

Picture the scene in the flickering candlelight: the dining room full of startled gentlemen in their fine laced clothes, the servant in his great turban, panting, his eyes rolling in not unpleasant excitement, Grand starting up with a cry of "Sacred Blue!" or words to that effect, spilling his wine, and the Le Gallais servants crowding from all directions to stand outside the open door and watch the white men's reception of this interesting news item.

Poor Grand rushed into the night. None of the other guests came with him, for he had not requested them to do so. It was obvious to all that this was a moment which called for the most exquisite tact. But on his way home, having had time to think a little, the Swiss recollected that he did not have his sword with him. He stopped at the house of his friend Major Palmer, borrowed the necessary weapon, and also brought Palmer along to act as second for the duel which was under the circumstances *de rigueur*. After all this it was distinctly a letdown, when he arrived home, to find that the villain had escaped.

Yet the cage was by no means empty. Upstairs, Catherine was wringing her hands and weeping noisily. This, however, was unimportant; her husband had no time to discuss matters with

Catherine. In the entrance room was a throng of men to deal with; not only his own Indian servants, but quite a number of Europeans. Inexplicably, sitting resignedly in the jemadar's grip was—no, not his betrayer Philip Francis, but Philip Francis's good friend Mr. George Shee, looking very silly. It was all most peculiar. Standing in a crowd about the group were Mr. Shore, Mr. Archdekin, Mr. Ducarel from across the road, and Mr. Keble from next door.

A surprising number of persons seemed to have been in Francis's confidence on the subject of this seduction. A veritable mob of gentlemen had been hovering about all the evening on the outskirts of the scene, like the male chorus in *Faust* who wait in the wings while Marguerite, onstage, is being tempted. In short, neighbors and friends there were in plenty, but of Francis Mr. Grand could find no trace, unless one counts the ladder.

This ladder played an important part as evidence in the court proceedings, later on. From the report we learn that it had been made that very day, fruit of Francis's and Shee's combined genius. An affair of split bamboo which was light and collapsible, it could be used, and in fact *was* used, to scale the wall which surrounded the Grand dwelling. Francis and Shee, after designing it and ordering it manufactured by a carpenter in Shee's employ, had dined. Then, having made all their plans, they set out gaily with the ladder and carried it to the Grands'. They arrived well after Grand had set out for his card party. This of course was deliberate timing and not lucky chance.

It is evident that Catherine did not expect any visitors, and had prepared herself for a quiet, solitary evening. She sent her ayah to fetch a candle, announcing that she and the woman would sit up together until her bedtime amusing themselves with talk and parlor games. The ayah lingered belowstairs to cut some betel nut for herself, after having transmitted the order for the candle. A male servant went out of the house to the storeroom, in the back, to get the candle. On returning through the courtyard he saw the ladder leaning against the inner side of the wall and naturally paused to examine it.

In the house, in the meantime, the ayah returned with leisurely step to her *memsahib's* room. There she found the door locked. When she tried it and got no response she presumed Catherine was angry with her for some reason. The country-bred French girl was probably capricious and spoiled. The ayah went below again, philosophically enough, to join the other servants until her mistress's storm of temper should blow over.

Out in the courtyard, the manservant with the candle studied the strange contraption against the wall and decided it was suspicious. He called the jemadar, who agreed that it was very suspicious indeed. In fact, the jemadar carried it away and locked it up. They were still standing in the yard discussing the matter when they were interrupted by agitated noises and squawkings among the servants in the house. Then a European, Francis himself, suddenly loomed up in the dark and accosted them. Had Catherine, then, rejected him? This seems very likely, considering the brevity of all the foregoing proceedings *chez* Grand.

The Indian servants, who of course knew all the Europeans in the colony, recognized the intruder. That Francis was an important man they were aware, but he had no right in their master's courtyard nevertheless, and he spoke with a peremptoriness which under the circumstances they did not like. "Give me my thing," he said, in broken vernacular.

The servants hesitated, glancing at each other.

"I will give you money," said Francis. "I'll make you great men."

He delivered quite an oration, all in all, now demanding his ladder, now telling them who he was and how important. He might possibly have talked his way out of it at this rate had not Mrs. Grand added her voice to the clamor by calling from her window, ordering the servants to let the sahib go away. That settled Francis's fate with the men. Never let it be said that they had obeyed a mere woman. Laying forceful hands upon the member of the Supreme Council of the East India Company, the Indians dragged him into their master's house and sent a messenger to Le Gallais's card party.

After that everything seems to have got confused. The jemadar clung to his captive's arm, but the captive struggled. It was dark in the house; everyone on the staff was far too excited to think of supplying candles. Then Francis suddenly whistled piercingly, and Shee, who had heard the uproar from the beginning and prudently rushed across the road to collect Shore and Ducarel, led a rescuing party of Europeans through the front door. In the scuffle the jemadar seems to have lost his grip for a moment. He grabbed and caught hold again, but when the lights went up at last he found himself clutching not Francis but Shee. Francis, practical as always, had retired from the scene and gone home.

The jemadar must have been furious. He was certainly in no mood to release the deputy captive, though plenty of people begged him to. One by one and then all together, the white gentlemen attempted to cozen and bribe him, to no avail. George Shee actually went so far as to give him three gold mohurs, which the jemadar accepted without letting go. So there they were, still arranged in the same group, when Grand came home. It was not an easy situation to laugh off, any way one looks at it.

Still, Shee, supported by his companions, did his best to laugh it off with appropriate nonchalance. In eager chorus they explained everything to the master of the house. It had been nothing more than a prank, they said, a boyish prank. Francis had been a bit the worse for wine, and everyone knew how he was when he was that way—sportive. The visit had not been arranged in advance: the lady of course knew nothing about it. There had been neither seduction nor rape. The lady was blameless. Everyone was blameless. Mr. Grand was uninjured. Everyone was uninjured. It was all nothing, absolutely nothing. The best thing Mr. Grand could do would be to shrug shoulders, accept apologies, and forget.

Mr. Grand would not accept this point of view. Mr. Grand's honor was smirched and he would have satisfaction. In spite of all the gentlemen's blandishments—and to tell the truth they had not really expected to succeed in convincing him—he sent off Palmer forthwith to the secretary's house with a challenge to a meeting.

There was nothing at all surprising in this challenge. It was quite conventional, but Mr. Francis's reaction *did* mildly astonish the group, hardened though most of them were to misbehavior. To quote Grand's version:

"His reply was laconic and easy. It was couched on these terms: That conscious of having done me no injury, and that I laboured under a complete mistake, he begged leave to decline the proposed invitation, and that he had the honour to remain my most obedient, etc., etc."

Even we, posterity, feel some surprise. We may find it difficult to appreciate all the subtle shades of an affair of honor, but we know the general outlines. Gentlemen of those days were not supposed to refuse such a challenge. No one among Francis's apologists, and he has many, has ever really explained this breach of etiquette. Junius was not inalterably opposed to dueling; we have for witness the famous occasion later, when he challenged Hastings.

I think the explanation lies in snobbery. Francis considered Hastings a worthy opponent, a social equal, whereas Grand was not. Grand was just a funny Frenchman or something of the sort, who couldn't even talk good English, let alone keep the affections of his wife. To fight a duel with such a figure of fun would lower a man. The fellow had been encouraged too much, that was it, in this ridiculous settlement where every Jack thought himself as good as his master. Standards relaxed in Calcutta, but he, Philip Francis, would not be a party to this ridiculous performance. The very thought of it made him cross.

Later he was accustomed to swear on his honor as a gentleman that Grand had no grievance against him anyway, technically speaking. There had been no adultery, nothing to warrant a duel. Admittedly Francis had made illegal entry into the house; admittedly he had entertained the worst intentions. But the lady had been coy, though no doubt that was because she was terrified of discovery and not from disinclination. Besides, he argued, there had simply been no time to seduce her, because of the ayah's interrupting knock on the door.

Unfortunately for Francis, these protests were ineffectual. In the suit for damages which Grand promptly brought against him, judgment was against Lothario. And, to use an old-fashioned phrase, how! Mrs. Grand's honor must have been of a rare and wonderful sort, for its worth to Mr. Grand was estimated at fifty thousand sicca rupees. In sterling that would be more than five thousand pounds, a tidy sum today, and it was far tidier in 1779.

"Who can find a virtuous woman? for her price is far above rubies." The Justices must have decided it was not a time for niggling adjectives. Virtuous or not, Mrs. Grand sold at a high figure.

George François Grand, having made his fortune thus unexpectedly, put it in his pocket and tactfully withdrew from the scene, though not forever. He was to turn up again at intervals in Catherine's life, for unlike Baron von Imhoff, who settled and used to advantage the money he got for his wife, Grand did not prosper in his other investments. And yet he *did* found the indigo industry in India, from which others have reaped fortunes.

Three months after the trial Francis claimed his dearly bought property from her father's house at Chandernagore, whither she had fled, and installed her in a house at Hooghly, upriver from Calcutta. Considering the circumstances, according to the usage of the day, this was exactly what he should have done. In fact, with the exception that he refused Grand's challenge, his actions throughout this whole affair, reprehensible as we may think them, were at least thoroughly conventional. Junius was never a man to fly against convention in the larger sense of the term. That is, he was a conventional seducer. Society does not really condemn such sins as most society commits: Calcutta people recognized this law-abiding trait in Francis and appreciated it. A more antisocial type than Junius might have taken Mrs. Grand into his own house and told the world to go hang. Not so Francis.

"If *certain connections* should be formed," he had once written in a list of self-admonishments, "to keep at a distance." This, to all intents and purposes, he did with Mrs. Grand, and it is interesting to observe that Catherine was not brutally condemned, any more than was Marian, by Calcutta society. Some ladies even continued to call on her. Not Mrs. Hastings, however. It would perhaps be too much to expect Marian to have done so.

Junius did not get off merely with the payment of that savage fine. Much to his fury, Hastings harped on the matter whenever he got a chance in council, and in company with Barwell he even sent a report of it home to the Court of Directors. Who were they, Junius demanded, to take exception to such an affair? Hastings, who had taken Imhoff's wife, and Barwell who had got mixed up with bad Mrs. Bonner! Talk about the pot calling the kettle black-arsed!

We don't know if Catherine was happy, living in sin with Francis. Nobody seems to have taken the trouble to inquire. That she remained under his protection for more than a year seems to prove it, but then she had little or no choice in the matter. Her father probably nagged her, telling her that she could count herself lucky, after behaving so badly, to have someone to pay her bills. As for Francis, he seems to have been content with his beautiful prize, though the loss of all those rupees must have irked whenever he thought of them. A series of notations in his journal soon after his mistress was installed shows that he got some of his money's worth, at any rate:

September 9: Go up to Hughely, where I propose to stay till we hear decisively from England. . . .
September 17: O, Cara Phillide, rendi mi il cor.
September 29: Quae spiravit amores.
October 12: In the evening returned to Hughely.
October 16: At Hughely.
October 17, Sunday: Ditto: Ridet hoc, inquam, Venus ipsa, rident simplices nymphae. . . .

From this point on the paths of the two outstanding brides of Calcutta, 1777, diverge sharply. Both had long lives still ahead of them, but they did not remain in the same city, nor even on the same Continent. Let us first see what became of Marian.

She returned to England nearly a year ahead of Hastings, in 1784, because they were both convinced that she was too delicate to stand the strain of another Calcutta summer. There was a brief flurry during the voyage, for she thought she was pregnant at last, after having given up hope of ever bearing a child to Hastings. She wrote the news to him and he was joyful until her next letter told him that she had miscarried. Hastings missed her sorely. Through all their life together he remained devoted to his wife, and it was a happy day for him when he rejoined her in England.

They were treated at first with great cordiality by court and company. Hastings felt he had every reason to expect a peerage, and Marian was gay and charming, and thought London a wonderful place. She saw no reason why she should not glitter in England as bravely as she had done in India. Fanny Burney, who met her, several times spoke of her high spirits and her charm. The little brown wren could not but betray a natural distrust of this peacock. Marian had attractive manners, however—Miss Burney admitted as much—"and attentions to those she wishes to oblige. Her dress . . . was like that of an Indian princess, according to our ideas of such ladies, and so much the most splendid, from its ornaments of style and fashion, though chiefly muslin, that everybody else looked under-dressed in her presence."

As things turned out, Marian would have done better not to have put so many others in the shade. She should not have glittered so bravely at Charlotte's court. Probably she did not realize that impeachment was hanging quite so close over her husband's head. Then the blow fell. The court never turned its back or reversed the royal family's conviction of the innocence of Hastings, who had married the friend of Mrs. Schwellenberg, but the company was another matter. Hastings was impeached; the seven years' ordeal began. And Marian was to learn through bitter trial how unwise she had been to blaze with jewels, wife as she was to a man responsible, if Burke was to be believed, for "violent sales, fraudulent purchases, confiscations, inhuman and inutterable tortures, imprisonment, irons, whips, fines, general despair. . . ."

Most of the tittering, wellborn audience assembled in Westminster Hall at the opening of the Hastings trial believed Burke. To believe him was the fashion: Francis had done his work well. There was in the public's enthusiastic acceptance of the accusations a certain element of pride, pride as it were in self-castigation. They were British, thank God. As justice-loving Britons they would not shrink, they felt, from punishing even so loftily placed a man as Hastings. In their burning zeal they could hardly wait to punish him. "If thy right eye offend thee, pluck it out." And if, as seems probable, many of the audience mistook their motives, and acted from submerged jealousy rather than a true passion for justice, we must place a part of the blame on those famous jewels of Marian's.

Besides, Burke delivered his lines so well! Who could resist him? Certainly not the *ton* of London, who knew only what they were told and judged by the manner rather than the matter of the telling. "The ladies in the galleries," wrote Macaulay, "unaccustomed to such displays of eloquence . . . were in a state of uncontrollable emotion. Handkerchiefs were pulled out; smelling bottles were handed round; hysterical sobs and screams were heard: and Mrs. Sheridan was carried out in a fit."

Ultimately, of course, it all settled down, well before the final vindication of poor Warren Hastings. Seven years is a long time, too long for feverish excitement to endure against the cold douche of fact. Cleared of the charges, the erstwhile governor general was free to retire to Daylesford, the family's former estate which he had always wanted to recover and had at last acquired. The only trouble was that now he had no money with which to keep it up. He had very few worldly goods left, especially for a man who had occupied the tremendously powerful position Hastings had held. He was old. His name was clear and he had his adored Marian, but he had spent his entire fortune in the defense, and his chance of a peerage had gone glimmering. (Francis, however, went into Parliament, acquired a title, and enjoyed the friendship of the Prince of Wales.)

It seems fitting that Marian's jackdaw-gathered jewels should have been used to pay for her husband's vindication. One by one during those years of trial they were brought out and sold. One famous diamond actually went back to India and was bought there. During the careful years at Daylesford, too, her long-guarded hoard was very useful. Nobody ever found out quite how much Marian had managed to salt away during that era of splendor in Calcutta, but there was enough, somehow, to settle a little fortune on her son when he married, to eke out here and there during Hastings's lifetime, and to keep his wife going in a frugal but aristocratic sort of way through her long widowhood.

In his old age Hastings had been deeply respected by everyone, and so was Marian, who lived so long she outstayed all memory of her tactless youthful display of wealth. She became a county gentlewoman, a typical English lady, with nothing vulgar about her, nothing extreme, not so much as one jewel in her venerable white hair. As a widow she lived and died discreetly. Today she lies in Daylesford courtyard with her husband, Joan to his Darby, quiet and respectable as if there had never been scandal about Von Imhoff, or envy in India, or vicious lampoons and caricatures of her in London pamphlets; as if she had never played with pearls and kittens in a bowl. Whereas Catherine . . .

Now let us turn back to Catherine, whom we left at Hooghly, snug in Francis's house and arms. Grand was gone and her needs for the present were taken care of, but she may with reason have worried about her future. After all, there could be no question of Junius doing the right thing by her. He was very much a married man with five children in England.

Moreover, it was becoming increasingly evident, even before the duel, that Calcutta would not be big enough to hold both Hastings and Francis much longer. One of them would have to go, and it was only in his more foolishly sanguine moments that Junius thought, nowadays, that it would be Hastings who would be forced out.

We don't know what it was like when they parted. We can only imagine tearful scenes and reproaches, culminating in Francis's offer to buy his lady love a passage to Europe, and perhaps a small annuity as well, so that she might start life anew. Perhaps it was not like that at all, but we don't know. We only know that she did go to Europe, before Junius himself set sail, and that there does not seem to have been any serious promise between them to meet again. It is my belief that Catherine was wild with joy at the prospect of seeing fabulous Europe. All her life (such as there was of it, she being only seventeen at this time) she must have dreamed of England and France as youth in Europe dreamed of romantic India. Did she weep as she kissed Junius good-by? If so, I think they were merely tactful tears.

The voyage to the Promised Land turned out to be a long, exciting one. At the Cape of Good Hope there came aboard Mrs. Grand's ship (a Dutch one) one Mr. Thomas Lewin, a young man who had for some time been private secretary to the governor at Fort St. George (Madras), and was carrying dispatches of some importance to England. As the ship put into Cádiz she was attacked by two French warships, and Mr. Lewin had to tear up his dispatches and throw them out the porthole. Whether or not Mrs. Grand was in his confidence at this time, they were certainly friends from Cádiz on. They traveled together to Lisbon and then to England, and set up housekeeping together in Fitzroy Square, where the beautiful houses must have only recently been built around the little park. Sometimes when crossing the square I think of Mrs. Grand's pretty face peering through the glass of her carriage as it rolled across the cobbles there and deposited her at one of the Adam doors.

Well, then they went to Paris, and there Mr. Lewin seems to have left Catherine, after settling an annuity on her. (He was only twenty-eight, but he had already made his fortune in India and was quite ready to spend it.) There is no hint that he ran away from her, or she from him, but it is impossible to figure out just what she did do after that, until she comes onstage again as large as life in the role of Talleyrand's mistress. It was rumored that she went to live with relatives in Paris. Sir Philip Francis in his dotage told his second wife that she did so, and that he saw her from time to time but never renewed their old intimacy. Some of the people who wrote about Talleyrand have given their versions of Madame Grand's whereabouts during the Revolution, and one of these goes on to tell about a young English naval officer who went to Paris to recover her property for her. Or was it her property? Was it not that of a nobleman who was at the time her protector? Since the entire tale may well be apocryphal, it seems idle to wonder.

There are other stories, of course. As soon as she married

Talleyrand many men claimed to have known her in the Biblical sense. It is a way men have. Some may have been telling the truth. An uncle of Sterne's "Eliza," an Anglo-Indian, is supposed to have kept her for a time. There was an elderly *roué* who boasted to his niece that he had been pursued by Mrs. Grand years before, when she was a daughter of joy in Paris, and that she had dined with him clad only in her long golden hair. But then he was so old he may have got his names mixed up.

Undoubtedly Catherine was a beautiful woman, but some of her charm was also in her soft, innocent manner, like that of a gentle little girl. Her large eyes with dark brows and lashes, her wonderful hair, her grace, her pleasing, simple gaiety—small wonder so many catty stories collected about her, especially after she made good beyond a harlot's wildest dreams, in marrying a man who became a prince. Today's reader studying her portraits need make no effort, as he must with Mrs. Hastings's pictures, to understand her beauty. It triumphs over fashion.

The story of her second marriage begins in mystery. Somewhere she met Talleyrand, probably during the Revolution. She was living with him when he came to Paris from Hamburg in 1796, and soon after their arrival she was arrested on suspicion of being a spy. Talleyrand wrote to Barras, the director, to get her released, protesting that it was ridiculous to have thought her capable of any interest in politics. "C'est une Indienne," he said indignantly, "bien belle, bien paresseuse, la plus désoccupée de toutes les femmes que j'ai jamais rencontrées."

The former priest had at that time been excommunicated for six years, for the crime of freethinking. It is said that he lent his assistance in the negotiations which preceded the signing of the Concordat, and that in return for his sympathetic help the Pope, in 1801, removed this ban of excommunication, allowing him to revert to the secular state. At least, Talleyrand himself claimed that he was allowed thus to revert, though later the Pope was angry that he had married. There are two theories as to how

Talleyrand happened to marry at all, after having lived irregularly with Mrs. Grand for many years without evident distress. The first theory is the romantic one that he longed to make an honest woman of her and planned well in advance, with great cunning, to gain the Pope's favor. Thence the Concordat. I do not think we need take this theory too seriously.

The other tale sounds more reasonable. Talleyrand was now Foreign Minister, and Catherine presided at his official receptions. For a long time she remained in happy ignorance that such an arrangement was not quite the thing, but ultimately there were so many indignant complaints from ambassadresses, and so many comments from envoys about the extraordinary customs of the French, that Bonaparte took action and commanded Talleyrand to put the woman out of his house.

Catherine, through the intercession of Josephine, obtained an audience with Napoleon. Kneeling at his feet, she wept and pleaded until he modified his orders. Talleyrand, he said, must marry her, or the original command still stood. Whereupon they were married, very quietly, on September 10, 1802.

A third version of the story is that Talleyrand married Catherine in defiance of Bonaparte's order that the relationship be dissolved. Maybe so. Certainly Bonaparte's subsequent behavior does not contradict this tale. He was very rude to her, and after his coronation always made trouble about her attending court. But then Bonaparte was usually rude to women, so that proves nothing.

As might be expected, the wits of Paris let their fancies roam freely on the subject of Talleyrand's wife. The greater part of their anecdotes make mock of her for her stupidity, and there can be no doubt that she often exhibited extreme simplicity of mind. Not only did she look babyish, even at the age of forty, but she had the mentality of a child. Modern Americans would call her a dumb blonde. But it is not unlikely that she deliberately exaggerated her stupidity, knowing that a woman who is mentally inferior to the average man automatically pleases him by tickling his vanity. Her type is universal and always with us. It is not recorded that Madame ever failed to take care of herself, or went hungry or badly clothed. As long as she lived by her wits she lived well. Could she, then, really have been so slow-witted?

Moreover, we must remember that the saga of Madame la Princesse (her husband was raised to the rank of Prince of Benavento in 1806) wrote itself in the malicious atmosphere of Napoleon's court. The little stories served to amuse many a *salon*. It became the fashion among the wits to think up new idiotic remarks and credit them to the princess, as today we credit all malapropisms to Mr. Goldwyn. Many of the tales were certainly fabricated.

It would be pleasant to be able to say that our heroine, safely married and still lovely at the age of forty, lived happy ever after. In a way, perhaps, it would be true. But she had her troubles, even after the fairy-tale story of her wedding.

To begin with, Mr. Grand cropped up, penniless in spite of Francis's rupees and the indigo venture. His appearance in Paris so soon after Catherine's second marriage *may* have been coincidence, but not many people who knew him would have believed that. His arrival, and his fairly prompt departure with a job in his pocket, created a host of new rumors. Had Madame really been divorced from Grand before she married Talleyrand? In the confusion surrounding the whole question, which includes the argument about Talleyrand's secularity, one loses track of what might matter, and by what law the marriage was or was not valid. One's head spins. Actually, poor Catherine may not have been worried about divorce and remarriage, but only about Grand; he must have been an embarrassing echo of the past in any case. Fortunately, Talleyrand had many contacts, and was not averse to using them. Ten days after the Talleyrand marriage, the Batavian Republic nominated Mr. G. F. Grand "to the station of Privy Councillor of the Government at the Cape of Good

Hope." To the Cape he went and at the Cape he stayed, married for the second time, and settled down and wrote his memoirs. He received a salary (for which he did no work) of something under £170 a year. This was not much, admittedly, for a man who once got fifty thousand sicca rupees in one stroke, but Grand managed on it. The lot of a cuckold is sad, but it need not be poverty-stricken.

After that crisis Madame Talleyrand got on well enough in her new station. The gossip went on; the anecdotes collected; more and more her husband ignored her, though he was never unkind. When she was fifty-three he set her aside altogether. Thereafter she maintained a separate establishment. But there was no divorce; she retained her proud married name and kept her rank and luxury. Her beauty faded at last. The princess grew stout and ruddy; even, it must be confessed, somewhat pompous. No doubt she felt she had a right to complacency. After all, in spite of her notorious stupidity, in spite of the long-ago disgrace in Calcutta, she hadn't done too badly. She had amassed a fortune; she had become a princess.

One wonders if, when she looked back at her life, she ever thought of Marian Hastings, who had been great in the days of her own littleness, who had queened it in India while she trembled in her obscurity, who had sailed serenely through the dangers of scandal, though she herself was caught in the mire. In those days Philip Francis must have filled her pretty ears with poison against the Hastings. But Catherine was invincibly good-natured, quite capable of remembering Marian without spite.

Would Marian have been as good-natured as Catherine? It seems doubtful. They were women of very different temperaments; it is odd that they should have been linked as closely as they were in Calcutta through circumstance and Junius.

Take it all in all, Catherine came out ahead. I confess I feel a little pang of pity for Marian when I think of the way she was tamed by life. She did love her jewels so much. And the Princess

Talleyrand, who had no great overpowering love for baubles, possessed among her other valuables when she died a casket of jewels worth forty thousand pounds. When I think of that I have a vision of her as a kitten, dancing on pearls.

Marian gave up her treasures and made atonement for all her sins, because although she was shrewd and grasping in youth, she became a good woman. Catherine, who was never really very bad, became a good woman in a much more roundabout way, by virtue of the Concordat, and Napoleon's twisted humor, and the obliging complacency of the Batavian Government. Catherine kept her jewels. . . .

Sometimes it must be very difficult, if one is a strict moralist, to regard history without feeling discouraged.

The Business

THIS, OUR LAST CASE, is a paradoxical choice, for it is about sexual misdemeanors which had important consequences yet which never took place at all. It was an affair (not an *affaire*) which was mixed up with the Bedchamber Plot, during Victoria's first year as Queen.

Not often in the history of kings do we come across an anecdote which depends for its point upon negative rather than positive sinning, but the pathetic story of Lady Flora Hastings does just that. She was a genuinely virtuous lady. One would have thought her safer in Buckingham Palace than she could have been anywhere else in England, at a court noted throughout Europe for its innocent bread-and-butter atmosphere. Courtiers, still breathless after the vicissitudes of life with Victoria's various wicked uncles, were having to learn all over again the simple childhood lessons of propriety.

This must have gone hard with some of the gentlemen, but they comforted themselves, no doubt, by reflecting that nothing is altogether new and that Britain had lived through earlier phases of prudery and recovered. There had been Oliver Cromwell and his Puritans. George III was no libertine; libertines yawned in his service. Yet after Cromwell there had been Charles II; after George III came George IV. Now they had Victoria, the girl Queen. Chafing under the bonds of her gentle influence (which I imagine as resembling pink or blue baby ribbon) they reflected that even Victoria, sooner or later, would have to marry and relax.

Their trials were to get a good deal worse, however, before they got better. In fact, they got so bad that Victoria, when her popularity was threatened, married rather more precipitately than she would otherwise have done. It was not the least like most hasty marriages, brought on by straightforward scandal. Nobody's chastity was involved. On the contrary, it was a case of too much virtue, all around, which led to trouble for the Crown.

On March 14, 1839, a British gentleman named Hamilton Fitzgerald, who was living in Brussels, opened a letter from his niece Lady Flora Hastings at Buckingham Palace, noting with surprise that it was a long one. This meant it was a very long letter indeed, for it was a period when correspondence in general was far from terse.

Whatever, he wondered briefly before reading it, could Flora have to say that called for so much space? Though she was a nice enough girl, if "girl" be a proper word of those days for a respectable spinster of thirty-three, her position as lady of the bedchamber to the Duchess of Kent could not by any stretch of the imagination be called exciting. At least that is what Mr. Fitzgerald mistakenly thought.

Under young Victoria, Buckingham Palace housed a very quiet court. The atmosphere, if not quite that of a nursery, yet resembled a schoolroom's more than an ordinary royal household's. The Queen was only eighteen and was still assiduously learning her task under the careful tutelage of her Prime Minister, Lord Melbourne. As for Lady Flora's mistress, the Queen's mother, her relations with her daughter were rather strained. Everyone knew how eagerly Victoria had seized on the chance, the minute she learned she was Queen, to shake off the duchess's influence and show her independence. It was not surprising that she should have done so, perhaps, the duchess, a true German, having rather overdone her duty as disciplinarian. Not that Victoria ran wild; she was always much too steady a little person for that. But she quietly and firmly removed herself from beneath her mother's wing, and rather pointedly retained Baroness Lehzen, her old governess and her mother's avowed foe, as best friend and *confidante*.

There *was* one other manifestation of power at her mother's expense. The Duchess of Kent's adviser and good friend Sir John Conroy was sent away from the palace and pensioned off. Further than that, however, Victoria did not go in curtailing the duchess's privileges. The mother of the Queen had a free choice of attendants, one of whom was Lady Flora, daughter of the Dowager Marchioness of Hastings and Countess of Loudoun, who was an old friend of the duchess's. The Hastings family was a proud one, and Lady Flora had her share of that pride. Like all the other women in waiting at Buckingham Palace, she was aware of the struggle for power that prevailed between her mistress and Lehzen, and the fact that the duchess's star was in eclipse did not affect her ardent loyalty. All the ladies who took their meals together, who treated each other as courteously as if they never disagreed in any way at all, were lined up on one side or the other in this struggle. It was a state of affairs not uncommon in palaces.

Mr. Fitzgerald was a man's man. He had never troubled his head with domestic chitchat from the bedchambers of Buckingham Palace. Presumably his niece talked these matters over in confidence with her mother and sisters when she came home on visits—she had just been home, as a matter of fact, now that he thought of it—but trifling scandals about Lehzen's tricks, or precedence at court meals, could not be expected to hold the attention of a serious gentleman like himself. Mr. Fitzgerald sighed patiently and set himself to read his niece's letter.

His superior calm did not endure beyond the first page.

> *My dear Uncle [Lady Flora had written], Knowing what a very good-natured place Brussels is, I have not a hope that you have not already heard a story with which I am told London is ringing; but you shall at all events have from my own pen the account of the diabolical conspiracy from which it has pleased God to preserve the Duchess of Kent and myself; for that it was intended to ruin the whole concern, though I was to be the first victim, I have no more doubt than that a certain foreign lady, whose hatred to the Duchess is no secret, pulled the wires, though it has not been brought home to her yet. I told you I was ill when I came to town, having been suffering for some weeks from bilious derangement, with its agreeable accompaniments, pain in the side, and swelling of the stomach. I placed myself immediately under the care of Sir James Clark, who, being physician to the Duchess as well as to the Queen, was the natural person to consult. Unfortunately he either did not pay much attention to my ailments, or did not quite understand them, for in spite of his medicines the bile did not take its departure. However, by dint of walking and porter I gained a little strength; and, as I did so, the swelling subsided to a very remarkable degree. You may, therefore, guess my indignant surprise when, about a fortnight since, Sir James Clark came to my room, and announced the conviction of the ladies of the palace that I must be privately married, or at least ought to be so—a conviction into*

*which I found him completely talked over. In an-
swer to all his exhortations to confession, "as the
only means of saving my character," I returned, as
you may believe, an indignant but steady denial
that there was anything to confess. Upon which he
told me that nothing but my submitting to a medical
examination would ever satisfy them, and remove
the stigma from my name. I found the subject had
been brought before the Queen's notice, and all
this had been discussed, and arranged, and denounced to me, without one word having been said
to my own mistress, one suspicion hinted, or her
sanction obtained for their proposing such a thing
to me. From me Sir James went to the Duchess, and
announced his conviction that I was in the family
way, and was followed by Lady Portman, who con-
veyed a message from her Majesty to her mother,
to say that the Queen would not permit me to appear till the examination had decided matters. Lady
Portman (who with, you will grieve to hear, Lady
Tavistock, are those whose names are mentioned as
most active against me) took the opportunity of distinctly expressing her opinion of my guilt. My beloved mistress, who never for one moment doubted
me, told them she knew me and my principles, and
my family, too well to listen to such a charge. However, the edict was given. The next day, having obtained the Duchess's very reluctant consent, for she
could not bear the idea of my being exposed to such
an humiliation (but I felt it right to her, and to my
family, and to myself, that a point blank refutation
should be instantly given to the lie), I submitted
myself to the most rigid examination, and I have
the satisfaction of possessing a certificate, signed by*

my accuser, Sir James Clark, and also by Sir
Charles Clarke, stating, as strongly as language can
state it, that "there are no grounds for believing that
pregnancy does exist, or has ever existed." I wrote
to my brother, who, though suffering from influenza, came up instantly.

It would be too long to detail all his proceeding,
but nothing could be more manly, spirited, and
judicious than his conduct. He exacted and obtained from Lord Melbourne a distinct disavowal of
his participation in the plot, and would not leave
town till he had obtained an audience of the Queen,
and which, while distinctly disclaiming his belief
of any wish in the part of her Majesty to injure me,
he very plainly, but respectfully, stated his opinions
of those who had counselled her, and his resolution
to find out the originator of the slander, and bring
him or her to punishment. I am quite sure the
Queen does not understand what they betrayed her
into. She has endeavoured to show her regret by
her civility to me, and expressed it handsomely with
tears in her eyes. The Duchess was perfect. A
mother could not have been kinder, and she took up
the insult as a personal one, directed as it was at a
person attached to her service, and devoted to her.
She immediately dismissed Sir James Clark and refused to see Lady Portman, and would neither re-
appear or suffer me to re-appear at the Queen's
table for many days. She has crowned her goodness
by a most beautiful letter she has written to poor
mamma, whom the accounts, kept from her while
there was a hope that matters might not become
public, would reach today. I am told there is but
one feeling as respects me—sympathy for the insult

offered to one whose name should have been a pro-
tection to her, and that in many places the feeling
is loudly expressed that a public reparation should
have been offered me by the dismissal of the slan-
derers. This does not, however, appear to be the
view of the Ministers; and as, personally, I wish for
no revenge on them who have insulted me, I can-
not say I much regret it, though I doubt whether
they are quite judicious as respects the general feel-
ing. As respects Parliamentary majorities, they are
with regard to the ladies. And poor Clark, who has
been the woman's tool, could hardly be sacrificed
alone. The Duchess has stood by me gallantly, and
I love her better than ever. She is the most gen-
erous-souled woman possible, and such a heart!
This business made her very ill. It shattered me,
too, very much, and I am wretchedly thin; but
under Doctor Chamber's good management, I am
getting round and hope soon to be well. Hastings
says he has not yet done with the business, nor
never will while there is any thing left to sift.

Good bye, my dear uncle. I blush to send you so
revolting a tale, but I wished you to know the truth,
the whole truth, and nothing but the truth—and
you are welcome to tell it right and left.

Your affectionate niece,
Flora Eliz. Hastings

Surely never before had such an affront been offered a lady of
the bedchamber. Lady Flora knew something about the subject,
for her grandmother also had been a lady of the bedchamber, if
briefly, to the sisters of George III. Like her grandmother, she
herself had borne the train of a queen at her coronation. The
Hastings family was ancient and proud, and Lady Flora's brother

the marquis naturally felt the insult even more strongly than did his sister.

No, the insult was unprecedented in the annals of British court history. Once during the reign of Charles II, at a very different sort of court, a newborn baby was found on the ballroom floor after a minuet, and actually all the attendants had gone through some form of showing perplexity as to where in the world it came from, before its Spartan mother, a maid of honor, was apprehended. (When questioned she always maintained stoutly that the father was another maid of honor, this being perhaps the first mention made of Lesbianism in official English history.) Grotesque as the incident may seem, it is evident that the courtiers of the Restoration must for once be given credit for courtesy and delicacy where Victoria's attendants lamentably failed.

Lord Hastings, then, was livid with rage about "the business," as he always referred to it, and rushed to London as soon as Lady Flora's distressed report reached him in the north. The letter she wrote to Brussels, which I have just quoted, was a considerably softened and shortened version of what actually occurred. She may have regretted the explosive effect the business had on her male relatives and so deliberately toned down the account after her earlier experiences with an angry brother; for the same reason she gave Mr. Fitzgerald too optimistic a picture of what the public was saying and thinking of her. She was a dying woman, though an indignant one. Doubtless she felt too tired to fight it through.

Not so Hastings. He came raging into London, determined to have satisfaction of somebody, preferably a man he could call out and fight a duel with, but he could not find an adversary. Everywhere he turned he met the same bland smooth surface—professed ignorance, haughty secrecy, flat refusals to incriminate people whose rank, it was implied, should protect them from irritating people like himself. Lord Hastings must have felt as frustrated as a sparrow trying to fly through a plate-glass window.

Let us leave him struggling with the maddeningly suave Melbourne while we trace out, through Lady Flora's and Sir James Clark's statements and depositions, what actually took place.

Lady Flora returned from Loudoun Castle in January. On the same day she arrived she hurried to consult Sir James Clark, who was physician to the duchess as well as the Queen. Lady Flora was not feeling well. For nearly two months she had been suffering from bilious attacks, and was worried by the fact that her abdomen was swollen. In addition to this, she occasionally felt severe pain in her side, which the fashion of the day must have aggravated through the tight lacing which was customary. It must also have emphasized the swollen appearance of her stomach. The easy Empire style of dress, with high waistline and flowing skirt, had gone out. Dresses were now designed to show off a supple waist. To emphasize this slenderness the rest of the figure was exaggerated. Ladies wore off-the-shoulder necklines and enormous puffed sleeves, as well as large deep bonnets. Everything was planned to look somewhat larger than life except the waist, which was compressed by tight stays. Unlike the Restoration maid of honor who was able without giving alarm to take her place in a minuet at the last moment of pregnancy, an early Victorian lady had very little chance to conceal her interesting condition, if such condition prevailed. Lady Flora, had she wanted to disguise her swollen stomach, could not have done so, but it does not seem to have occurred to her that such concealment should have been necessary. She was a modest maiden lady with a clear conscience.

That is what made the shock all the worse when it happened. Sir James may have leaped to conclusions as soon as Lady Flora first consulted him, physicians being notoriously evil-minded, but for a little while he kept his thoughts to himself. Instead of talking, he gave the patient various medicines for her bilious attacks and some liniment for the swelling. Lady Flora averred that the medicines didn't help very much, but that exercise did. She took long walks, she began to feel better, and she thought the swelling subsided to some extent. She stopped worrying.

In the meantime the season was approaching when Parliament was to meet, and there were several routine changes in the royal household. Lady Tavistock came into waiting on the Queen for a week or so, and when she departed Lady Portman took her place. These two ladies, looking at Lady Flora with unaccustomed eyes, leaped to the same conclusions that Sir James had already reached. Perhaps they put their heads together and talked it over. Perhaps it was the doctor who first stirred them up. Or perhaps, as Lady Flora and her rather silly mistress the duchess always firmly believed, it was all a plot engineered by Baroness Lehzen to discredit the duchess in the sight of the Queen and get her thrown out, like Sir John Conroy. Today, far from the battlefield, this last interpretation seems rather too elaborate for credence. It is more likely that Lady Flora simply looked pregnant, and that the Queen's ladies went on the warpath about it, as other ladies have been known to do under similar circumstances.

Sir James seems to have had a lot to learn about diplomacy. After a good deal of whispering with ladies in corners, and indignant statements by all and sundry that something should be done about it, and asking of advice, and letting more people in on the talk, he made up his mind at last to speak plainly to Lady Flora. (In the defense he later published, he said that Lord Melbourne had spoken of the business to him, in confidence, as early as the first of January, but this statement is difficult to reconcile with the other dates mentioned.) One Sunday, accordingly, on the sixteenth of February, he talked to Lady Flora.

"Have you been privately married?" he demanded.

Lady Flora was flabbergasted. She scarcely had time to deny it when the physician rushed ahead to explain and accuse. He was brusque, probably all the more brusque because he was embarrassed. He asked the question, he said, because her figure had excited the remarks of the ladies of the palace. "To my emphatic denial," wrote Lady Flora, "he became excited, urged me 'to confess,' as 'the only thing to save me,' stated his own conviction to agree with that of 'the ladies,' that it had occurred to him at the first and that 'no one could look at me and doubt it,' and remarks even yet more coarse."

The poor woman seems to have rallied swiftly to self-defense, though perhaps it would have been better to grow angry instead of merely protesting that the swelling had lately gone down. She offered as evidence of this the fact that her dresses had become less tight.

"Well, I don't think so," said Sir James. "You seem to me to grow larger every day, and so the ladies think."

Sir James in retrospect gave in vindication of his stubbornness the significant state of Lady Flora's health, which did not appear bad. Apart from the pain in her side, he argued, she seemed quite well, and was able to carry out her normal duties, which fact fitted in perfectly with the theory of pregnancy. Anyone, he insisted, might have made the same mistake.

The two accounts differ more in tone and degree of detail than in substance. Sir James always claimed to have been gentle and as delicate as a man could be. Lady Flora said he was rude and coarse. Sir James said that he put his next suggestion—i.e., an examination to settle the argument—in the most tactful possible way. Lady Flora said he couldn't have been worse; he assured her that nothing but a medical examination would satisfy the ladies of the palace, and if she refused he would have to tell Lady Portman on her. (The implication was that the Queen would then be sure to share Lady Portman's opinion.) Sir James said Lady Flora refused to allow the most rudimentary form of examination; that he wished merely to put his hand upon her abdomen with her stays removed, and that she flatly refused. Lady Flora in her accounts never mentioned such shameful things as stays. "I said, feeling perfectly innocent, I should not shrink from any examination, however rigorous, but that I considered it a most indelicate and disagreeable procedure, and that I would not be hurried into it."

Sir James makes much of her request for time. What was he to think, he asks pathetically, when the woman would not send immediately for the other doctor she chose to be present, and submit then and there to an examination? The hostile ladies were constantly at his elbow, nagging him; Lady Flora seemed to be playing for time; the thing was obvious, or seemed so.

Lady Flora now recollected her duty to her mistress. What, she asked, did the duchess have to say to all this? Sir James admitted that the duchess did not as yet know anything about the business. But he had greater authority on his side, and he felt quite confident of his position. Lady Flora, retiring with at least some honors of the battle, was soon dashed to discover that the Queen herself was taking a hand in the matter: ". . . it was her Majesty's pleasure, that I should not appear until my character was cleared by the means suggested. . . ."

She held a hasty consultation with the duchess, who wanted her lady of the bedchamber to go on refusing to submit to an examination. But Lady Flora realized nothing else would ever settle the matter, and next day, after summoning another physician, Sir Charles Clarke, the disagreeable ceremony took place, "in the presence of my accuser, Lady Portman, and my own maid." It was on Lady Flora's insistence that Lady Portman was there. The examination didn't take very long, nor was it as brutal or as public a proceeding as the victim's terse description would imply. Medieval would be a better adjective.

The grim little party met in the antechamber to Lady Flora's chamber. Lady Flora and her maid retired to the bedroom and called to Sir Charles when she was ready. Properly chaperoned by the maid, he did what was necessary. He came out in a very short time, declared that Lady Flora was not pregnant, and evidently added that furthermore she could never have been preg-

nant because she was *virgo intacta.* Then he requested Sir James
to come in and see for himself. Sir James hung back, protesting
that Sir Charles's word was enough. Sir Charles insisted—wisely,
it would seem—and Sir James, consenting, was convinced.

It looked like a complete victory for Lady Flora, who composed
herself to receive apologies all round. That evening Lady Portman offered her share. "She acknowledged that she had several
times spoken a great deal to the Queen on the subject, especially
when she found it was her Majesty's own idea." She added, however, that it had been her duty to behave as she had done, and
that she would have done the same no matter who had been the
suspicious party. Lady Flora replied stiffly that what surprised
her was that anyone who knew her people could have believed
such a thing. She forgave Lady Portman, though she could not
promise ever to forget. She looked around expectantly then, waiting for some sign of remorse from Lady Portman's august mistress,
the Queen. Was there to be no retribution?

Strangely, nothing of the sort seemed to be forthcoming. It
was then that Lady Flora wrote to her brother and he came pelt-
ing to town. In the interim nothing happened save that the
Duchess of Kent discharged Sir James Clark from his post as her
physician. Clark remained, however, physician to Her Majesty.
Could the Queen really think, demanded Lord Hastings, that the
affair was finished?

There seemed so much to do, so much to resent, so many
people to call out, that he scarcely knew where to begin. He consulted his good friend Lord Winchelsea, who said he should first
demand from Melbourne himself an explanation of the business,
so Hastings immediately wrote off to the Prime Minister.

Melbourne tried to dismiss the matter in genial, careless fashion. It was nothing to get excited about, he implied. He himself
knew little about it, merely that Lady Tavistock had told him
something, upon which he had desired the ladies of the court to
be quiet, himself not placing any belief in it.

Hastings would not be soothed so easily. He wanted audience of Her Majesty herself, he declared, to express his horror and disgust at the whole of the transaction, and to ask who were the originators of the plot. Melbourne expressed grieved surprise at such crass intentions. Should not the business be kept as quiet as possible, he said, for everyone's sake? Had not enough harm been done? Consider the youth of the Queen! Consider the delicacy of the affair! If Hastings must do something, said Melbourne, let him go and talk it all over with Wellington, like a good chap. Wellington was leader of the Government's opposition.

Hastings accordingly tried to find Wellington, but the duke was not at home. . . .

On February 26, Hastings was still in London, still trying to get satisfaction. His confidence in Melbourne as arbiter had long since waned. Melbourne, he knew, was a friend of Lehzen's; if Lady Flora's suspicions were correct and Lehzen was at the bottom of all this, Melbourne's do-nothing policy was explained. If it wasn't Lehzen—— But Melbourne must be forced to do something in any case. Hastings determined to corner the wily Premier. He wrote a crisp letter with a threat in it. He had now waited in town seven days, he pointed out, hoping to see the Queen, but there had been as yet no word from the palace. If he did not get a reply by the next morning he would have no recourse but to publish all correspondence pertaining to the business. "I repeat, that the whole business has been *base* and *cruel*, and reflects *dishonour* and *discredit* to all concerned in it, from the highest to the lowest; and I cannot find words sufficiently strong to convey the sense of my disgust and *contempt* for the conduct of all who have figured in this business."

He could not believe, he continued, that the Queen would have behaved as she had done without the "baneful influence" which surrounded the throne. Wellington, whom he had managed at last to interview, advised him to leave matters "for the sake of avoiding the painfulness of publicity." It was a time-worn argument, one feels, which seldom failed to frighten people away from courses which might be awkward for the Throne, but Hastings refused to be frightened. On the contrary, he twice repeated his threat: he would seek publicity rather than shun it if Her Majesty continued to ignore his demands. The public could draw its own conclusions as to who had behaved badly.

That did it. Melbourne replied immediately, without taking advantage of the twelve hours' grace Hastings had allowed him. The Prime Minister's manners seemed mysteriously to have improved too; he sounded much friendlier, not nearly so stuffy as he had been before. He was much disturbed. He hadn't realized Hastings was waiting for an audience with the Queen; in fact, he wasn't sure, even yet. . . . *Was* Hastings waiting? Was all this necessary?

Hastings replied briefly, ignoring the plaintive tone of Melbourne's letter. Yes, he was waiting.

Lord Hastings had his way, and saw Victoria. It is doubtful what he expected to gain from a personal audience with the Queen. In later years she would have known how to awe and placate an angry man on such a subject, but she was then a very young woman, whose opinions depended upon her advisers. The formal apology she made had to be accepted for exactly what it was worth, and no more. She made no offer of a public gesture. As a loyal subject Lord Hastings could not claim to be other than gratified with her gracious behavior, but he was determined to get more satisfaction than that out of the formidable setup at Buckingham Palace before he was through. Inevitably the story of his sister's ordeal was spreading through London in all the grotesque variations malice could contrive. Still, for the moment he had done all he could. On the surface everything at the palace was well. He had seen his sister, as he said, "reinstated in her proper place at the Royal table." One can well imagine the anxious politeness with which she was being treated on every hand by ladies who a week before had wanted her stoned out of town.

Returned to Donington Park, Lord Hastings did not rest. (His influenza had long since been forgotten.) The rumor must be traced through all its devious paths, back to whatever villainous person had first sent it out. It was his bounden duty as a brother and a Hastings to avenge Lady Flora. Let's see; what names had Melbourne mentioned? Lady Tavistock's had been the first, had it not? Hastings sat down and wrote to the Marquis of Tavistock.

"From the length of time I have known you, from the respect and regard which I have ever entertained towards you as a man of the highest honour and integrity . . ."

He told Lord Tavistock what he had done to date about the business, and how he happened to be writing such an unpleasant letter. ". . . it is to know from *her* [Lady Tavistock] from *whom* this accusation first originated that I write to you, and that I may know what part each person has taken in the business. I think I know more about it than some persons imagine, but I will not act upon my suspicions only. That Lady Portman has taken a very active part in it, there can be no doubt, from the manner in which she sought my poor sister's forgiveness, *after having in-flicted the deepest injury she could upon her.* . . . Though my conscience acquits me of not having done *all I can* in the busi-ness, yet I know that my poor sister will have the painful ordeal to go through of *every* version which the public may give of this story, and that I myself must submit to the same, and *am* at this moment submitting to the same *unfair* judgment, *till I publish* everything connected with the business . . . (such determina-tion I told Lord Melbourne, by letter, I had come to); and have only refrained from so doing in the hope that my poor sister might be spared the pain of the publicity of this matter. May I then ask, *was not* Baroness Lehzen the first person who origi-nated this foul slander, and mentioned it to Lady Tavistock; and if she *be not* the individual, who was?"

Lord Tavistock replied immediately. Lord Hastings's letter had annoyed him very much, he said, but he appreciated the spirit in which it was written. Himself, he had known nothing about the affair until after the worst had happened. He didn't want to talk to his wife about it, because it would distress her greatly, and he was sure she had been influenced by only the best motives in speaking to Lord Melbourne. He added in postscript that he would not speak to his wife until he had Hastings's reply, but he was evidently too agitated to refrain, after all, from speaking to her, and a second letter was sent off the next day, with the following report:

Lord Tavistock had had some conversation with his wife, without telling her about Lord Hastings's letter, and the case so far as she was concerned lay in a nutshell. Lady Tavistock "was informed of the opinion that had unhappily been entertained" with respect to Lady Flora's state of health, and was asked to speak to Lord Melbourne. First she thought of speaking direct to Lady Flora, but "this feeling was overruled . . . by considerations" which Lord Tavistock felt he need not go into. He had not asked his wife where she got her information, and, furthermore, he didn't think she would tell him if he did ask. Of course she must take the responsibility of having mentioned the affair to Melbourne. Lord Tavistock earnestly hoped Hastings wouldn't press him to do more than he had done. He was *sure* his wife wouldn't tell. Anyway, she was not to be blamed; the physician had been just as wrong as anybody, and certainly Lady Flora's appearance . . .

"It has been an unfortunate business," summed up Lord Tavistock artlessly, "but I am persuaded that the best intentions prevailed. . . . Your feelings have been naturally roused and your suspicions excited, but after the danger you have lately witnessed of forming opinions rashly, I hope you will do nothing publicly, except upon the fullest consideration and with the best advice."

To these extraordinarily maddening letters Lord Hastings retorted with what sounds like commendable restraint. (We do not know, of course, how many previous essays he threw into the wastepaper basket.) They were, he said, unsatisfactory. He was now writing to Lord Portman, and if he didn't get any more out of him, he would publish *all*. He asked the two important questions once again: By whom was Lady Tavistock requested to name this business to Lord Melbourne? By whom was she informed of the opinion entertained of Lady Flora's health?

Lord Tavistock was sorry, but Lady Tavistock wouldn't tell and felt she had nothing to reproach herself with. After thinking it over and listening to rather a lot of conversation from her husband, however, she deigned to come off her perch long enough to write a statement repeating the ambiguous phrases she had already uttered.

There must have been agitated correspondence going on all this while between the Portman and Tavistock families, for the Portmans were well primed when their turn came round. It was as well for them; Lord Hastings was much stiffer on the subject of Lady Portman than he had been with Lady Tavistock; after all, she had been there when the actual insult was offered, and she had been vindictively insistent on its taking place. Lord Portman pointed out, more in sorrow than in anger, that immediately after the affair his wife had put off her departure from Buckingham Palace on purpose, waiting to face Lord Hastings when he rushed from the country in his sister's defense, but that he had angrily refused to see her. If Lord Hastings now wished to interview Lady Portman, said Lady Portman's husband, he would be glad to receive him either in town or at their country house.

To which Lord Hastings replied that he was still unwilling to put foot under the Portman roof. At any rate, what would be the use? "I only ask you to look at the garbled statements and the lies which daily fill the papers, and answer me as a man of honour and a gentleman . . . whether I have not a perfect right to inquire into Lady Portman's conduct on this occasion; or am I to remain suffering the taunts and false statements of the world till April [when Parliament again convened], then only to be told by Lady Portman that she is sorry for what has passed, and no more?"

Like Tavistock, Lord Portman replied in dignified pain, but enclosed a formal statement signed by his wife.

Now Lady Flora's mother joined in the fray. She wrote direct to the Queen, reminding her of the honorable records of Loudouns and Hastingses for many generations back. It was an excited, incoherent letter, the letter of a sorely shocked and wounded old lady, tacitly asking for public vindication. "My husband served his country honourably . . . my own family . . . my grandfather . . . with so many claims on my feelings of old —although now unfashionable—aristocracy, it is impossible to suppose me capable of disrespect or want of loyalty towards your Majesty . . ." But nevertheless, the marchioness implied, something more than a private grudging apology from Victoria seemed to be indicated.

Melbourne replied for the Queen in lofty tone. "The allowance that her Majesty is anxious to make for the natural feelings of a mother upon such an occasion, tended to diminish that surprise which could not be otherwise than excited by the tone and substance of your Ladyship's letter." Her Majesty, he continued, had hastened to seize the first opportunity to apologize. What more could anyone want? Lady Hastings promptly told him what she wanted: that Sir James Clark be removed.

Melbourne went up like a rocket. "The demand which your Ladyship's letter makes upon me is so unprecedented and objectionable, that even the respect due to your Ladyship's sex, rank, family and character, would not justify me in more, if indeed it authorizes so much, than acknowledging that letter for the sole purpose of acquainting your Ladyship that I have received it."

This exchange really threw the fat into the fire. Nothing, they felt, now prevented the Hastings family's appeal to the public by the most direct possible medium, the press. They had long since taken advice of counsel, which was uncomforting: "the facts of the case did not afford any ground for legal proceedings on the part of Lady Flora Hastings and her family." The ball was thrown to Mr. Hamilton Fitzgerald, lately arrived from Brussels with fire in his eye.

Having read his niece's letter, as he later explained, he was at first disinclined to take the business seriously. Had not Lady Flora assured him that her brother had already done everything anyone could do, that her innocence was proved, that the public was sympathetic to her, and so forth and so on? Mr. Fitzgerald was fairly easy in his mind for the rest of that morning, but when he went out later in the day and began to make inquiries among his friends his composure evaporated.

"Everyone there knew of it before I did," he commented later in understandable annoyance, nothing being more irritating, as we all know, than such a state of affairs. Letters poured in from all quarters containing injurious reports. According to these, the vigorous proceedings of Lord Hastings were unknown except in his own circle and at the palace. The poor man was being abused in the London clubs for not having acted with sufficient spirit. Infamous stories were circulating about his sister. Family friends were discovering to their cost how impossible it is to manage the world or to persuade it to let go once it has got its teeth into a juicy scandal. Whenever Mr. Fitzgerald, racing about Brussels, tried to trace some such story to its source he got the same infuriating reply: "I cannot give up my authority; I must beg of you not to quote me, but I assure you the report is very generally believed."

"It was said," wrote Mr. Fitzgerald, "that the present was, at least, her second error, as when she left the palace last year she was certainly pregnant." Bets were laid as to when she would have to bolt from the palace, he said wryly. "At Vienna it was believed on the 15th of March, that she had remained on her knees an hour begging mercy of the Queen, and that Lord Hastings, having as a Peer forced his way into the Royal presence, had upbraided her Majesty, who made him no answer, but curtsied and retired when his tirade was over."

There speaks the very voice of Scandal, imaginative lady that she is. It would be difficult to surpass the apparent authenticity of that touch about the curtsy.

Hamilton Fitzgerald hurried to England and found that his friends had told the truth; they had even understated the unpleasantness of the situation. The Hastings family themselves were not in town and were as yet unaware of many stories now being told about them. The inference was always that Lady Flora was guilty but had been spared by the humane Queen. There was nothing to check this belief, Lady Flora's uncle decided, but the Duchess of Kent's prompt dismissal of Sir James. Grimly Fitzgerald set himself to learn the worst. With passion and no slightest trace of the humorous philosophy which most men of today would use to alleviate similar trials, he did his duty, making the rounds of the city incognito, listening in on conversations in taverns, clubs, and even private parties.

"At those respectable houses, where men of business pass their evenings, and discuss the news and speculations of the day, I found public opinion was universally against Lady Flora. The general idea was that she had been treated with unnecessary harshness; that she should have been got quietly out of the way; that such things occur every day in palaces; that people who place their daughters in them must take the consequence of doing so. It was often said that her brother would not have been so quiet if he had known 'that more than he liked would have come out if the thing had not been hushed up.' "

Really, shocking as the idea may be, one cannot help but reflect that the Hastings family might actually have suffered less if

Lady Flora *had* been pregnant, instead of merely honorably mori-
bund of a cancerous liver.

Having duly considered the situation and looked over the
correspondence, the family, in the name of Hamilton Fitzgerald,
published the entire bag of tricks. This action was taken on the
twenty-fourth of March, and provoked a violent reaction. The
Hastings family had done an unconventional thing, a thing condemned by many people in their class, those to whom publicity
itself was worse than any private crime no matter how great.
Added to the fact that the Hastingses had deliberately publicized
such a delicate matter was the disloyalty to the Queen thus implied. But not everyone, even in the aristocracy, felt like this;
most people, when they knew the facts, were on Lady Flora's
side.

A wider question was indirectly affected by the business. Her
people in general felt disappointed in the Queen, and for a time
abandoned their sentimental admiration of the young girl who
so picturesquely wore a heavy crown. She became unpopular.
The public observed, and did not like, the spectacle of smug un-
relenting cruelty. A young healthy woman had done grave wrong
to an older ailing one, and did not have the grace to admit it
when her mistake became apparent. Was it argued that Victoria was badly advised? Then one must blame the advisers, and
they were Whig ladies. And it was a Whig Government, already
not too popular, which ruled at Whitehall. Thus the controversy over Lady Flora's figure, trifling as it had seemed at first,
began to threaten the Government of England.

The Queen was stubborn; the Queen was defiant. She would
not dismiss Sir James. Lehzen's possible guilt was not so much as
mentioned. The Queen's temper was not too good just then in
any case; she was holding long, serious discussions every day with
Melbourne about a choice of bridegrooms, and her decision was
wavering, though it came back every now and again with notice-

able frequency to her cousin Albert, the young Prince of Saxe-Coburg. It was all very vexing, and now here were the Hastings family being disagreeable. Victoria thought it most unfair. She made no attempt to conceal her displeasure with Lady Flora.

"With one exception," wrote Lady Flora in her diary, "an enquiry after Lady Forbes's children, her Majesty showed Lady Flora no notice from the 24th of March, the date when Mr. Fitzgerald's letter was published, until the 9th of June, when her Majesty sent to ask how she was."

Soon the matter of Lady Flora's figure entered the realm of high politics. On May 7 the Government passed a bill with a majority of only five; it became obvious that they would have to resign. To Victoria this seemed disastrous. She would lose her adored Melbourne, on whom she depended heavily. She sent for Wellington, but he pleaded his extreme age in refusing to act and named Sir Robert Peel for his substitute. The Queen did not like Peel, and she liked him less when he told her while forming his Cabinet that some of her household ladies, most of whom were Whigs, should be replaced, according to accepted custom, by ladies from Tory families.

This touched a sore point with Victoria. The Tories were angry with the Queen because of Lady Flora, and the Queen was angry with the Tories for the same reason. Hand herself over to her enemies? Victoria dug her heels in; she would not change her household. She would never change her household. In vain did Peel reason with her. In vain did Melbourne advise her to give in. Victoria maintained that her bedchamber arrangements were her own affair and had nothing to do with the public interest. In the end, Peel respectfully bowed out. He could not form a Cabinet, he said, if the Queen would not give in on this matter. Melbourne came back; the Government remained in office.

Victoria won that battle, but Lady Flora had the last word after all; she died. It happened on July 5, 1839, in Buckingham Palace. One of her final requests, a very urgent one, was for a post-mortem, so that the unhappy mystery of her swollen abdomen might be settled and her reputation definitely cleared. It was then discovered that her liver was diseased so badly that all the organs of the stomach were involved.

The poor lady was to be buried from Loudoun Castle, and her brother came down from the country to accompany the body on its journey. Victoria sent a carriage to join in the procession to the station in London, but the populace actually hissed it, and threw stones. At Loudoun Kirk five thousand people attended the funeral. Onlookers wept when the old Dowager Marchioness tottered painfully to the graveside to look her last on the coffin of her martyred daughter. The next Sunday the local preacher spoke openly of the circumstances which had led to Lady Flora's death. Feeling had never before run so high against the Queen.

Small wonder, then, that the preparations for Victoria's marriage were speeded up. A royal wedding is always popular, and perhaps as a matron, thought Melbourne, the Queen might be less fiercely virtuous. Albert was summoned. Even on the night before he arrived, three full months after the death of Lady Flora, somebody threw stones at the palace and broke a few windows. Decidedly, it was high time the Queen was married.

Summing It Up

WELL, THERE THEY ARE, and a pretty sorry spectacle they make for anyone who happens to be a romantic, though I found them an interesting lot notwithstanding. Misgivings now assail my conscience. Have I possibly been guilty of stacking the cards, committing the worst sin known to science, selecting my evidence to bolster up a theory? I swear I haven't. I can't make an exact cross-section of history, or sample it as if I were doing a Gallup poll, but I have ranged without prejudice, to the best of my ability, through the centuries.

Let us be fair and careful, however. Before closing, we might go at this thing the other way; reverse the process of reasoning and see what we get out of it. If some of these characters had not loved as they did, but had found other objects for their passion, would it have made any difference to the world at large?

It's no good speculating further about Sappho; that would merely be piling one conjecture on top of another. Nor do I feel anything would be gained by investigating alternative programs for Nzinga. Frankly, Nzinga's inner life defeats me; I simply don't know how she felt about people. The Chevalier d'Eon, a special case, likewise defies our methods, and some of the others will be difficult to play the game with for one reason or another. But we can have a try.

Let's suppose that Helen of Troy had been worse behaved. If she had taken matters into her own hands, if she had tried for once to influence Fate instead of lying back with a complacent smile, repeatedly permitting people to carry her off, what might have come of it? I believe she would have approached Hector if she had dared, and told him that she loved him and that she was fed up with Paris and ready to be abducted. We are told she was irresistible. Hector, presumably, would have forgotten his wife Andromache and his son, and obediently run away with Helen. That fresh scandal would have caused considerable flurry among the attacking Greeks. Menelaus might have challenged Hector to a duel, and if there had been a fair fight (though with those tiresome meddling gods always butting in, one never knows), Hector, who was the better man, would certainly have won. Would Troy, then, have been saved? I don't think for one minute that it would. The besieging army had invested too much time and matériel to let the war lapse at that point. The thousand ships were already launched; the topless towers of Ilium were doomed. So much for Helen's influence. . . . I am inclined to be a little catty about Helen, I am afraid.

Had Antony and Cleopatra failed to click, we would have been much the poorer for want of Shakespeare's play. Moreover, humanity would not have gained peace; the dreary march of hostilities could not have been halted just at that time. Rome was bound to quarrel with Egypt, for she couldn't afford to let such a fabulously wealthy colony slip out of her grasp. Octavian did not intend to allow Caesarion to grow up at a safe distance, developing kingly ambition at his leisure. Cleopatra, however, might have had a better life had she chosen a husband who didn't drink. But even if she had done so, even if the hypothetical husband had put up a better show than Antony did against Octavian's forces, he and she and all of Egypt were bound to be incorporated in the Roman pattern sooner or later. Cleopatra, courageous and hungry for power, lived and died as she would have chosen. I can scarcely imagine her a softly smiling old lady, the Egyptian equivalent of Whistler's mother.

The details of Henry VIII's attachments had little to do with the crazily cruel life he led. Less than any other man was he affected by marriage. Perhaps if he had married Katharine Parr before Katheryn Howard—— But that could not have happened. Henry had to become a beaten man, weary of sensuality, before he would turn to Katharine Parr's dull safety. If Jane Seymour had lived she might have made the story less revolting. On the other hand, things might have been worse if she hadn't died. Henry would have been got at by scheming courtiers who were always ready and waiting to poison him against whatever wife he had at the moment. Not even conjecture or the game of might-have-been can mitigate the horror that was Henry VIII.

Marie Françoise, Princess of Savoy, seems a rather pallid personality next to him. She changed husbands in midstream, to be sure, and if the Church had not obligingly come to her rescue, the lady would have been a bigamist, an incestuous bigamist at that. However, the Church helped her out. Marie Françoise was saved, and after all the excitement had died down it was pretty obvious that none of it made much difference to Portugal anyway. The Princess of Savoy is quickly forgotten as we turn to look instead at her contemporaries the Königsmarks, roistering away in North Europe like the hearty extroverts they were.

Did the Königsmarks matter? Two of them did, there is no doubt of that. Karl Johann caused only a few weeks of scandal in London's streets, but Philipp Christoph and his sister Aurora made their mark on world affairs. If Philipp had not fallen in love with Sophie Dorothea of Celle, her son George II of England might have been a nicer man. *Might* have been, but I am dubious about it. He was the son of George I, and his mother loved him none the better for that. If she had not taken a lover, if she had not been imprisoned, if her son and daughter had not been cut off from all communication with her, even so it is likely that George II would have developed into the lout he was. Philipp, had he not fallen fatally in love with Sophie Dorothea, would have drifted away to other love affairs, possibly to marriage and a settling down in Sweden. It is unlikely, however, that he would have died in bed, even so. He was a Königsmark.

On the subject of Aurora there is no possibility of conjecture. Aurora collected fewer regrets than most women of her time, for she always did just as she liked. She never married. From among her lovers she picked out Philipp's good friend, the elector Frederick Augustus, and lived with him, if not for the rest of her life at least for a long time. Their son grew up to become famous as Marshal Saxe. Aurora and Frederick Augustus used to quarrel often and enjoyably. Once when he was accusing her of infidelity (the elector himself had more than a hundred illegitimate children, but consistency is not carried to extremes by such men) he quoted the proverb, "Caesar's wife ought to be above suspicion."

"Doubtless," said Aurora, "but I must confess I can't quite see how it applies. You are not Caesar, and I am not your wife."

I have tried earnestly to envisage Lord Nelson under other circumstances than the ones we know. It all adds up to nothing. Whatever one does with him, he remains the intrepid admiral. Abolish Lady Nelson, marry him to Lady Hamilton or somebody else, leave him unmarried, do what you will; none of it makes any difference. He was a genius of an admiral; let it stop there.

However, our other eighteenth-century heroes and heroines, Mr. and Mrs. Warren Hastings and the Princess Talleyrand, are not of the same unalterable stuff. Warren Hastings depended very much upon his wife. He was a marrying sort of man too; he would have married somebody else if Marian had not been aboard when he made his long journey out to India as a recently bereaved widower. Only suppose it had been Mademoiselle

Worlée instead! Would she have been less frail, I wonder, if she had been married to a clever man with a good position, like Hastings? He was too old for her, but so was Junius. However, I don't think it would ever have happened. Mademoiselle was not his type.

As for the other Hastings, Lady Flora, it is quite impossible to suppose she could have led another sort of life than the one bestowed upon her by Fate. Only the narrow Whiggish minds of Victoria's ladies in waiting, only the ignorant Queen herself would have made such an appalling mistake. Let us not add to the sum of their miscalculations.

There they are; I rest my case. Out of these thirteen people, four achieved a certain measure of happiness or content. What, you may ask, does it signify? Nothing very much, perhaps, save that I would like to put on record somewhere the following revised proverb:

ALL CONQUERS LOVE